New H   bililty

Volume II

In Memoriam Dr. Trevor Williams

As an internationally renowned scholar of sport sociology and disability sport and a member of the IPC Sport Science Committee, Dr. Trevor Williams was involved in the preparation of VISTA´99. Sadly, he passed away shortly before the Conference. In recognition of his invaluable contributions to the disability sport movement the editors and the Sport Science Committee dedicate the Conference Proceedings to him.

Gudrun Doll-Tepper/Michael Kröner/Werner Sonnenschein (eds.)
in cooperation with
the Sport Science Committee of the International Paralympic Committee

New Horizons in Sport for Athletes with a Disability

Proceedings of the
International VISTA´99 Conference
Cologne, Germany, 28 August-1 September 1999

Volume II

Integration/Development/Recruitment
Organization/Administration
Media/Marketing/Sponsoring

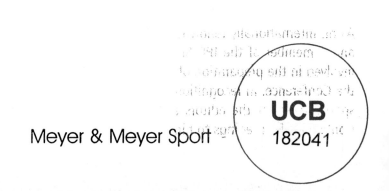

Meyer & Meyer Sport

British Library Cataloguing in Publication Data
A catalogue record for this book is available from the British Library

New Horizons in Sport for Athletes with a Disability, Vol. 2
Gudrun Doll-Tepper/Michael Kröner/Werner Sonnenschein (eds.)
ISBN 1-84126-037-1

© 2001 by Meyer & Meyer Sport (UK) Ltd
Oxford, Aachen, Olten (CH), Vienna, Québec,
Lansing/Michigan, Adelaide, Auckland, Johannesburg, Budapest
Member of the World
Sportpublisher's Association
www.w-s-p-a.org

Layout and Editing: Neil King
Cover Design: Birgit Engelen
Printed and bound in Germany by
Mennicken, Aachen
e-mail:verlag@meyer-meyer-sports.com
ISBN 1-84126-037-1

Contents

Volume I

3 Sport Performance – Technical Developments / Equipment

4 Sport Performance – Sports Medicine

5 Classification

6 Ethics

Volume II

7 Integration/Development/Recruitment

8 Organization/Administration

Prefaces

Introduction

Preface

When, in November 1997, the International Paralympic Committee (IPC) resolved to move its headquarters to Bonn, the decision was met with broad approval by Germany's sport policy makers and sport administrators. But the move was not only acclaimed at the political and administrative levels, it also roused considerable interest amongst the national sport science community, as teaching and research in sport-related rehabilitation and sport for the disabled have a long and well-established tradition in the universities of our country. The German Sport University in particular has played an important role in developing such programs since the late 40's.

It was therefore not surprising that on the occasion of a visit of IPC President Dr. Steadward to Cologne, in the presence of representatives of the Government of the Federal State of North Rhine-Westfalia and of the German Sport Federation of the Disabled, the idea was conceived to organize a scientific conference on sport for athletes with a disability at our University. The event was planned so as to coincide with the official opening ceremony of the new IPC headquarters.

The further discussion with Dr. Steadward and the Chairperson of the IPC Sport Science Committee, Dr. Doll-Tepper, led to a conference concept which was of particular appeal to both parties: We agreed to take up and continue the "theory meets practice" approach introduced by the 1993 VISTA Conference in Jasper/Canada which had set the stage for a highly effective and fruitful dialogue between scientists, coaches, athletes and administrators on key issues of competitive sport for persons with a disability. Since the IPC is considering the institutionalization of the VISTA Conferences in the future, the essential elements of VISTA '93 – the major topics, the criteria for the selection of presenters and the ample space for discussion and analysis – were maintained, thus creating the basis for a consistent frame of reference and comparison for what we hope will develop into a permanent state-of-the-art forum for Paralympic sport.

In adopting the VISTA concept we were guided by the conviction that (high) performance sport can be a means of positively influencing the self-concept of persons with a disability and their acceptance in able-bodied society. Overcoming a disability in athletic contest contributes to the mobilization of new strength and spirit and thus sets the stage for mental health and self-determination. At the same time, it fosters recognition by, and integration into, the non-disabled world. The public visibility of top athletes and the dedicated work of their organizations are instrumental in this process.

I trust that VISTA '99 has contributed to this cause.

Professor Dr. Walter Tokarski
President
German Sport University

Preface

In September of 1999, the German Sport University Cologne embraced the concept of VISTA '93 to host a conference for world renowned scientists, coaches, athletes and administrators in the area of sport for athletes with a disability. The outstanding success of the Cologne event, named VISTA '99, confirmed the value of maintaining and repeating this world-wide congress as the knowledge which has had a notable impact on disability sport science and the training, technique, and performance of athletes world-wide, along with the administration and organization of relative programmes and sport opportunities.

It was unanimously recognized by participants at VISTA '99 that the regular staging of these conferences every four years will prove, indisputably, to result in positive, beneficial consequences on the future of the disability sport movement in every corner of our globe. Whenever we can assemble to share our knowledge and experience and to discuss in an open forum the issues that surround any and all disciplines surrounding disability sport, we stand to gain – substantially. It is the invited speakers and congress registrants who by imparting their background, experience and expertise to the attendant assemblage, make a difference to the future development of disability sport throughout the world.

For this reason, the hosts of such significant events are due homage and appreciation. Accordingly, I would like to express my sincere thanks on behalf of the International Paralympic Committee (IPC) to the German Sport University, to our own Sport Science Committee and to the International Council of Sport Science and Physical Education (ICSSPE). Vista '99 would not have been possible without the financial support of the government of the Federal Republic of Germany, the government of the Federal State of North Rhine-Westfalia, the German Research Council (Deutsche Forschungsgemeinschaft) and the IPC. Among the many organizers who were required to successfully stage Vista ´99, several individuals are deserving of particular mention, including Prof. Dr. Joachim Mester who was Rector during most of the time spent in preparing for the Conference; Prof. Dr. Walter Tokarski, who assumed responsibility for the event subsequently to his election to Rector; Prof. Dr. Gudrun Doll-Tepper, President of ICSSPE and more specifically Chairperson of the IPCSSC in which function she assumed the role of chief liaison between the IPC´s scientific and technical expertise and the conference organizers; and the staff and volunteers of the German Sport University Cologne whose assistance was essential to the organization of the event.

The IPC is proud of the growth of its membership; the inclusion of its representatives on the International Olympic Committee commissions; the recent and overwhelming success of the XI Paralympic Summer Games Sydney 2000; the establishment of its central world-wide Headquarters in Bonn, Germany and installation of professional staff. We have strengthened our Sports Department and continue to plan for a Paralympic Hall of Fame Museum as well as an Ambassador Program to celebrate the achievements of our athletes and preserve Paralympic history. Much of our success is due to the outcome of conferences such as Vista ´99.

We look forward to the next Vista conference; in the meantime, the Proceedings that follow are yours to absorb and enjoy.

Professor Dr. Robert Steadward
President
International Paralympic Committee

Introduction

Disability sport has made enormous progress during the past decades. Athletes with a disability have experienced greatly improved acceptance and increased interest amongst the public and the media. However, despite this encouraging trend, scientific study of important issues pertaining to disability and sport is still less than satisfactory. Both in a disciplinary and a cross-/interdisciplinary perspective, such research has not yet been developed to its full potential, and existing findings are frequently not accessible. Therefore, scientific dialogue and communication are increasingly critical for the further development of disability sport.

Following the successful example of VISTA '93 in Jasper/Canada, VISTA '99 in Cologne offered an excellent forum for this kind of exchange of knowledge and ideas. One of the main goals of the VISTA conferences is to bridge the gap between theory and practice and to encourage interdisciplinary discussion. The VISTA concept is unique because it brings together leading scientists, coaches, athletes and administrators in the area of sport for athletes with a disability from around the world and creates an atmosphere of appreciation of different and controversial points of view and expertise.

It was on the occasion of the VISTA '93 Conference that the Sport Science Committee of the International Paralympic Committee (IPCSSC) was established. The Committee aims to enhance the knowledge about Paralympic sport by intensifying cooperation and communication among athletes, coaches and sport administrators on one side, and medical personnel and researchers on the other. The Committee's tasks include a needs assessment and the development, evaluation, dissemination and application of a body of knowledge about Paralympic sport relevant to 1. the initiation and continuation of sport participation, 2. sport performance, and 3. retirement from sport. This mission is achieved through activities directed towards the integration of theory and practice and the promotion of sport science edu-cation. The Committee comprises sport scientists from different disciplines as well as an athlete representative and the Medical Officer of the IPC. On the basis of this expertise, the Committee was strongly involved in the preparation and realisation of VISTA '99 and in the reviewing process for the proceedings. We would like to express our gratitude and appreciation to all Committee members for their extraordinary contribution to the success of the Conference.

Following the example of VISTA '93, the 1999 Conference focussed on current key issues of Paralympic sport. These were:

- sport performance (including exercise physiology, advances in training techniques, technical developments/equipment, and sports medicine),

- classification,

- ethics,

- integration/development/recruitment,

- organization/administration, and

- media/marketing/sponsoring.

It was our objective to have these topics discussed by a balanced field of invited experts from the Paralympic Movement - balanced in terms of the professional and athletic backgrounds of the presenters, the different disabilities represented, different sports, male and female participation and, last but not least, the different regions of the world. As the proceedings show, the results of this recruitment policy were - all in all - quite satisfactory. There were, however, some trends in the distribution of speakers which we feel deserve comment:

As distinct from VISTA´93, there was a remarkably strong participation in the area of "organization/administration". Eighteen out of 65 presenters, i.e. more than 25%, chose to present in this area. Many of these presented papers on the future structure and organization of the IPC. There appears to be an enormous interest in discussing the needs and possibilities of standardizing procedures and of improving co-operation within the Paralympic Movement - an interest which is obviously caused by the unprecedented dynamic development of disability sport in recent years.

This impression is reinforced by the fact that the second largest program section, with 15 presentations, was the area of "integration/development and/or recruitment". Here again, it appears that the rapid expansion of the Paralympic structures has led to an increased demand for critical assessment of existing policies and procedures. It is probably no accident that gender issues played a major role in this discussion; in the program they merited a separate session and were part of various other papers.

A further indicator of the current situation of transition characterizing the Paralympic Movement is the large number of representatives from developing countries who attended VISTA´99. Their concerns were also treated in a specific program session, with discussions producing both encouraging examples of progress and the awareness of almost insurmountable disadvantages, especially with regard to the growing problem of "technical boosting".

On the other hand, contributions on exercise physiology, training techniques and sports medicine were not quite as numerous as we had expected. Although the papers which *were* submitted, cover very important areas of disability sport, a more comprehensive representation would have contributed to an even better balance.

It appears that at the present time the organizational consolidation of

Paralympic sport and the harmonization of its policies and procedures are perceived as more pressing problems than issues of performance optimization.

In conclusion, it needs to be emphasized that these proceedings are a true reflection of the "theory meets practice" approach of the VISTA conferences, an approach which is inclusive both in terms of presenters and of concepts. It is for this reason that papers vary with regard to scientific content and form. With this observation in mind it can be said that VISTA´99 was an excellent forum of analysis and debate between the different partners and groups involved in disability sport. This kind of dialogue should be continued and intensified.

We wish to extend our sincere gratitude to everyone who was involved in the VISTA '99 Conference. With these proceedings, we hope to contribute to an improved knowledge of the field of disability and sport, with special emphasis on the Paralympic Movement, to create a better understanding of the developments and challenges in this field and to encourage more people around the world to become active in disability sport as an integral part of sport in science, education and culture.

Professor Dr. Gudrun Doll-Tepper
Michael Kröner
Werner Sonnenschein

Presentations

Integration / Development / Recruitment

The forgotten athletes - a critical appraisal of IPC sports competition of World and Paralympic Levels

Colin Rains

Colwick, United Kingdom; Vice-President CP-ISRA

It would come as a surprise to many if it were alleged that we had groups of sports people who were being denied competition. Yet it is possible that we are guilty of doing just this. We are in many ways lessening the chances for certain groups of athletes and yes there is ample evidence that this is the case. It is not an overt preventing of competition, it is occurring in different ways and through different methods all of which seem to be acceptable. However when looked at in its widest context and not in isolation, it amounts to nothing more or less than possible discrimination.

Here are just a few examples: In 1988 at the Seoul Paralympics approx. 15 % of the competitors were what we would now class as the more severe competitors. In Sydney, using the system that is in place that percentage will have dropped by 9 % on the present analysis.

Before we go any further let me just define what for this paper I am considering as severely disabled - they are the cerebral palsy classes 1, 2 and 3 and the tetraplegic groups from ISMWSF and the B1 group from IBSA. Any analysis of Pan Disability events at Paralympics or Multi Disability World Championships will confirm that this group of sports people have lost many events and therefore many opportunities for competition.

Now let me return to discrimination. Not an easy word to use and much more a difficult concept to analyse and verify. We appear to discriminate in many ways. I hasten to add that this is not knowingly to discriminate but imperceptible, and through a number of avenues it cannot be described as anything other than this.

In what sort of ways are we guilty?.We prevent opportunities as soon as we legislate that this group or that group cannot compete because of what? They do not fit into an Olympic ideal; they have not sufficient numbers to make up the requirement for a competition; we must reduce our numbers because there are too many medals and this gives the wrong message to the TV or to the public at large; and we could go on...

Pick up one or two of these myths, for this is what they are: Olympic ideal - the last thing that we should be conscious of is the Olympic ideal. We are the Paralympics, not the Olympics, and it was Fernand Landry who warned us both at VISTA '93 and before that at his keynote address in Barcelona in 1992:

> *"there is nothing in the Olympic movement now in force that characterizes athletes in such absolute terms as to serve as a basis for the thinking that conceptually the Paralympic movement does not fit into the broader concept of Olympism and the Olympic movement ..."* (F. LANDRY, VISTA '93)

Yet even as recent as the minutes of an IPC EC Meeting, the comment was made that

> ..."*we must reduce the medal tally .... The Olypmics have only 300+ medals but we have 500+ ...*"

So what, we are different and our sports people are different!

Again,

> *"but many of the events are not suited to TV and the public conception of disability..."*

No, they may not be, but all our Paralympic aspirants have worked to their highest levels to achieve and who is to say that less able is not able? Who is to say that the more disabled athletes are not as dedicated as those who are less disabled? Much of this is immotive and we can argue the rights and wrongs of any case what we cannot justify is organisational and administrative issues taking precedence over sports justification and sports implementation.

Now I am not naive to say that there are no limits, that there are no rules that have to be followed and implemented. What I feel I am justified in advocating is that each athlete in each group or class must have the opportunity and the right to be given the chance. There is evidence that this is not the case, and even for our Games next year in Sydney there is evidence that some athletes have not been given a fair and equal chance to at least enter. It may be that subsequently it will not be possible to compete for certain reasons but we cannot and we should not deny the right for opportunity.

Before I leave this point: How can an athlete in a class where at one point in time, there are insufficient numbers to fill the class and therefore fulfil the requirement of competition, how can that athlete and his/her class ever come back into the consideration? How can development over a four year Paralympic period ever be considered in order to build up those numbers? How can an emerging nation or federation be encouraged to enter such an athlete in whatever event, if the event has already been removed some years earlier because of insufficient numbers? Our rules at the moment mean that there could be an 8 year wait before any lost event could be reintroduced.

Into this group of disadvantaged sportsmen and women I now introduce women themselves as a group. All that has been said for the more severe group applies equally to the events for women. The Games at World and Paralympic levels have lost almost all the possibilities for women to compete - in the last World/ Paralympic Games less than 13 %.

I move now to my second issue. I believe that if we scratched the surface we would discover that, despite our aims within the Paralympic movement and despite our articles of government where we clearly emphasise the importance of these minority groups, if we really dig deep enough, we are guilty in one way or another of raising barriers for these groups. Again these are not deliberate, they are not intentional, but how many times when considering taking a group away for competition do we consider the extra needs of the severely disabled and weigh these against financial implications: If we take that athlete, then we take also an extra care staff, or extra chairs or baggage. This is not only an international problem; it is fundamentally a national one.

As has been said, the extra event for these athletes extends the programme, the events take longer, there is a need for additional work on the pool side, or there are extra chairs on the transport system. If we have reduced the number of classes that I am considering, have they gone elsewhere for competition? Yes, I believe that some have. We have seen an increase in boccia, in wheelchair rugby, in goalball, but that has not accounted for all the reduction. Where have all the women athletes gone? I hear some say, well it is a national trend that women do not participate to the same degree as do men. Statistics show that women take part in other physical activities and they are not necessarily competitive. There is only a grain of truth in that analysis. What has happened is almost a replica of the problem with the more severly disabled groups, there has been a lack of initial numbers and consequently the sports events have been reduced. Where are they now? They are not even offered or if they are, they are combined in order to try and provide fair and equal competition.

I think we must question the fundamental attitude of us all to these issues. As members of clubs, groups, or federations we are actively promoting opportunities. I have just come from the European Championships for athletes with cerebral palsy. I belong to a federation that actively promotes opportunities for these specific groups of sports people. I know from the entries that we receive that the athletes exist if the chance to compete is offered. As members of international federations, I wonder just how many times we actively promote activities for women, for the more severe athletes even at the expense of the more able.

Can I suggest one or two ideas in conclusion? Let us review the sports programme of our national groups. How many times do we provide specific activities for minority groups? Within our development programme, can we identify specific opportunities for these groups. Is it possible to encourage the sports clubs to look into their various activities and promote even at the expense of others, e.g. a women's group?

I appreciate that there are cultural and religious differences amongst us, but in so many small ways opportunities can be identified and certain barriers taken down, or at least moved aside. In some places our potential sports people are institutionalised. They live in the centre or commute daily. This creates some problems for clubs and federations, but problems are created to find solutions – have we considered this? Is it possible for us to consider a rationing system to encourage participation? Only recently I heard that the South African Rugby Union is considering a quota system within its organisation in order to encourage black players.

Within our Paralympic system we have operated a quota system. What if it were applied to national federations in order to ensure that minority groups actually came to compete. Is there an argument for considering amendments to rules in order to allow for minority groups to compete at the highest level, the Paralympics? That may encourage more to come and may have the effect of building up the numbers which is what we want to do.

Strategic approaches to vertical integration and equity for athletes with disabilities: An examination of a critical factors model

Ted Fay

State University of New York at Cortland, Cortland, NY, USA

Introduction

The purpose of this article is to present the findings of a much larger comprehensive study entitled: **Race, Gender, and Disability: A New Paradigm Towards Full Participation and Equal Opportunity in Sport** (FAY 1999). This study examined the integration histories of three respective sport governance structures with regard to a specific identity group. A critical change factors model (CCFM) was designed and developed by the author as an interpreting tool from which to examine the extensive case histories of African-American males in professional baseball, women in US based intercollegiate sport, and athletes with disabilities in Olympic/Paralympic sport. An **Organizational Continuum** (ESTY, GRIFFIN & HIRSCH 1995) was also utilized as an explanatory instrument to illustrate how far a particular governance structure and/or organization has progressed with respect to being an inclusive entity.

A further intent of this study was to develop a set of propositions which could serve as a foundation for the development of recommendations for the continued integration of individuals with disabilities into the United States Olympic Committee and its related national sport governing bodies. The problem, as defined and identified in this study, specified that race, gender, and disability are often found to be the primary determinants in disputes involving equity issues in a given society and specifically in sport, in sport governance structures, and in sport organizations as being part of a particular culture.

The struggles to achieve racial and gender equity in the United States
have been researched, analyzed, and discussed from many
perspectives. The historical context of these struggles remain relevant
as members of various identity groups (i.e. African-Americans,
Hispanics, and women) continue to strive for full inclusion in society,
the workplace, and the sportplace (CARR-RUFFINO 1996;
DELGADO 1995; ESTY, GRIFFIN & HIRSCH 1995; LAPCHICK
1998; SABO 1997; SHROPSHIRE 1996). The same, however, cannot
be said about the documentation of the struggles of people with
disabilities in American society or specifically in sport (DEPAUW &
GAVRON 1995). By expanding the identity (ID) group paradigm to
include race, gender, and disability issues, this study can potentially
offer increased understanding to researchers and practitioners about
equity issues facing individuals with disabilities from the perspectives
of 1. society as a whole; 2. strategies needed to incorporate more
diversity in the workplace and sportplace; 3. competencies needed in
managing increased diversity in sport organizations; 4. compliance
with legal mandates; 5. reallocation of scarce funds/resources
(distributive justice); and 6. education and training needed in changing
core belief systems.

Sport, as a defined part of an overall culture, is not exempt, distinct, or
immune from the effects of societal issues related to diversity and the
corresponding demands by specific identity groups for greater equity
(COAKLEY 1998). Historically, sport as an aspect of American
culture, has been presented as playing a contradictory role in serving
either to maintain the status quo (segregation or limited integration) or
conversely, aiding significant change (integration) on the playing fields
and in the decision-making structures of American sports
organizations. To date, the focus of sport historians and sociologists
has been primarily on African-American males and women in their
respective struggles to be more fully integrated into the practice and
management of sport in America (EITZEN & SAGE 1993; COAKLEY

1998; RADER 1996; SAGE 1998; SHROPSHIRE 1996).

Conversely, a lack of research has contributed to the confusion and a lack of awareness of where sport for athletes with disabilities fits with respect to existing mainstream sport structures in the United States. There is virtually no evidence to support that any in-depth research has been conducted which intentionally examines and compares the histories and issues facing all three identity groups (e.g., race, gender, and disability) in their struggles for integration and equity in sport (FAY 1999).

Olympic/Paralympic sports, historically and currently, are still the only significant area of opportunity for athletes with disabilities to participate in at an elite level. Little to no opportunities exist for these athletes in scholastic, college, or professional team sports. Wheelchair tennis, alpine ski racing, and wheelchair road racing are examples of individual sports that have developed international and national circuits for athletes with disabilities that offer prize money for the winners.

In 1998, two legal actions profoundly changed the dynamics over the debate of whether or not athletes with disabilities should be allowed to achieve further integration into sport in America. The US Congress passed the Ted Stevens Olympic & Amateur Sports Act of 1998 which inserted the term "Paralympic" into the text of the previous Amateur Sports Act of 1978. Its intent was to reflect the need for the future integration of athletes with disabilities into the United States Olympic Committee (USOC) structure (STEVENS 1998). The second landmark decision involved Casey Martin action against the Professional Golfers Association (PGA) based on the Americans with Disabilities Act of 1990 (ADA) which granted him the "reasonable accommodation" to be able to ride an electric cart during PGA tour events (BLAUVELT 1998). More legal action is anticipated from athletes with disabilities similar to the civil actions taken in numerous gender equity cases in intercollegiate athletics which used the federal regulations of Title IX to support their cases. The summary of findings of this study provide a blueprint from which to predict organizational response to potential challenges to the status quo within the Paralympic sport movement in the United States.

Summary of Findings

The examination of integration was focused broadly at the participant, managerial, and executive levels of each sport governance structure and organizations identified in this study. A theoretical framework was employed which combined critical, equity, and systems theories in order to analyze and explain how integration has been either facilitated or resisted within the context of an organization. The analysis also included the identification of an interdependent set of relationships between a hegemonic majority within a sport organization and those of specific identity groups as based on race, gender, or disability (SAGE 1998).

This research consisted of four distinct phases. In the first phase, a theoretical model was developed to assist in conducting a historical as well as a comparative analysis of two longitudinal case histories of the integration of African-Americans in Major League Baseball (MLB) and women in intercollegiate athletics. This new model, entitled the Critical Change Factors Model or CCF Model, was constructed based upon a synthesis of three primary theories (i.e. critical social theory, equity theory, and open-systems theory). The incorporation of these theories aided in identifying ten specific factors that were perceived as precipitating or being conducive to individual, organizational, and cultural change.

Critical social theory, as presented specifically through the work of Coakley (1998), Gruneau (1983), and Sage (1998), served as one of the principal theoretical underpinnings of this study. In particular, the subperspective of hegemony - pluralism in sport as presented by Sage was incorporated throughout the study. Equity theory as expressed through the concept of distributive justice (HUMS & CHELLADURAI

1994a, b; TOMBLOM & JONSSON 1985, 1987) served as the second theoretical pillar of this study. Within the context of the third theoretical pillar of open-systems theory, four additional subperspectives were incorporated as presented in Pfeffer and Salancik's resource dependency theory (1978), Gouldner's norm of reciprocity (1960), Mintzberg's power theory (1983), and Mintzberg and Quinn's strategy process (1992). Additional insight for the CCF Model was drawn from 1. recent research dealing with diversity in the workplace; 2. unpublished monographs relating to the integration of athletes with disabilities and the Paralympic Movement; and 3. the author's own personal experience.

An examination of two longitudinal case histories was conducted detailing over 100 years of racial integration in Major League Baseball and gender integration into organized collegiate sport. Secondary data such as books, monographs, articles, and other archival sources were used to develop each of these histories. Each history was categorized into specific eras based on key breakthrough and/or critical events relative to organizational change and changes in the patterns of integration. Data were analyzed through the use of descriptive statistics and qualitative methods. Empirical findings were presented based on both the specific eras of a given historical analysis and on the overall current state of each identity group with respect to Major League Baseball and intercollegiate sport as sponsored by the National Collegiate Athletic Association (NCAA). Specifically the nature and level of integration of each of the identity groups were assessed with respect to the three stratification or organizational levels of working, middle, and executive classes.

The Critical Change Factors (CCF) Model was then employed to help illustrate the viewpoints and controlling actions of the principal decision-makers within MLB and intercollegiate athletics during each of the transitional stages of an ID group's progress along the Organizational Continuum (OC) model. Particular interest was given to the type and levels of resistance to change displayed by individuals within the sport organizations identified to undergo initial or further integration. Equal concern was given to the examination of the issues of resistance to change (breakthrough and integration) linked to key stakeholders from within the ID groups and their supporting segregated sport structures. This resistance was further compared and contrasted to the roles of key individuals and organizations involved in helping support and facilitate the achievement of integration through the different stages of the OC model.

Once outlined as a preliminary set of ten factors, the CCF Model was then linked to a conceptual model which illustrated the stages an organization would move through as it changed from a totally segregated workplace environment to a fully inclusive organization. This model called the Organizational Continuum (OC model) was drawn from the literature on workplace diversity (ESTY, GRIFFIN & HIRSCH 1995, p. 189). This model consisted of six distinct stages in which an organization moved from being a monocultural to a multicultural organization. This OC Model presents organizational change in regard to integration of ID groups in six stages.

From Monocultural ————————————▶ To Multicultural

Exclusive Club (EC)	Lip Service To Inclusion	Tokenism (T)	A Critical Mass (CM)	Tolerating/ Accepting Diversity (TAD)	Valuing Diversity (VD)

Exclusive Organization ————————————▶ Inclusive Organization

Fig. 1: Organizational continuum on workplace diversity (from Esty, K., Griffin, R. & Hirsch, M.S.: Workplace Diversity. Holbrook, MA: Adams Pub. 1995 p. 189)

The OC model helped to establish benchmarks upon which conclusions about the levels of integration and inclusion within respective sport governing organizations were based. The "current state" of identified organizations was also evaluated based on the three stratification levels (i.e. working class, middle class, and executive class) as presented in Sage's hegemonic – pluralistic model of culture and organizations. Although the OC Model is most often displayed as a horizontal progression demonstrating a mono-cultural to multicultural shift within an organization, it also can be presented in a layered or vertical dimension showing the disparities regarding integration/inclusion at each stratification level (i.e. working class - athletes, middle class - coaches/administrators, and executive class - CEOs and Board Chairpersons).

Several cautions must be raised regarding the use of this model within this study. First, all organizations and specifically the sport governance structures and sport organizations presented in this study were not necessarily inherently exclusive clubs at their inception with regard to the exclusion of any of the respective identity groups of this study. The identity groups of this study may also have been or are represented by some organizations (i.e. Negro League franchises, AIAW member colleges and universities, and/or disability sport organizations) which could be defined as supporting the concept of exclusion through virtue of creating and supporting a segregated model of sport.

The organizational continuum is not presented as a representation of reality. Instead it should be looked at as an "Ideal Type" with which the real experience of organizations may be compared. It may be implied from the model that an organization is likely to move in an ideal or uni-directional evolution from an exclusive to inclusive organization. The OC Model needs to be seen, however, as a multi-directional model wherein an organization can experience leapfrogging of a particular stage or the slipping back from one stage to another depending on specific and unique circumstances.

Key secondary sources were utilized by this study which were drawn from three national studies (i.e. the **Racial Report Card**, the **WSF - Gender Equity Report Card**, and Acosta & Carpenter's longitudinal studies on women in intercollegiate sport) which helped to establish the "current states" of integration within MLB and the NCAA. In so doing, the first two of four research questions of this study were addressed in this phase of the study.

Q1 asked: What is the current status of each of the identified subgroups in this study within their corresponding sport governing organizations (i.e. African-Americans in MLB, women in NCAA Division I sports) at the participant, managerial, and executive levels as defined by an "access" paradigm?

Q2 asked: What, if any, similar critical change factors can be found to exist in each of the integration histories and case studies of the identified subgroups (African-Americans in MLB, women in organized collegiate sports) in this study? How do these identified critical change factors relate specifically to issues of integration and full inclusion of members of each of these subgroups into previously segregated sport organizations and structures?

Critical Change Factors Model

A set of ten critical change factors (CCF) were identified to provide a framework to assess the commonalties of how breakthrough events occurred and what ripple events were sustained. These themes were selected for their potential broad application across identity groups and different sport governance structures identified in each of the integration histories. These factors included:

-**Fl:** a change/occurrence of major societal event(s) affecting public opinion toward ID group;
-**F2:** a change in laws, government, and court action in changing public policies toward ID group;
-**F3:** a change in level of influence of high profile ID group role models on public opinion;
-**F4:** a change in the level and nature of mainstream mass media's

portrayal of the ID group;

-**F5:** a change in the critical mass of ID group athletes attaining high athletic achievement;

-**F6:** a change in attitudes of key leaders in power elites who act as catalysts for breakthroughs;

-**F7:** a change in perceived or real economic value of ID group as assets to the ruling power elite;

-**F8:** a change in the beliefs about the medical & intellectual stereotypes of the ID group;

-**F9:** a change in hiring practices toward ID group related to managerial and leadership roles; and

-**F10:** a change in use of strategic processes by the power elite to effect greater integration.

Each of the factors was then applied to each of the specific eras identified within the integration histories of Major League Baseball and intercollegiate sport to determine whether all, some, or none of the listed factors were present at or near the time of identified benchmark events. The relation of a given factor to issues of integration was coded using a bi-polar construct (Yes - No) to indicate both the existence of and the effect of specific critical change factors during a historical era. It was also determined that a simple matrix would not work to adequately present a sound qualitative assessment of existence and effect of the given factor. This notation system was further modified to characterize the complexities in the longitudinal process and the maintenance of factor shifts. This was important to understand that once a factor emerged and a shift occurred, regression, reversal, or the diminished effect of a factor could be appropriately noted.

Competitive Analysis

In the third phase of this study, an examination of whether or not a set of common change-related factors could be determined for the two ID groups based on race and gender was conducted through the use of a comparative analysis.

Q3 asked: Is it possible to develop a unified critical change factors model (CCFM) from an examination of the various integration histories -which can be applied to different sport organizational environments or are the factors unique to a given sport environment, sport organization, or identity group?

As with each specific integration history, the ten specific critical change factors were examined as to whether they had a common precipitating effect on the process of organizational change with respect to mitigating racial and gender stratification in Major League Baseball and organized intercollegiate sport. A comparative analysis of racial and gender stratification was provided in which historical and current evidence was presented outlining the current state of both ID groups relative to each stratum (i.e. working, middle, and executive class). Data were presented which reflected the "current state assessments" of each identity group relative to their progress along the OC model.

Empirical findings using the CCF model were then compared in order to search for parallel practices and experiences in the histories of African-Americans in Major League Baseball and women in organized collegiate sport. One of the outcomes of this analysis was to determine whether or not each of these critical change factors was generalizable to other identity groups facing similar stratification and equity issues. The CCF Model was further modified to reflect a hierarchy of principles (factors) of change in racial and gender integration in sport. This was accomplished by adding four qualifying statements to the CCF Model relative to each factor. These statements were as follows:

- **I:** a factor is sufficient to cause change;
- **II:** a factor is necessary, but not sufficient to cause change;
- **III:** a factor is supportive, but not necessary or sufficient to cause change; or
- **IV:** a factor can be counterproductive.

Strategic Management Process

The fourth and final phase of this study, related to the determination of what strategies or processes of strategic management, if any, have been utilized which might help facilitate the most equitable form or pattern of integration and inclusion.

Q4 asked: Can a CCF Model serve as a means of developing propositions for a series of recommendations by which the United States Olympic Committee, through a strategic management approach, might facilitate greater opportunity and inclusion for individuals with disabilities into its member national sport governing bodies more rapidly than the processes experienced and utilized by Major League Baseball and the NCAA?

The broader question is, whether or not, the application of insights to the strategic management process of the integration of a minority (i.e. identity) group into specific sport organizations are generalizable regardless of a specific identity group or case example. Implicit to the concept of acceleration of greater opportunity and inclusion, is a companion concept of achievement of "higher levels" of integration within sport organizations.

Built into the overall design of this study was the principle of generating a theory-to-practice model that could be applied by sport practitioners. This was presented through an application of insights to a strategic management process of the integration of identity groups into sport organizations. It was theorized that the primary decision-makers within an organization would be better equipped to deal with such problems armed with a deeper understanding of the political, economic, multicultural, and social contexts in which they functioned.

A review of supporting social and open-systems theories was presented as a foundation upon which to build a specific strategic process oriented to each sport governance structure (i.e. MLB and the NCAA).

Specific suggestions regarding strategic applications relative to Major League Baseball and NCAA sponsored intercollegiate athletics were made following an open-systems approach to strategic action. The application of a strategic management approach was also applied to a third case example comprised of athletes with disabilities along with individuals involved in the management of sport for these athletes. A framework of four phases was employed consistently across cases including:

-   **I:**   output - including an ideal future vision;
-   **II:** throughputs - including actions, implementation, and documented change of an organization;
-   **III:** inputs - including a current assessment and strategy development; and
-   **IV:** feedback - including key success factors.

The output phase included an in-depth SWOT analysis of each governance structure with respect to given **S**trengths, **W**eaknesses, **O**pportunities, and **T**hreats (HAINES & MCCOY 1995; MARX & THEROUX 1996). An analysis of how each governance structure has used strategic processes as a general operating practice as well as a specific approach to issues of integration was also conducted. Included in this analysis was a series of specific recommendations by which the USOC, through a strategic management approach, could, in fact, facilitate greater opportunity and inclusion for individuals with disabilities into its member national governing bodies.

Conclusions

The findings of this study demonstrate that integration in Major League Baseball and intercollegiate athletics remains primarily at the participant or athlete level and that hiring practices of minorities and women by these organizations at managerial or executive level positions remain at token or lip service to inclusion levels. The current state assessment revealed that the most significant advancement by either group with respect to integration has been African-American players in MLB. Black players have achieved a level of supercritical mass (CM) in MLB when illustrated on the OC Model, while female intercollegiate athletes are just beginning to approach critical mass. Women in intercollegiate athletics are slightly ahead of African-Americans with respect to integration at both the managerial and executive levels of their respective sport governance systems. The levels of integration and the progression along the OC model are consistently inversely proportional for both African-Americans and women with respect to vertical integration. The data are stark and very graphically revealing when superimposed on the OC model. The findings of this study reveal that neither identity group has yet to achieve a level of integration which reflects an organizational environment that promotes a level of tolerance and acceptance of diversity (TAD) at a minimum or the valuing of diversity (VD) at all participant, management, and executive levels at a maximum.

A systems theory based model of integration/inclusion of identity groups into heretofore segregated sport organizations provided insight into the various critical factors or influences which must be taken into consideration by all stakeholders involved in organizational change. Based on an analysis of previous research, this study provided a potentially more sophisticated model from which to analyze the historical and existing practices of Major League Baseball or NCAA member institutions relative to progress towards a more accepting and valuing environment of inclusion.

The integration of the conceptual frameworks of CCF and OC models allows one to develop a more in-depth qualitative assessment of the current state of the integration of identity groups in sport than can be gained from aggregated descriptive statistics by themselves. In employing these models, the author made a conscious distinction that the progression along the OC to the final two stages of tolerating/accepting diversity (TAD) and valuing diversity (VD) cannot be stated to have been achieved if integration exists at one stratification level only (i.e. working class).

The integration histories and descriptive analyses used in this study show conclusively that African-Americans in Major League Baseball and women in intercollegiate sports operate in very stratified and hegemonically controlled environments. The prevailing economic value of the integration of athletes (i.e. the working class) towards critical mass without a corresponding effort to foster similar levels of integration at the management or executive levels reinforced these findings. Due to spatial limitations, it is impossible to present the full extent of the findings relative to African-Americans in professional baseball and women in intercollegiate sport. For the complete study and the full context of the summary of findings of this study, please contact the author.

Each of the ten critical change factors were found to exist, and to relate specifically to issues of integration and full inclusion of members of each of these subgroups into the previously segregated sport organizations and structures (i.e. MLB and the NCAA). In applying the CCF Model to MLB, the most consistent principles necessary for change were 1. the impact of a world war (**Fl**) on an emerging public sense of moral correctness against overt segregation; 2. the threat of new public policies and laws (**F2**) on civil rights might be applied to MLB; and 3. a strongly held value by an initiating owner/CEO coupled with a logical economic self-interest (**F6** and **F7**) in acting as a catalyst for change. Although these factors have been deemed to be potentially sufficient by themselves to cause change, the historical evidence indicates all four factors were strongly present when Jackie Robinson broke the "color line" with the Brooklyn Dodgers in 1947, thus reintegrating Major League Baseball in the 20th century.

The single most overriding principle or factor with respect to change in the integration of African-American players in MLB is that of owner/CEO financial self-interest. This is contrasted by the apparent lack of financial incentive or self-interest for franchises in MLB to hire minorities in management positions, while at the same time it has an overwhelming primary interest in acquiring the best on-field talent regardless of a given player's racial identity. Given the weight of historical data amassed for this study, it is difficult to characterize Major League Baseball as other than a white male hegemonic institution which continues to implicitly maintain an environment of white privilege (i.e. supremacy) off the playing field and beyond the dugout. Power and control could be described as a form of "plantation economics" in which athletic talent is constantly exploited in order to achieve owner wealth and prestige.

In applying the CCF Model to intercollegiate sport, the most consistent principles necessary for change have been: 1. the impact of a world war (**F1**) on an emerging public sense of moral correctness against the overt suppression of women; 2. the mandate of new legislation and laws (**F2**) on intercollegiate athletics; 3. the impact of negative public relations by the mass media (**F4**) regarding issues of gender equity and its ensuing impact on the competition process of recruitment of female students; and 4. concern by college presidents to contain the threat of large punitive damages resulting from legal action as a logical economic self-interest (**F7**). Although three of these four factors have been deemed to be potentially sufficient by themselves to cause change, the historical evidence indicates the fourth factor (**F4**) has recently become a strong influence present when respective colleges and universities have made decisions to meet Title IX compliance standards.

The single most overriding principal or factor with respect to change in the integration patterns of female athletes in intercollegiate sport is that of the potential for financial judgements against a university or the NCAA itself. This viewpoint is contrasted by the apparent lack of equal incentive or self-interest for institutions of higher education to hire women in coaching, administrative, and executive level positions. There also is not a similar economic incentive in acquiring reaching proportionality between men's and women's sports. Nearly all women's sports are typically non-revenue generating enterprises and therefore represent a drag on the overall resources of a respective college athletic department. This is also exacerbated by the current pattern of the cutting of men's non-revenue sports to make way for new women's sports, while maintaining the disproportionate investment in men's revenue producing sports of football and basketball. Given the weight of the historical data amassed for this study, it is difficult to characterize the National Collegiate Athletic Association and its collective membership as other than a predominantly white, male hegemonic enterprise which continues to implicitly maintain an environment of male privilege (i.e. sexism) at all stratification levels.

Many common critical change factors were found to exist in the integration histories of each identity group studied that revealed the continued presence of an established and entrenched white male hegemony. A new finding, however, revealed that not all factors were of equal importance relative to breakthroughs and the sustaining of integration. In applying this hierarchy of principles to the ten factors of the CCFM, three factors (**F1, F2**, and **F7**) stood out as sufficient in themselves to cause change regarding initial racial and gender integration in sport at the foundational level of social stratification (i.e. the working class-athlete level). It was not evident, however, that these factors are sufficient by themselves to facilitate vertical integration at the middle class (i.e. management) or executive class levels. Integration can be accelerated if certain additional critical factors or prevailing conditions are in place. Five factors (**F3, F4, F5, F6**, and **F10**) appeared to be necessary, but were not sufficient by themselves to help create change at any of the three social stratification levels. Historical evidence revealed that an organization needs favorable leadership (**F6**) which has a proactive strategic vision (**F10**) and is willing to challenge the prevailing conventions of the status quo. Racial or gender pioneers (**F3**) needed to be highly successful in order to act as antidotes against embedded stereotypes. Seven factors (**F1, F2, F3, F4, F7, F9** and **F10**) were determined to have the potential to be also counter-productive.

Factors (**F8** and **F9**) were deemed supportive, but not necessary or sufficient to achieve integration at any of the three social stratification levels (i.e. working, middle, and executive). It can be argued that these factors become more important and therefore, more critical and necessary, when one assesses the vertical integration of these supra-organizations with respect to achieving more diversity and equity in middle management and executive leadership. It is evident, however, that regardless of how many critical factors might be present, effective and time-sensitive systemic change at all three organizational levels is dependent on the understanding and use of strategic processes (**F10**) by the managers of organizations such as MLB and the NCAA.

The historical evidence relative to the racial stratification in Major League Baseball and gender stratification in intercollegiate sport described very similar organizational environments as predicated on the maintenance of the hegemony of an embedded, white, male, privileged power elite. It is not a sheer coincidence that the power elites of both of these supra-organizations (i.e. MLB and the NCAA) appear to look and act in similar ways with respect to issues of racism and sexism. A comparative analysis supported the characterization of both structures as being conservative, highly stratified organizations which embrace change very slowly and reluctantly whether initiated internally from their representative members or externally as potentially influenced by the prevailing social contexts of racial and gender issues of a given era.

Relevance of Study to Paralympic Movement

It was a declared purpose of this study to provide a "bridge" or transition point for a practitioner from theory-to-practice. Specifically, the findings from the scholarly analyses of this study regarding race and gender integration need to be converted into a more practically grounded approach in order for a middle or executive level sport manager to be enabled to use the analyses more effectively. It was necessary, therefore, to attempt to justify the assumption that strategic management processes are, in fact, the means which can best assist a manager to guide (i.e. manage) a process of organizational change. Ultimately, the use of strategic processes by the power elite in each of these respective supra-organizations can help affect the greater acceleration of "higher levels" of integration.

Based on the three case examples in this study, it is evident that to change embedded resistance and barriers to inclusion held by the existing members of an organization or supra-organization several things need to occur. Critical stakeholders from an organization led by an initiating manager (internal) in cooperation with the assistance of external advocacy groups must focus through the means of education and training on changing the beliefs and perceptions (**F6**) of resisting the power elite.

Societal and political events can be taken advantage of (**Fl**) and regulatory (**F2**) factors can be used to help shape the overall context from which a strategic process is created and engaged. The attitudes, beliefs, and behavior of key stakeholders (**F6**) within an organization at each stratification level, as well as in its related industry partners, are very critical to the process of change. The "will" or commitment to change the embedded beliefs or organizational "value" systems based on the behavior of key leaders in the power elite (**F6**) is essential to the success of any significant and sustainable organizational change. Change in perceptions can be facilitated through a number of problem-solving approaches, both formal and informal, which also confront the issue of managerial initiative as defined by a manager willing to take a proactive or hands-off approach.

Depending on the circumstances (i.e. timing) and contextual environment (i.e. who are in key stakeholder positions), both approaches have merit in being able to achieve particularly unpopular or futuristic ends. Informal power networks also play a critical role in moving people who are "riding the fence" and are looking for direction from key stakeholders towards adopting "the viewpoint" of perceived power brokers on a hot-button issues such as diversity in hiring practices. The use of rewards (both symbolic and material) as reinforcements for attitudinal change would also emphasize the influences brought to bear by an initiating or resisting manager. Practically, this is a slow and complex process in which it is likely to be necessary to replace the resisting individuals over time through attrition by means of retirements, resignations, or firings.

The clash of external and internal forces within each of the respective environments of MLB, the NCAA, and the USOC will ultimately determine the specific strategies which are evolved and articulated. Of particular interest to this study is the potential impact of each of the ten critical change factors on the implementation and success of a strategic or ad hoc integration process. In the case of MLB, the integration of talented African-Americans helped change the balance of power (i.e. the Dodgers, Braves, Giants, and Indians of the late 1940s and 1950s and the Reds and Pirates in the 1970s) and helped increase game attendance for the winning teams. The NCAA and the United States Olympic Committee (USOC) continue to be more responsive to the potential punitive consequences of federal regulations if integration is not adequately addressed based on federal standards (i.e. Title IX and the Amateur Sports Act of 1978) as evidenced by strategic action following changes in federal laws and several unsuccessful defenses of the status quo in civil lawsuits.

Using a standard construct of a "systems approach" to strategic planning and implementation (**F10**) from which to create a comparative analysis of each of the case examples, the following conclusions were drawn: The United States Olympic Committee through its annual and quadrennial High Performance Review Process is the most practiced and invested in strategic management principles of the three supra-organizations. The National Collegiate Athletic Association employs an equally sophisticated strategic process and structure within its national organization; however, it does not have the same influence and control to implement this process on a more regional (i.e. conferences) or local level (i.e. colleges and universities).

A commitment to a theory-based systems approach by the power elite in a sport organization can help facilitate a more comprehensive change in a shorter span of time than if this process is left to a more ad hoc approach. The final critical change factor (**F10**) in the CCF Model remains necessary, but not sufficient in or of itself, to effect change. Used in a combined strategy of an understanding of the value and influence of the nine other factors, internal (i.e. managers and executive leaders) and external (i.e. watchdog and advocacy) forces can effectively challenge the prevailing and dominant hegemonic forces of an organization or supra-organization.

Strategy, in and of itself, cannot produce change. Strategic processes can and will also be used by the power elite within an organization or supra-organization to continue to resist change. Strategy, therefore, has no inherent attachment to "good" or "bad" purposes within an organizational structure. Ultimately, it is the process through which action can be managed in which specific measurable goals and principles can be achieved. It appears evident that a commitment to a theory-based systems approach by the power elite in a sport organization can help facilitate a more comprehensive change with respect to integration of identity groups in a shorter span of time than if this process is left to a more ad hoc approach.

Ultimately, the use of strategic processes by the power elite of an organization can help affect the greater acceleration of "higher levels" of integration of ID groups within each of these respective supra-organizations. The relevancy of the longitudinal histories of African-Americans and women and the value of the theory-based CCF Model appears to be very strong and appropriate on the process of inclusion of athletes with disabilities into the USOC and its related NGBs. A broad question remains regarding what general set of recommendations can be gleaned from these three case studies for managers who may be confronted in the future with integrating a mono-cultural organization.

If one knows the general character of mono-cultural organizations and their "defenses", and one can identify critical change factors which have helped other organizations overcome these defenses in the past, then he or she should be able to develop some unique recommendations which will help a manager confront a particular situation. Due to spatial constraints, the following six recommendations have been greatly condensed. The reader can contact the author for a copy of the full text.

Recommendations

Sport managers and the executive leadership within sport organizations may wish to consider the following six recommendations. These recommendations are intended to serve as strategies for moving sport governance structures and their respective sport organizations along the OC model to becoming more tolerant, accepting, valuing, and inclusive organizations with respect to individuals based on race, gender, disability and/or other identity characteristics that are commonly used to stereotype and marginalize groups of people. Although the strategies in this study are aimed principally at practitioners in the field, they maybe deemed to be of value to policy makers, special interest groups who are advocating for greater social justice in sport, and members of the identity groups who are seeking inclusion into previously exclusive and/or tokenly integrated sport organizations. Although three specific case examples of sport governance structures were used for this study (i.e. MLB, NCAA sponsored intercollegiate sport, and the USOC and its related NGBs), these recommendations are intended to be more universally applied to any sport organization in any segment of the industry which is facing similar issues.

Recommendation 1: Involvement at all stratification levels

To quote a well worn phrase used in shooting sports, a "ready, fire, aim" approach to problem-solving or ad hoc strategy planning is both wasteful and counterproductive. Given the histories of power struggles among in-groups and out-groups, a new climate of trust, respect and cooperation must be created in each of the sport governance structures of this study. Too often key decisions are made without the full knowledge and input of all the primary stakeholders. The recommendations put forth must be inclusive of not just the policy makers (executives and administrators) and the service providers (directors & coaches), but also must conspicuously value the perceptions and ideas of the athletes (development through elite levels).

Ideally, everyone in an organization needs to be invested (i.e. involved) according to their level of expertise in the strategic management process. This does not mean that an organization must function as a "committee of the whole" in which rules of consensus are employed. Rather, it means that an astute manager/leader needs to tap existing expertise from all stratification levels, plus involve an organization's consumer base (i.e. so-called critical publics).

Organizations (i.e. MLB, the USOC, and the NCAA) which provide sport as entertainment (i.e. as a commercialized product) to a definable clientele or "critical public" (i.e. the fans and viewers) must add the perceptions and ideas of these stakeholders as having important value. Strategic management processes are potentially the most effective and sustaining pathways to more inclusive organizations. The "devil is in the details" as any organization or sport governance system becomes committed to actively implement meaningful, and lasting organizational change.

Recommendation 2: Commitment to distributive justice principles (changing the will)

The enterprise of change is no less than a profound cultural paradigm shift where the embedded hierarchies of privilege and control must seek clear and measurable means to redistribute wealth, power, and access to finite resources. Stakeholders at all stratification levels, both internal and external to an organization, must become familiar with the basic principles of distributive justice. A strong and encompassing mission statement supported by clearly defined and measurable goals and objectives regarding the value and form of diversity within an organization needs to be articulated. A substantial organizational commitment at all stratification levels (i.e. working, middle, and executive classes) to a strategic management approach to organizational change must be stated publicly and sustained through the vigilance of external watchdog and advocacy groups.

Recommendation 3: Transcending the barriers of limited resources (real or perceived)

Executives and middle managers in sport organizations undergoing change need to find new and better ways to identify and obtain the critical resources needed to accommodate the inclusion of identity groups within their sport environments. These managers also need to develop the potential existing available resources. In the cases of the NCAA (gender) and the USOC (disability), this may mean expanding their existing fundraising and corporate marketing strategies to identify new donors or explore new market niches. This represents a neglected and potentially powerful idea.

Inclusiveness is most often dealt with from the perspective of being a moral value, as being worthy in itself. Perhaps, change can be accelerated by inducing the realization among managers, that, with changing demographics and value positions, inclusion has the potential for demonstrable financial returns. This could be defined as "enlightened self-interest." Individuals with disabilities and their families are, for example, extremely loyal to corporations which actively hire and promote people with disabilities. As a potential consumer group, over 54 million individuals with disabilities represent a virtual untapped market. Paralympic sports have the potential to become a new niche market.

Recommendation 4: Training and education

To facilitate integration, each of these sport governance systems needs to develop effective strategic processes to help promote greater diversity and equity within their respective member organizations. To do so, there needs to be committed centralized leadership in each of these governance structures which helps chart the course for other members, institutions, and franchises to emulate.

As part of a training and education process, middle and executive level managers need to develop critical negotiation and mediation skills involved in the development and management of greater diversity in the workplace. To accomplish this, workplace diversity training needs to occur throughout an organization at all stratification levels. This training should consider incorporating and utilizing the CCF and OC models. The representation of in-groups and out-groups in this process becomes paramount. Ultimately, a group of key stakeholders will decide the distribution or re-distribution of power and finite resources. Without the presence of out-group members, the potential for decisions reflecting the status quo or "business as usual" remains high.

Recommendation 5: Transparency and systemic interaction

Each of the sport governance systems in this study needs to publish a strategic plan for vertical integration that is subject to public scrutiny through the mass media. Part of this plan would require a clearly articulated system for resource development; the development of a hot list of candidates from the ID group to aid in vertical integration; and greater representation and democratization within a given sport governance system inclusive of ID group members.

Recommendation 6: A new way of leading - openness and accountability

Any strategic initiative launched by these governance structures will require a more open process of verification of the implementation and maintenance of higher levels of integration from independent, external sources. Without these mechanisms providing critical feedback to a variety of invested stakeholders, an open system of integration becomes a closed system which reinforces the status quo of hegemony and tokenism. The power elite within sport organizations must become committed to a new way of leadership predicated on openness and accountability.

Directions for Future Research

There continues to be a need for further study with regard to the nature and levels of the integration of traditionally marginalized identity groups (i.e. race, gender, and disability) into the sport industry. New research models need to be developed which analyze integration and inclusion of individuals from a spectrum of identity groups into all aspects of sport. In addition, further study is urgently needed in developing new conceptual frameworks (taxonomies) which link the critical relationships among all levels of the sport performance pyramid from the unofficial games of the sandlot to the most elite levels of a given sport. Incumbent in these new frameworks would be the inclusion of collateral support networks such as the sporting goods industry, facilities, sport agency, and sport marketing firms which fuel the sport enterprise.

There also need to be more qualitative studies involving stakeholder interviews of athletes, administrators, and leaders within sport organizations to help determine the levels of tolerance, acceptance, and valuing of identity groups who have achieved some limited integration in a given organization. Additional qualitative studies would be helpful in examining the critical versus circumstantial pathways to success which members of a particular identity group have taken to become included in traditionally not inclusive sport environments. Athletes with disabilities have a rich history of athletic achievement, however, it remains almost virtually silent due to the limitations of oral rather than published histories. The history of the experiences of athletes with disabilities in sport, similar to the ones developed for this study on race and gender, needs to be written to help demonstrate that the segregation of sport by disability is similar to that of the segregation of sport by race and gender. By doing so, the public awareness of sport for athletes with disabilities can be vastly increased.

Given the complexities and demands on workplace diversity, future research needs to be more complex, inclusive and comparative in its design and approach. One of the underlying principles of this study was to actively link the challenges facing individuals from diverse identity groups as based on race, gender, and disability as being profoundly similar. More research is required in looking at an expansion of critical theory to accommodate a new body of knowledge (i.e. critical disability theory) to take its place alongside critical race and critical feminist literature. A new movement within some higher education institutions to develop "disability studies" as a curricular option similar to African-American studies and women's studies will need more research into all dimensions of American culture with respect to individuals with disabilities.

Other studies need to be developed which can assess the relevance of existing assessment models and strategies which focus on analyzing vertical integration and inclusion in professional sports and/or in college athletics for the purposes of developing a comparable assessment model related to disability. Such studies could be followed by further research into the development of a standard assessment procedure and instrument to assess and evaluate the degree of and levels of participation and integration/inclusion of athletes with disabilities into the organizational structures and operations of NGBs, DSOs, multi-sport Organizations and the USOC itself.

This new research would add significantly to the current body of knowledge and level of understanding regarding the inclusion of athletes with disabilities into the elite sport movement as organized through the USOC and its respective NGBs and DSOs. This research would also lead to the development, linking and networking of key resources – clearing houses and resource banks which have long been absent. It is hoped also that this research could have practical impact on the field of sport management by emphasizing the relationship with current research in the more general field of workplace diversity and/or organizational change which could be relevant to sport organizations.

Future Significance

What then is the potential significance of this comprehensive study to the field of sport management? Joy DeSensi, past NASSM president, stated in her address to the annual Conference of the North American Society for Sport Management (1994) that there was a void of sport management research utilizing a multicultural approach to examining issues of diversity in sport organizations. She expressed that:

> *"The oppression of all people, through racism, sexism, class-ism, ageism, able-ism, homophobia, and any other form of discrimination, contributes to the establishing of serious barriers for everyone. My hope is for a true multicultural understanding within sport and especially on the part of our sport managers administrators, as well as the educators preparing these professionals"* (DESENSI 1994, p. 73).

DePauw and Gavron (1995, p. 206) reinforced DeSensi's remarks by stating bluntly that "ethnicity, race, and class and their relation to disability sport have not been studied."

It is hoped that this study has directly addressed the concerns of DeSensi and DePauw and Gavron. The significance of this study may also rest on the fact that it was designed to speak directly to the managers, administrators and executive leadership involved in sport management. Specifically, this study is meant to be a call to arms that "good practice" can be enhanced through "good theory". A theory-based model grounded in the application of strategic management processes can make a difference in creating more inclusive environments. Ultimately, this study attempted to develop a new paradigm towards full participation and equal opportunity in sport that is inclusive of individuals based on race, gender, and disability. For a copy of this 468 page study including a 75 page bibliography, please contact the author.

References

ACOSTA, R.V. & CARPENTER, L.J.: Women in intercollegiate sport: A longitudinal study - nineteen year update. Brooklyn, New York 1996

AMATEUR SPORTS ACT OF 1978: PL 95-606, 36 U.S.C.A. 391

AMERICANS WITH DISABILITIES ACT OF 1990: United States Senate. 42 U.S.C.A. 1201 et seq.

BLAUVELT, H.: Martin adjusts to life on the tour. In: USA Today (1998), p. IOC

CARR-RUFFINO, N.: Managing diversity: People skills for a multicultural workplace. Los Angeles, CA. 1996

COAKLEY, J.J.: Sport in society: Issues and controversies. 6th ed. St. Louis, 1998

DELGADO, R. (ed.): Critical race theory: The cutting edge. Philadelphia 1995

DEPAUW, K. P., & GAVRON, S. J.: Disability and sport. Champaign, IL. 1995.

DESENSI, J. T.: Multiculturalism as an issue in sport management. In: Journal of Sport Management 8 (1994), 1, p. 63–74

EITZEN, D. S. & SAGE, G.H.: Sociology of North American sport. 5th ed. Dubuque, IA. 1993

ESTY, K., GRIFFIN, R. & HIRSCH, M.S.: Workplace diversity, Holbrook, MA, 1995

FAY, T.G.: Race, gender, and disability: A new paradigm towards full participation and equal opportunity in sport. Doctoral Dissertation. University of Massachusetts, Amherst 1999

GOULDNER, A. W.: The norm of reciprocity: A preliminary statement. In: American Sociological Review 25 (1960), 2, p. 161-178

GRUNEAU, R.: Class, sports, and social development. Amherst, MA 1983

HAINES, S.G. & MCCOY, K.: Sustaining high performance: The strategic transformation to a customer-focused learning organization. Delray Beach, FL 1995

HUMS, M.A. & CHELLADURAI, P.: Distributive justice in intercollegiate athletics: Development of an instrument. In: Journal of Sport Management 8 (1994), 3, p. 190-199

HUMS, M.A. & CHELLADURAI, P.: Distributive justice in intercollegiate athletics: The views of NCAA coaches and administrators. In: Journal of Sport Management 8 (1994), 3, p. 200-217

LAPCHICK, R.: 1997 Racial report card. Boston, MA 1998

MARX, R. B. & THEROUX, J.: Principles of management: A modular text. Needham Heights, MA 1996

MINTZBERG, H.: Power in and around organizations. Englewood Cliffs, NJ 1983

MINTZBERG, H. & QUINN, J.B.: The strategy process: Concepts and contexts. Englewood Cliffs, NJ 1992

PFEFFER, J. & SALANICK, G.R.: The external control of organizations. A resource dependence perspective. New York 1978

RADER, B.G.: American sports: From the age of folk games to the age of televised sports. Upper Saddle River, NJ 1996

SABO, D.F.: Women's Sports Foundation Gender Equity Report Card 1997. East Meadow, NY 1997

SAGE, G.H.: Power and ideology in American sport: A critical perspective.2nd ed. Champaign, IL 1998

SHROPSHIRE, K. L.: In black and white: Race and sports in America. New York 1996

STEVENS, T.: Ted Stevens Olympic and Amateur Sports Act. 36 U.S.C.A. 2205 et seq. 1998

TITLE IX REGULATIONS, 45 C.F.R. Part 86 (1975) codified 106 (1991)

TOMBLOM, K.Y. & JONSSON, D.S.: Subrules of the equality and contribution principles: Their perceived fairness in distribution and retribution. In: Social Psychology Quarterly 48 (1985), p. 249-261

TOMBLOM, K.Y. & JONSSON, D.S.: Distribution vs. retribution: The perceived justice of the contribution and equality principles for cooperative and competitive relationships. In: Acta Sociologica 30 (1987), p. 25-52

The integration and inclusion of world class disability sports programmes

David McCrae

UK Sport Disability Project, Glasgow, United Kingdom

History - Where Have We Come from?

In most of the world's countries, disability sport has evolved, for the best part, outside of "mainstream sport" and has been organised under a heading which centred on disability, (i.e. amputees, spinal injuries, visual impairments, etc.). These associations / organisations would often be run by a volunteer force with tremendous enthusiasm; however they are less likely to have a full-time or professional input to them. The quality of expertise accessed by these organisations would often be diluted. Today there are examples from various countries around the world of almost every possible permutation available of organisations from completely inclusive and integrated to almost completely isolated from other aspects of sport. The presentation will examine these possibilities.

Integration/Inclusion (What Do We Mean?)

Definitions

To integrate - "combine (parts) into a whole, bring or come into full membership of a community";
to include - "have or treat as part of whole, put into a specified category";
inclusive - "including what is mentioned, including everything".

The very definitions of these words and the range with which the definitions can be interpreted, give us an idea of the range of models of integration and inclusion which are available to us in disability sport.

Why bother?

Our performers, in whichever nation they are, are demanding the best input from coaches, sport scientists, technicians, medical staff, and indeed core management of sports. Standards are now such within the Paralympic Movement that the athletes also deserve the very best input we, the administrators, can give them. The standards at all levels of competition continue to rise with almost alarming speed and if athletes are to stay at the top, they require the very best focussed input from whichever services are required. Due to this level of competition, the very best input might just give the performer the "edge" to win.

Social inclusion is now high on the agenda of many senior nations in the Paralympic Movement in the governance of their countries as well as sport. Sport can affect those concerned in the political world as well as within the sporting world.

Practical Examples

Australia - Athletics Australia

Athletics Australia takes responsibility for elite track and field athletes with a disability. Its overall operation has performance and development responsibility. Within the development arm of Athletics Australia lies schools, junior, and disability. Within that structure a disability advisory committee is chaired by the Development Manager of Athletics Australia and representatives from each of the disability groups are part of that committee. Other representatives from the Australian Paralympic Committee, the Australian Institute of Sport national coach and an athlete representative are also key to that committee. The performance arm of Athletics Australia, in its competition structure, includes Paralympic events within its Grand Prix circuit and indeed also organises the national championships for athletes with a disability. This highlights a range of examples of inclusion within the Athletics Australia structure.

United Kingdom - UK World Class Performance Programme

The World Class Performance Programme within the UK is funded by the income of the national lottery. It supports national governing bodies of sport within the UK and in the Paralympic area has a range of models of inclusion of these. All except one elite sport programme are 'sport-specific' regardless of Olympic or Paralympic. This exception is that of the British Paralympic Association, whose programme focuses on the generic preparation and actual attendance of the Sydney 2000 team at the Games. Awards are allocated by the government sport agency, UK Sport, and programmes are delivered themselves by the sports. Paralympic sports currently in the World Class Performance Programme are: Athletics, swimming, equestrian, judo, cycling, sailing, wheelchair basketball, table tennis, goalball, wheelchair rugby, shooting and powerlifting. Different models include:

Swimming - The Amateur Swimming Federation of Great Britain takes responsibility for elite swimming for people with disabilities within the UK. It is the national governing body of sport in Great Britain and treats Paralympic swimming as a discipline of its work (i.e. part of/including diving, synchronised swimming, masters, water polo, Olympic, and Paralympic).

Sailing - The Paralympic sailing disciplines (Sonar and 2.4) are fully inclusive in the Royal Yachting Association World Class Performance Plan. The athletes are not even named as Paralympic, only as the name of the discipline which happens to be a Paralympic boat.

Table tennis – The British Table Tennis Association for Disabled People is a disability association specifically for that sport and is given current responsibility to administer the plan in the absence of an appropriate UK body able to administer a plan (mainstream).

Goalball - Goalball is treated as a sport within its own right with a World Class Plan and is given support from a service unit within the Sports Council for its financial and administration purposes.

Scotland - a small country that makes it work

In Scotland, many athletes who are part of Great Britain teams are also within a structure in their smaller nation, Scotland, which has one organisation with responsibility for people with disabilities - Scottish Disability Sport. This agency also caters for development, young people etc. The agency has very strong partnerships with the mainstream governing bodies of sport within Scotland, in particular in Paralympic terms, the Scottish Athletics Federation, and the Scottish Amateur Swimming Association. Scottish Disability Sport runs on a very small grant award from Sportscotland (government agency) and the very best Paralympic athletes are included within the Scottish Institute of Sport athlete services programme.

Critical Success Factors

The critical success factors for all of these examples can be crystallised as follows:

- Standards of performance must be high.
- The athletes themselves must be ambassadors of the sport they represent.
- The quality of the programmes undertaken must be seen as on a par with any mainstream counterparts and in particular where they are inclusive within these bodies.
- The credibility of athletes, performers, coaches etc will be crucial to the sustainability of any programme.

In the speaker's view this most definitely produces better performance. It does the following:

- concentrates the quality of support to the athletes
- gives the athletes respect which matches the level of performance
- gives them access to a greater quantity and higher quality of service
- encourages infrastructure improvement within organisations and therefore a higher degree of sustainability.

Conclusions - Why?

As we become more professional in this field, accountability will always become an increasing factor. World standards are rising and if we, as nations, want to continue and indeed to sustain our funding for the future, the very best outcomes must be achieved. The "stage" must be the very best for our athletes. They deserve to be able to perform on that stage. Our countries want to be the best, to top the medal table and obtain every "edge" we can get. It is vital to maintaining this degree of professionalism. Our athletes want to be the best, they want to succeed, and they want to have the top medals around their neck.

Acknowledgements

Many thanks are extended to UK Sport, to Chris Nunn of the Australian Institute of Sport, and to Scottish Disability Sport.

Inclusion - the Canadian experience

Ray Allard, Rebeccah Bornemann

Sport Canada, Ottawa, Canada

Preliminary Note

The issue of the inclusion of athletes with a disability is a complex one; even the language used to describe experiences is inexact and used differently in different contexts. For the purposes of this paper, we will use the word "inclusion" to describe a process whereby athletes with a disability become fully-participating members of a sport organization, with access to programs and services on par with their mainstream counterparts. "Mainstream" will refer to the traditional or "able-bodied" sport system.

The majority of inclusion activities in Canada have focused on Paralympic sport. For this reason, most of the following discusses the inclusion of Paralympic-stream athletes into the mainstream sport system. Where appropriate, other scenarios are considered.

Throughout the main body of text, there are names of programs that appear in bold letters. Brief overviews of these programs are provided in an appendix at the back.

Introduction

The Canadian federal government's support to amateur sport organizations dates back to the early sixties with the introduction of the **Fitness and Amateur Sport Act** and the establishment of the Fitness and Amateur Sport Branch. From the outset, funding for mainstream National Sport Organizations (NSOs) was provided from the Sport Unit of the Branch, while support for disability-based NSOs was from the Recreation Unit. Thus two parallel sport systems were established, one for mainstream sport-based organizations, the other for disability-based sport organizations that served athletes with a disability.

Over the years, fitness and amateur sport has been the responsibility of several departments through various government reorganizations, and the two parallel sport systems continue to exist. The same government branch - Sport Canada, within the Department of Canadian Heritage - is today responsible for supporting both systems (Fig. 1).

The reorganization of the government responsibility for sport clearly played a role in inclusion. Other factors, including two government-wide initiatives, were largely responsible for starting the process of inclusion. **The National Strategy for the Integration of Persons with Disabilities** (NSIPD or National Strategy) was introduced in 1991. In 1993 a "program review was launched, designed to identify and eliminate areas of duplication in federal government programming, thus streamlining the system. Together with the decision of the Canadian Wheelchair Sports Organization in 1993-94 to "get out of business" by lobbying for, and achieving, the inclusion of athletes in their areas of responsibility into mainstream sport organizations, these programs provided the driving force behind inclusion.

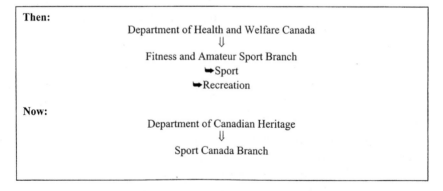

Fig. 1: Federal Government Departments involved in sport

Since 1991, programs and services for athletes with a disability have been gradually transferred from disability-based NSOs to mainstream NSOs. In the late eighties, disability-based NSOs received funding from the federal government for programs and services for all 21 summer and winter Paralympic sports in which Canada was represented. Today that number has been reduced to approximately six sports funded through disability-based organizations, with mainstream NSOs currently providing programs and services to the remaining fifteen Paralympic sports. In addition, just six disability-based organizations are funded for their programs and services, including the non-Paralympic affiliated Canadian Deaf Sports Association and Canadian Special Olympics, Inc. This paper will discuss the Canadian inclusion approach and experience. It will explore the process to date, and discuss our successes and challenges for the future.

Influencing Factors

A number of factors have influenced the inclusion process for athletes with a disability into mainstream sport organizations. These range from environmental to organizational influences; some have been planned, others serendipitous. All have had an impact (Fig. 2).

The National Strategy for the Integration of Persons with Disabilities was a five-year program launched in 1991. With an overall budget of $157.8 million, the goal of this interdepartmental federal government program was to address barriers to participation in all aspects of society for Canadians with a disability. While a small proportion of this funding was directed into sport inclusion projects, this funding support helped to serve as a catalyst to encourage inclusion.

Federal government reorganization has also played a role in the support of inclusion. The 1993 program review aimed at reducing administrative cost and duplication of programs and services throughout the federal government resulted in the parallel mainstream and disability-based sport systems coming under fire. Thus Sport

Canada was encouraged to step up its program inclusion initiatives currently underway with aid of the National Strategy.

> **Federal Government**
>   - reorganization
>   - national strategy for the integration of persons with disabilities
>   - program review
>
> **Funding**
>   - funding and accountability framework for athletes with a disability
>   - Athlete Assistance Program
>   - new funding for sport
>
> **Community Involvement**
>   - disability sport (CWSA and CIAD)
>   - mainstream sport (Athletes CAN)
>
> **Growth of the Paralympic Movement**

Fig. 2: Influencing factors

In addition, responsibility for amateur sport moved from the Department of Health and Welfare Canada to the Department of Canadian Heritage in a major government-wide reorganization in 1995. The mandate of the Department of Canadian Heritage is "Strengthening and Celebrating Canada," with an emphasis on promoting the diversity within Canadian society. Support for athletes with a disability, as well as the inclusion agenda, fits well within this mandate. Sport for athletes with a disability is supported within the department, and the successes of and concerning athletes with a disability are given good visibility.

Funding from the federal government for projects has also had an impact on the inclusion process. The National Strategy provided funds for inclusion projects with different sports (such as swimming and tennis), thereby enabling the necessary handover processes to occur.

Another initiative funded partly by the National Strategy was the **Committee on Integration of Athletes with Disabilities** (CIAD). Under the direction of Rick Hansen (of the Man in Motion world tour, and former Paralympic athlete), CIAD is a commission of the International Paralympic Committee, and has been in existence since 1990. The mandate of CIAD is to gain inclusion of selected full medal events for athletes with a disability in major international competitions. The Committee on Integration of Athletes with Disabilities was funded by the federal government for a two-year period and was successful in creating events for athletes with a disability in the World Athletic Championships and the 1994 Commonwealth Games, as well as raising the overall profile of sport for athletes with a disability.

Programs within Sport Canada for funding National Sport Organizations have further affected inclusion. Since 1995, there have been three major funding developments within the Canadian federal government for athletes with a disability. These are the **Funding and Accountability Framework for Athletes with Disabilities** (FAFAD), the **Athlete Assistance Program** (AAP), and the **New Funding for Sport** (NFS) program.

The Funding and Accountability Framework for Athletes with Disabilities (FAFAD) was introduced to provide funding to both disability-based and mainstream NSOs that provide programs and services for athletes with a disability. While similar to the **Sport Funding and Accountability Framework** (SFAF), introduced in 1995 for mainstream sport, FAFAD recognizes the unique aspects and diverse needs of sport for athletes with disabilities. The FAFAD provides a funding structure that is more in line with the mainstream sport system, and is used to determine which NSOs are eligible for funding and the funding ranges available to each organization. Between the two frameworks, the federal government currently funds a total of 40 mainstream NSOs and 6 disability-based NSOs.

The two funding frameworks share the same basic philosophy and operating principles. Of these, the development of accountability is an integral component of SFAF/FAFAD. All mainstream NSOs receiving funding must negotiate an Accountability Agreement with the federal government. The agreements are based on key objectives from the NSO's multi-year plan in areas of federal government priority for sport. The purpose of the accountability agreement is to ensure that public funding contributes to the achievement of federal priorities and policy objectives. Within these Agreements there are minimum expectations in five areas, of which the area of athletes with a disability is one. Thus mainstream NSOs that have not pursued inclusion to date are further encouraged to consider the prospect.

Another funding program operated through Sport Canada is the Athlete Assistance Program. The AAP provides direct support to qualifying athletes, including a monthly allowance, tuition credits, and access to National Sport Centres and other support services. While athletes with a disability have been able to access the program for some time, recent (1998/99) modifications have ensured that they are eligible for funding opportunities similar to those of their mainstream counterparts. These modifications also provide support to tandem cycling pilots and guide runners/skiers who qualify along with their visually impaired partner. This expansion of access has significantly increased the number of eligible athletes and the level of support available to each athlete. For example, prior to the program modifications, roughly fifty athletes with a disability received support through AAP. Today that number approaches 160 athletes.

The third federal government funding development was introduced in 1998. The New Funding for Sport program consists of three central components; athlete assistance, training and competition and coaching support. This new initiative focused its funding support on the federal government primary target, the high performance athlete, and was designed to augment and enhance the existing funding programs. Indeed, the above mentioned modifications to the AAP were made possible by the New Funding for Sport. All three types of NFS funding are accessible for programs and services for athletes with a disability, thereby expanding the dollars available to serve these athletes and making the idea of inclusion much more financially attractive to mainstream NSOs, as well as providing better support services for athletes with a disability.

The sum effect of these funding initiatives is that the federal government's support for athletes with a disability has increased from approximately $800,000 in the early 1990s to over $3,000,000 in 1999. While financial resources have been an unquestionably strong motivating factor in support of inclusion, certain environmental factors - both in Canada and internationally - have been important in encouraging the process.

For example, the work of the Commission for the Integration of Athletes with a Disability has heightened the awareness of sport for athletes with a disability and facilitated future inclusion discussions within the mainstream sport community.

Athletes from the mainstream sport system have also played a critical role in the inclusion process. In addition to supporting their colleagues with a disability in training and competitive settings, Canadian athletes have shown their support from an organizational standpoint. In 1992, athletes from various national teams concerned with the general lack of access to the decision-making process within sport organizations formed a national athletes' organization, now known as **Athletes CAN**. From the outset, athletes with a disability were welcomed into the group as equals. In fact, several athletes with a disability have helped the organization evolve into a legitimate entity representing the views and interests of all of Canada's high performance athletes. This in turned served to legitimize athletes with a disability not just within the context of Athletes CAN but also within the broader Canadian sport system.

Another influential environmental factor has been the incredible growth of the worldwide Paralympic movement. The increasing levels of competition evident from the 1988 Seoul Paralympics to the 1996 Atlanta Games have had a positive influence on the inclusion process. The technical leadership required to maintain Canada's performance standing at world championships and Paralympic Games encouraged disability-based NSOs to approach their mainstream counterparts for technical assistance in the areas of coaching and coaching development, training, competition opportunities, sport science and sport medicine. The positive reaction of the mainstream NSOs, together with the funding commitments of the federal government for sport for athletes with a disability, was very important to the inclusion movement.

Guiding principles

The increased funding, along with greater understanding and collaboration between the parallel sport systems created a positive climate for inclusion. The momentum established through the National Strategy, as well as the effort to keep pace with the growth of the Paralympic movement and the associated training and competition needs of the athletes have ensured the continuation of the process. Developments relating to inclusion have significantly changed the nature of sporting opportunities for athletes with a disability in Canada. The following guiding principles were developed by the federal government to help shape the evolution of sport for athletes with a disability, and to continue to advance the inclusion agenda:

- Adapted or modified sports for athletes with a disability would be supported through mainstream NSOs;

- Disability-based sport organizations would be encouraged to provide leadership and direction to advance the inclusion agenda;

- Mainstream NSOs would be encouraged to gradually assume greater responsibility for technical leadership, administrative and governance of sport for athletes with a disability;

- Other key partners within the Canadian sport system would be encouraged to form strategic alliances with NSOs to advance the inclusion agenda;

- Funding support would be directed to sports on the calendar of Major Games;

- Inclusion would be made a high priority in the allocation of funds through the various federal funding programs;

- Funding support would be directed to athletes with a disability, not necessarily to sport organizations for athletes with a disability.

Inclusion Projects

While Sport Canada has clearly promoted inclusion for athletes with a disability into the mainstream sport system, inclusion has not occurred in any one single way. With funding made available for such initiatives, inclusion projects began to unfold in the mid-1990s and continue to date. The process in each instance has been shaped by the particular situations of each of the groups involved, and each project developed differently. The following provides an overview of some of the projects, namely in swimming, cycling, athletics, tennis, and wheelchair basketball.

Swimming

Swimming/Natation Canada (SNC) has served swimmers with a disability for the past six years. This was the first inclusion project involving the transfer of administration, technical leadership, and governance from the sport community for athletes with a disability to a mainstream NSO. Funded under the National Strategy, the transition process was very formal and involved four disability groups (amputee, wheelchair, blind, and cerebral palsy). A Transition Team was established under the direction and leadership of the Canadian Paralympic Committee with representatives from the various disability groups, the federal government, and two athlete representatives. As was the case with most inclusion initiatives at the time, the Canadian Wheelchair Sports Association (CWSA) was the driving force behind the project (Fig. 3).

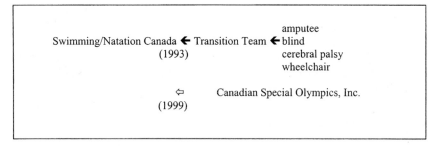

Fig. 3: Swimming inclusion

Following many months of Transition Team meetings and ongoing dialogue and negotiations with SNC, a formal fifteen page Memorandum of Understanding (MOU) was signed between the Canadian Paralympic Committee, acting on behalf of the various disability groups, and SNC. Thus control and responsibility of swimmers with a disability was transferred from the various disability groups to the mainstream NSO.

The MOU addresses in detail the following areas:

- Article I - Management and Administration: Constitution, by-laws and policies, organizational structure, membership, volunteers, operations, planning, funding, marketing and promotion, and communications.

- Article II – Technical: High performance services, i.e. national team, selection standards, athlete assistance program; domestic sport, i.e. coaching development, technical resources, competitions, rules, officiating, classification, anti-doping; and swimming community services.

- Article III – Partnership: Affiliations, communications, monitoring and evaluation.

It is also important to note that for the first two years following the signing of the MOU, the Chair of the Transition Team was a member of the Board, and the Transition Team was a Standing Committee of the SNC Board of Directors. This structure helped to ensure continuity of service, and a smooth transition of programming. This same individual has continued to serve on the Board as an elected member at large, well beyond the transition period.

Canada's performances at the most recent Paralympic Games and IPC World Swimming Championships suggest that the swimming integration project is an unqualified success. Management, administration, and especially technical expertise have benefited from the transition. However, the process is not without its critics. The transfer has been criticized in some circles for the reduction of the number of swimmers representing Canada at international meets, and for the lack of attention to the developmental aspect of swimming. Swimming/Natation Canada's response to its critics is that fewer international participants are a function of tough selection standards, which also apply to swimmers without disabilities. Furthermore, developing swimmers is a provincial/territorial responsibility, and Swimming/Natation Canada is working hard with its partners inside the organization to address this shortcoming.

It is interesting to note that the Canadian Special Olympics has also recently (June 1999) signed a Memorandum of Understanding with SNC. While this MOU discusses more a partnership between the two organizations rather than a "handover" of responsibilities (compared to the MOU signed between SNC and the Canadian Paralympic Committee), the seven-page document is extremely specific in outlining the responsibilities of each for the four-year duration of the agreement. Canadian Special Olympics will continue to provide programs and services, and will work with Swimming/Natation Canada to help ensure access for Special Olympic athletes to their programs as appropriate. This MOU between the Canadian Special Olympics and SNC comes as a result of Canadian Special Olympics' desire to develop national team programming for athletes with a mental handicap, and the solid reputation that Swimming/Natation Canada has developed over the last several years regarding their delivery of programs and services for swimmers with a disability.

Cycling

Compared to the swimming inclusion project, the cycling experience had little structure or formality. This initiative was led by the federal government, following the Atlanta Paralympics. After the 1996 Paralympic Games there were questions raised regarding the preparation programs of Canadian cyclists, as well as concerns about cyclists who had problems obtaining racing licenses from the Canadian Cycling Association prior to the competition.

An initial meeting was held with representatives from the Canadian Blind Sports Association (CBSA), the Canadian Cerebral Palsy Sports Association (CCPSA), the Canadian Cycling Association, and the federal government. The Cycling Association was very receptive to the notion of providing programs and services for cyclists with a disability. The head Canadian cycling coach at the Atlanta Paralympics was employed at the National Cycling Centre at this time, and was prepared to incorporate cyclists with a disability into his program. But the Canadian Cycling Association made it clear that, due to the relatively small number of athletes with a disability involved, it was not prepared to engage in any lengthy discussions on formal structure or a Memorandum of Understanding. Furthermore, the Canadian Cycling

Association would be willing to provide programs and services to cyclists with a disability provided that there was monetary support available from the federal government for these initiatives, and that the cyclists were members in good standing of the NSO, and were prepared to purchase racing licenses.

After several subsequent meetings, the federal government was satisfied that coaching and other technical aspects of the sport for cyclists with a disability would improve considerably under the direction of the Canadian Cycling Association. The federal government notified the Canadian Amputee Sports Association, the Canadian Blind Sports Association, and the Canadian Cerebral Palsy Sports Association that future Athlete Assistance Program matters and all future funding for cyclists with a disability would be dealt with through the Canadian Cycling Association (Fig. 4).

Canadian Cycling Association ←	Canadian Amputee Sports Association Canadian Blind Sports Association Canadian Cerebral Palsy Sports Association
(1997)	

Fig. 4: Cycling inclusion

Operating under this arrangement, cyclists with a disability have access to similar coaching, training, and competition opportunities as able-bodied cyclists. As in the case of swimming, however, there has been some criticism of the lack of work on behalf of developing cyclists with a disability. Nevertheless, it appears that attention is being devoted to this area. Prior to the move to the Canadian Cycling Association, three tandem teams competed in the CBSA 1995 National Cycling Championships. At the most recent CCA-Disabled Cycling National Championships, nine teams competed in the visually impaired events, a significant increase. The same success has not been realized for cyclists with cerebral palsy. Although several new cyclists have joined the program, growth in this area does not match that of visually impaired cyclists. This may be partly attributable to the rocky relationship between the Canadian Cycling Association and the Canadian Cerebral Palsy Sports Association; in the meantime all parties involved continue to try to resolve their differences.

Athletics

The Canadian Wheelchair Sports Association and the federal government have promoted and lobbied for the transfer of track and field athletes with a disability to Athletics Canada since the early 1990s. Until recently, Athletics Canada, due to several major internal problems, was not at all receptive to assuming responsibility for athletes with a disability. In 1997, after five years of discussion, Athletics Canada agreed to assume responsibility for wheelchair athletics with the signing of a Memorandum of Understanding with the Canadian Wheelchair Sports Association. A year later, the federal government was able to convince Athletics Canada to include amputee track and field athletes in the agreement.

This Memorandum of Understanding is a brief two-page document outlining the responsibilities of each party in the transfer agreement. The opportunities for Athletics Canada, objectives, implementation strategy, funding, and a four-phase inclusion process are addressed in more detail in a document accompanying the MOU (Fig. 5).

Fig. 5: Athletics inclusion

The initial two years of this arrangement have been difficult ones for both associations as they work through some funding issues. While Athletics Canada and CWSA debate these issues, progress on the transfer of blind and cerebral palsy athletes to Athletics Canada has been put on hold. Recently however, the federal government served notice that future applications to the Athlete Assistance Program for blind and cerebral palsy track and field athletes would only be considered through Athletics Canada. This tactic will hopefully inspire the associations in question to at least resume inclusion discussions. Amputee athletes are now served by Athletics Canada through informal agreement, as the Canadian Amputee Sports Association is not currently able to provide the necessary support.

Tennis

In July 1998 the Canadian Wheelchair Sports Association and Tennis Canada signed a formal Letter of Agreement. A simple two-page document, the intent of the letter was to define the relationship between the two parties to the benefit of wheelchair tennis athletes, coaches, and participants throughout Canada. The tennis inclusion project is often recommended to other interested parties as the approach to pursue during preliminary inclusion discussions.

Several factors contributed to the success of the tennis inclusion project. First, the Canadian Wheelchair Sports Association was very experienced in the inclusion process by this point, and had learned from shortcomings in previous projects. Tennis Canada was very receptive to the notion of serving athletes with a disability and made the project a priority. In fact, Tennis Canada and the Canadian Wheelchair Sports Association had worked very closely together following the Atlanta Paralympics in order to improve the quality of training and competition for wheelchair tennis players. Examples of cooperation included Tennis Canada assisting the Canadian Wheelchair Sports Association with coach selection, encouraging the member clubs to serve wheelchair tennis players, and helping to promote

Canada's wheelchair tennis program. The more formal agreement that later followed was reflective of an already healthy working relationship (Fig. 6).

Tennis Canada ← Canadian Wheelchair Sports Association
(1998)

Fig. 6: Tennis inclusion

Another contributing factor to the success of the inclusion project was that, just prior to approaching Tennis Canada, the Canadian Wheelchair Sports Association conducted a domestic audit to gain a better understanding of the current level of activity of wheelchair tennis in Canada. This was done to ensure that the developmental requirements of the sport (a weak area in some of the other inclusion projects) and future challenges for wheelchair tennis were clearly understood.

Once Tennis Canada was assured that federal government support would follow the wheelchair tennis players to Tennis Canada, a final meeting was held to discuss timelines for the transfer and both parties signed a Letter of Agreement. As was initially the case in the swimming inclusion project, the transition team - known as the Wheelchair Tennis Management Committee - remains intact and operates as a standing committee of Tennis Canada. The committee, through its chair, reports to the board of directors. The chair of the Wheelchair Tennis Management Committee is the same individual who had handled the transfer negotiations on behalf of the CWSA.

Although the agreement is a little more than a year old, both parties continue to be excited about the project. Tennis Canada is proud of its role in the inclusion process, and would like to be seen as a leader in the area of inclusion.

Basketball

As well as the tennis inclusion project has succeeded, the basketball inclusion project has struggled. Initially part of the Canadian Wheelchair Sports Association (CWSA), wheelchair basketball left its affiliation with the CWSA in the early nineties and struck out on its own, becoming an independent sports association and legal entity. For the next five years it mounted a strong lobby to obtain recognition and direct funding from the federal government for wheelchair basketball. The request was denied based on the federal government's position of funding only one NSO per sport in Canada, and on the guiding principle that adapted or modified sports would be supported through the mainstream NSOs.

Following the Atlanta Olympics, Basketball Canada went through a very difficult financial crisis that led to major program cuts and staff reductions. As it was experiencing difficulties serving its current athletes, it was in no position to expand operations. Basketball Canada took several years to reorganize. By March 1998, the organization had undergone a complete staff turnover, restructured its operations, moved its national office from Ottawa to Toronto, eradicated its deficit, and appeared ready to entertain discussions on inclusion with wheelchair basketball.

Although Basketball Canada seemed ready to advance inclusion, the wheelchair basketball association was still not in the least bit interested. During a preliminary meeting to discuss the prospects of some form of alliance, Basketball Canada presented a proposal recommending that the Canadian Wheelchair Basketball Association disband immediately and the sport of wheelchair basketball become part of Basketball Canada. The proposal was not well received. This initial meeting served to widen the gap between the two groups and prompted the Canadian Wheelchair Basketball Association to heighten its campaign for the federal government to recognize its independent status. The organization furthermore sought legal advice to advance its position.

Undaunted, the federal government continued to work with individual inclusion supporters within each organization in an attempt to soften positions and find common ground. After another year of negotiations and a critical vote by the Canadian Wheelchair Basketball Association to pursue affiliation with Basketball Canada - which led to the resignation of the President and the Executive Director of the Canadian Wheelchair Basketball Association - inclusion discussions between the two parties have resumed with the help of the federal government.

Current talks are centered on an arrangement that would permit the Canadian Wheelchair Basketball Association to maintain some formal structure and its involvement in technical matters and have a direct voice in Basketball Canada's decision making process. Under this approach, Basketball Canada would be the sole NSO recognized for basketball in Canada and thereby the only recipient of federal government funding, while wheelchair basketball would retain, for the time being, some of its desired autonomy. While the two organizations remain entirely separate to date, a document containing several Points of Agreement was signed in March of 1999 (Fig. 7). These points confirm the joint approach that the two organizations will take in working with the federal government, and outline areas for future potential cooperation.

Basketball Canada ⇔ Canadian Wheelchair Basketball Association
(1999)

Fig. 7: Basketball inclusion

Impact of Inclusion

The inclusion projects have had a strong influence on sport for athletes with a disability in Canada. Awareness of sport for athletes with a disability has been heightened by the process: Athletes CAN is an enthusiastic supporter of athletes with a disability, and many mainstream NSOs with responsibilities for athletes with a disability have become strong advocates on their behalf. This increased recognition within the sport community - in addition to the ongoing initiatives of the federal government - has helped to legitimize the movement, advance the inclusion agenda for athletes with a disability, and aid in the development of sport for athletes with a disability.

Athletes with a disability now have increased access to training and competitive opportunities, technical expertise, sport science and medicine support, and other support services. While the inclusion process is hardly six years old, the impact of these spinoffs is already evident in the performances of Canadian athletes. The quality and depth of the national team programs – particularly in athletics, cycling, shooting, swimming, and tennis - is increasing, which bodes well for future performances at Paralympics and World Championships.

The changing face of the sport community as more and more mainstream NSOs take responsibility for programs and services for athletes with a disability has had an undeniable impact on sport in Canada. The National Sport Organizations do not exist in isolation, but are connected to various other organizations, not least among them the major games organizations, such as the Canadian Paralympic Committee. The federal government supports these major games organizations as well as their single-sport (NSO) counterparts (through both SFAF and FAFAD), and while it is evident that the same inclusion model as that used with the NSOs would not be directly applicable to these major games organizations due to the differences in the types of services offered, there are opportunities in this area for further work in terms of inclusion.

Major Games Organizations

There are two principal ways in which major games organizations have been involved in the inclusion movement for athletes with a disability: in the inclusion of events for athletes with a disability within traditionally mainstream major games, as well as in the organization of Canadian teams for major games for athletes with a disability. In the first instance, Canadian sport officials have applied pressure to include events for athletes with a disability in mainstream major games in a number of ways; through the federal government, organizations like CIAD, or independently. The federal government has been instrumental in ensuring events at the Canada Games, while others have played a prominent role in the decision to include similar events in the Olympics, the Commonwealth Games, and les Jeux de la Francophonie.

The second way concerns the significant task of coordinating teams to participate in major games such as the Paralympics, World Special Olympics, and the World Games for the Deaf. Of the eight Major Games Sport Organizations supported by the federal government, three directly serve athletes with a disability: the Canadian Paralympic Committee (CPC), Canadian Special Olympics, Inc. (CSO), and the Canadian Deaf Sports Association (CDSA). Others, such as the Canadian Olympic Association and the Commonwealth Games Association of Canada have organized teams that have included athletes with a disability competing in demonstration events. The Commonwealth Games Association of Canada in particular showed a strong commitment to treating all team members equally.

The largest sport organization for athletes with disabilities in Canada is the Canadian Special Olympics, Inc. This organization has close to 20,000 athletes participating in eight summer and five winter sports. The CSO runs national team programs (much like the role played by NSOs), and organizes teams for major multi-sport games. Although the CSO has only recently begun to forge relationships with organizations within the mainstream sport system, it has been very active of late. In addition to signing the agreement with Swimming Natation Canada mentioned earlier, the CSO has established close working relations with the Canadian Figure Skating Association, the Canadian Speed Skating Association, Softball Canada, the Canadian Rhythmic Sportive Gymnastics Federation, and the Canadian Powerlifting Federation. To date, these relationships have focused on the exchange of technical information and leadership from mainstream NSOs and not on the transfer of program/service responsibilities, as has been the case with the sport-specific inclusion initiatives involving the other disability groups (cycling, tennis, etc.). There is consensus in the sport community that not all Special Olympics athletes would benefit from inclusion with the mainstream sport system at this time, and that the mainstream sport system is not currently well-equipped to take responsibility for all Special Olympics athletes, particularly those not in high-performance streams.

An added dimension to the community for athletes with a mental handicap is that there is a second organization in Canada providing programs and services for this population. The Canadian Association for Athletes with a Mental Handicap (CAAMH) is the national affiliate of the International Sports Federation for Persons with Intellectual Disability (INAS-FID), which is a member of the International Paralympic Committee. As such, CAAMH is more of a NSO (by virtue of the types of services offered) than a major games organization. However, they are active in only one region of the country, and furthermore have strong ties with CSO. The result of this situation is that a small number of athletes served by CAAMH - who may compete in the Paralympics - are also Special Olympics athletes, and so are accessing two sets of major games, each with their own competition protocols. The overlap between the Paralympic and Special Olympic communities presents an interesting challenge from the point of view of inclusion, consistency of treatment across disability groups, and equitable and appropriate support for all athletes.

Much like CSO, the Canadian Deaf Sports Association has a dual role coordinating international multi-sport games participation and national team programs in specific sports. In contrast to CSO, the CDSA has less interest in cooperation with the mainstream sport system. Like its international counterpart, le Comité International de Sport des Sourds (CISS), CDSA does not feel that it is part of the disability sport community, but rather part of a cultural and linguistic minority. Nor does CDSA wish for cooperation with the mainstream sport community: rather it is in the process of creating an alternative deaf-sport system, with sport-specific sport commissions being affiliated with CDSA. As the association denied affiliation status to the deaf volleyball commission after it had approached Volleyball Canada for technical expertise, it does not appear likely that any inclusion projects with CDSA would presently succeed. Furthermore, communication would be a challenge, as sign is the language used in all association interactions.

The Canadian Paralympic Committee, which focuses exclusively on coordinating and promoting teams for the Paralympics, is much more open to the idea of inclusion. Inclusion projects with the NSOs have already had a significant impact on the CPC; from the way it operates at Paralympic Games, to its membership. At the 1992 Barcelona Paralympics - prior to any of the integration projects with Paralympic sports - the Canadian mission was divided into four "teams": amputee, blind, cerebral palsy, and wheelchair. In contrast, the mission at the 1996 Atlanta Paralympics was organized by sport: athletics, cycling, swimming, etc. This change was reflective of the CPC's membership. Whereas the members used to be exclusively the disability-based NSOs (prior to April 1993, the CPC existed as the Federation of Sport Organizations for the Disabled, an organization with a somewhat broader mandate), today ten of the nineteen member associations belonging to the CPC are sport-based mainstream NSOs. This development has enabled the CPC to take advantage of the mainstream sports' expertise in technical areas such as qualification and selection standards (Fig. 8). Because of the increased inclusion in the Paralympic community, the growing overlap between the membership of the CPC and the Canadian Olympic Association (COA), and the already existing connections between the Paralympic and Olympic Games, the potential for inclusion initiatives with the Canadian Paralympic Committee is strong. In the fall of 1998, the CPC approached the Canadian Olympic Association with a proposal to have the COA assume responsibility for the Paralympic Movement in Canada, either as a fully functioning part of the organization (as in the case of the inclusion in the NSOs), or in a manner similar to the role played by the United States Olympic Committee (where their national Paralympic committee is a standing committee of the larger organization).

1992	1999
Canadian Amputee Sports Association	Athletics Canada
Canadian Association for Disabled Skiing	Canadian Amputee Sports Association
Cdn. Assoc. for Athletes with a Mental Handicap	
Canadian Blind Sports Association	Canadian Association for Disabled Skiing
	Cdn. Assoc. for Athletes with a Mental Handicap
Canadian Therapeutic Riding Association	Canadian Blind Sports Association
Canadian Wheelchair Sports Association	Canadian Cerebral Palsy Sports Association
Sledge Hockey Association of Canada	Canadian Cycling Association
	Canadian Table Tennis Association
	Canadian Therapeutic Riding Association
	Canadian Wheelchair Sports Association
	Canadian Yachting Association
	Federation of Canadian Archers
	Judo Canada
	Shooting Federation of Canada
	Sledge Hockey Association of Canada
	Swimming/Natation Canada
	Tennis Canada
	Volleyball Canada

Figure 8: Membership of the Canadian Paralympic Committee

The COA declined the offer, stating that it was premature for such a move given its current responsibilities for the 1999 Pan American Games in Winnipeg, and its ongoing preparations for the 2000 Olympics. The COA did, however, agree to leave the door open for future discussions following the Sydney 2000 Olympic and Paralympic Games.

In the meantime, the two organizations are working together to help prepare their teams for future games. An example of this cooperation is the established practice of document exchange on issues relating to the Paralympic/Olympic Games. The COA and the CPC also work together to brief core mission staff for the Games; cooperation in this particular area has increased steadily since 1992. Furthermore, as a measure of goodwill, the COA includes information on the Paralympics in a school kit that the COA produces prior to each winter and summer Olympic Games.

Federal government practices have also reflected the growing recognition and inclusion of athletes with a disability in a major games context. Beginning in 1992, the federal government began consistently holding receptions for Canadian medallists at games – both Olympics and Paralympics together. These high-profile events, hosted by the Prime Minister and (in 1996) the Speaker of the House, have underlined the federal government commitment to inclusion of athletes with a disability. Following the 1997 World Special Olympic Games, a separate reception was also held to recognize returning Canadian medallists.

Lessons Learned from Inclusion Initiatives

Inclusion has been extremely successful from the point of view of sport development in Canada for athletes with a disability. Strides have been made in terms of improved performances, heightened general awareness of sport for athletes with a disability, and increased sensitivity to the needs of athletes with a disability. Athletes with a disability are now included in major national discussions and projects as equals, and not simply additions. In turn, athletes with a disability have added value to the Canadian sport system. In addition to their impressive international performances and results, Canadian athletes with a disability serve on Boards of Directors of various NSOs and Major Games Organizations, they provide feedback to governments on policy development, and serve as positive role models for all Canadians.

The inclusion process has not, however, always been a smooth one. As discussed previously, some inclusion initiatives have been more successful than others, and certain themes continue to need to be addressed. Some of the major points learned from the inclusion experience include:

- the importance of raising awareness and sharing knowledge

- the role of funding in making initiatives work

- the need for cooperation between the organizations involved

- the necessity of a flexible approach.

Raising awareness played a key role in the inclusion process. The federal government encouraged sport organizations to seek out partnerships in various ways, one of which was to include a category on athletes with a disability in the Accountability Agreements with each mainstream sport organization. This approach encouraged NSOs to investigate the possibility of including athletes with a disability in their programs. Disseminating information about the success of Canada's athletes with a disability, and efforts to raise the profile of the Paralympic movement in Canada have also had a positive impact on the receptivity of mainstream NSOs.

Sharing information also facilitated the transfer of knowledge between organizations in the inclusion process. The needs assessment done by the Canadian Wheelchair Sports Association prior to its agreement with Tennis Canada helped the latter organization to better plan for domestic development of wheelchair tennis in Canada, as well as providing an opportunity to better know what the organization was "getting into."

Where inclusion has been successful, a continuing flow of knowledge and expertise also seems to have been crucial. In each of the inclusion initiatives some provision has been made to ensure that a transfer of knowledge occurred. In the case of both swimming and athletics, staff members from the disability sport community were hired to take care of the technical demands of the programs for athletes with a disability, and to help educate other office staff on issues specific to disability sport. While this approach has been largely successful, one evident drawback is that the designated staff member becomes over-relied upon, and the expertise is not disseminated. In the case of athletics, the staff member responsible for athletes with a disability has experienced conflicting loyalties between representing the disability dimension or the sport dimension first. Both of these organizations are currently faced with losing these staff members; it will be interesting to see how their situations evolve.

Second, funding played a critical role in the success of all of the inclusion projects. Concurrent with the federal government's move towards inclusion, the federal government began to downscale its involvement in the sport system. In this environment of fiscal restraint, mainstream NSOs were particularly reluctant to take on new projects. Once assured that funding would follow athletes, the willingness of mainstream NSOs to assume responsibility for programs for athletes with a disability was assured in each of the cases discussed previously. In the cycling inclusion project, the question regarding funding was asked in a very direct manner.

Third, cooperation between the organizations involved - both before and after any formal agreement - has been important for the inclusion process. The inclusion of wheelchair tennis in Tennis Canada, for example, went very smoothly, in part because of the close working relationship between the two organizations involved. Furthermore, their signed Letter of Agreement was a formalization of a transfer that had already practically occurred.

In contrast, problems with cooperation (for varied reasons) creates stumbling blocks to the inclusion process. Athletics Canada and the Canadian Wheelchair Sports Association have experienced problems around issues ranging from funding to international liaison. The Canadian Cycling Association is experiencing some challenges in working with the Canadian Cerebral Palsy Sports Association, whereas the CCA has been much more successful in establishing a good relationship with the Canadian Blind Sports Association. The fact that friction exists indicates that the inclusion processes with these organizations should be considered as "in progress" and ongoing.

Tension is also evident as the disability sport organizations experience difficulty "reinventing" themselves. Some disability-based NSOs (or key individuals in these organizations) are reluctant to "let go of their athletes"; a scenario that may account for some of the difficulty encountered between mainstream and disability-based NSOs in the inclusion process.

The fourth dimension that helped to determine the success of inclusion was the flexibility of approach and structure used for each of the projects. Because each initiative involved different sports, different organizations, different numbers of organizations, and occurred at different times, a single type of approach would likely not have been as successful. For instance, the formal process taken with swimming was necessary at the time. Since this was the first large inclusion project, the people involved wanted to ensure that all the details were taken care of and that the process was beyond reproach. This approach would not have worked with cycling; representatives from the Canadian Cycling Association were clear that they did not want a formal

Memorandum of Understanding. As is evident from the turbulence already experienced, a model where the athletes with a disability become incorporated into the mainstream sport organization's operations (such as with swimming), will not at this time work for wheelchair basketball. Flexibility has helped to promote and ensure the success of inclusion, together with all the associated benefits for the athletes involved.

Challenges for the Future

As we move forward, we continue to face challenges with regard to inclusion and sport delivery for athletes with a disability within the mainstream sport system. Some of these are related to the work still to be done; others are a measure of the success of inclusion initiatives to date.

One of the chief challenges is that the national sport system is currently in a state of change. Some of the sports for athletes with a disability are completely included in the mainstream sport system, while others remain separate, or are only partially integrated. This patchwork creates difficulty in terms of equitable treatment for all organizations, funding allocation and distribution, and ensuring that athletes have access to the services for which they are eligible. Fortunately the Funding and Accountability Framework for Athletes with a Disability is sufficiently flexible to allow for the funding to be attached to programs and services, as opposed to organizations.

Not all sports, however, can be expected to "fit" into the mainstream sport system as it is currently structured. Three Paralympic sports - namely boccia, goalball, and wheelchair rugby - do not have clear counterparts in mainstream NSOs. Unlike wheelchair basketball, which uses the same basic rules, court and techniques as stand-up basketball, each of these sports represent distinct games. It is not clear at this time how athletes in these sports can be best served, and what organizations would best meet their needs. A related issue concerns the future of the disability-based NSOs. Will they be able to take responsibility for these sports without "homes" in the mainstream sport system, become advocacy rather than sport technical organizations, or perhaps cease to exist?

Another dimension of the changing nature of the sport system concerns the planned merger of the Sport Funding and Accountability Framework (for mainstream sport) and the Funding and Accountability Framework for Athletes with a Disability. An additional challenge is to ensure that programs and services for athletes with a disability continue to be supported. Furthermore, certain NSOs (archery, shooting, and powerlifting) are currently funded for the services and programs provided to athletes with a disability through FAFAD, but not for those provided to mainstream athletes (through SFAF). These challenges continue to exist.

One major system-wide challenge is the promotion of disability sport at the grassroots or developmental level. Each of the NSOs who have taken responsibility for serving athletes with a disability has confronted this issue, with varying success. The national sport system is geared towards high-performance sport, and development (strictly speaking) is within the jurisdiction of the provincial organizations. An agreement at the national level, where the NSO takes responsibility for national team programs and services for athletes with a disability does not automatically compel the provinces to follow suit, yet development is key for the future of high performance programs. At present, it is up to provincial organizations to pursue inclusion, or for the NSOs to follow-up with their provincial counterparts (the federal government is at the stage of considering bringing the issue of inclusion to the table at Federal/Provincial/Territorial meetings). The result is that there tend to be pockets of development throughout the country in each of the sports.

Additionally, while great progress has been made in terms of gaining acceptance for athletes with a disability within the mainstream sport system, work still needs to be done to raise awareness and to heighten the expertise available to these athletes. Generally speaking, issues relating to disability sport need to appear on the agenda of some of the multi-service organizations (such as coaching, or ethics in sport) in the national sport system. A notable exception is Athletes CAN, the athlete advocacy organization that has embraced athletes with a disability as an integral part of their membership. Many unexplored opportunities exist in terms of research, sport science, and sport medicine for athletes with a disability.

One aspect of the disability sport community that makes it difficult to raise awareness is the lack of a strong united voice, or single organization to advocate on behalf of athletes with a disability. The predecessor of the Canadian Paralympic Committee, the Canadian Federation of Sport Organizations for the Disabled, partially fulfilled this role. However it has been an ongoing struggle for the various disability-based sport organizations to reach consensus and to effectively lobby as a group for athletes with a disability, both before and during the move towards inclusion.

An internal challenge has been within the federal government. When the inclusion initiatives started, one program officer at Sport Canada was largely responsible for all the files related to athletes with a disability. With the inclusion projects, program officers responsible for coordinating with mainstream NSOs also became liaisons – and in several cases, advocates - for issues relating to athletes with a disability in those particular sports. While this has been a huge advance in terms of integrating this dimension of sport into the everyday workings of the branch, there are still strides to be made.

The success of the inclusion initiatives has also created its own challenges. The ever-improving performances of Canadian athletes with a disability, and the increasing depth of the national team programs, means that Canadian Paralympic Committee has the potential to send its largest ever Paralympic team to Sydney. This obviously has financial and human resources implications for an organization already taxed by the comparable demands of the 1998 Nagano Paralympic mission.

Additional Considerations

While many of the challenges faced for the future of inclusion are directly related to the current state of the Canadian sport system, there are additional considerations that may also eventually have an impact on the process. At present, for instance, Canadian athletes with a disability do not compete in a number of sports on the international calendar. These include sports such as table tennis, wheelchair fencing, 7-a-side soccer, and ice sledge racing - all of which are on the calendar of the Paralympic Games. Should these sports develop domestically, it would be logical given current activities to encourage mainstream NSOs to be involved. However, it is difficult to foster awareness and acceptance when discussing hypothetical future developments.

An associated issue concerns the potential role of the sport system in the development of these new-to-Canada sports. Should the (mainstream) NSOs have any responsibility or obligation for fostering the growth of sports that are on the international calendar? Since the federal government typically supports high-performance sport, its role in providing necessary funding support for such endeavors is, as yet, undefined.

Another dimension of sport development concerns sports that are played in Canada, but not internationally. As individuals, or on a project-by-project basis, Canadians have been involved in the evolution of various sports; but again the role of the federal government is unclear. Wheelchair racquetball is one such sport in this category. The mainstream NSO has long had responsibility for wheelchair racquetball, but the program is suffering in part due to the lack of an international circuit. Pleased with the commitment of Racquetball Canada to athletes with a disability, the NSO has been funded through

FAFAD for the past few years. However, it is uncertain in what capacity this support will continue, particularly with the growth of other, more recognized sports. Other "spinoffs" of mainstream sport are possible, as acceptance of disability sport grows in the sport community.

Additionally, not all NSOs that could potentially be involved are partners in inclusion projects at present. In some cases, this is indicative of a lack of domestic development in a particular sport, in others a lack of interest on the part of either the mainstream or disability NSO. A contributing factor may also be the human resources necessary to encourage and facilitate the inclusion process. The flexibility of approach which has resulted in success is also rather labour intensive.

Future strategies for promoting inclusion need to take into account not only the direct challenges discussed in the previous section, but also the more peripheral aspects above. Not knowing how some of these related aspects will develop underlines the need for continued flexibility to be able to best support sport and athletes with a disability in the Canadian sport system.

Moving On

The progress of the inclusion projects is truly remarkable. In less than a decade, sport for athletes with a disability has evolved and developed in Canada, and the results and benefits are already evident. Athletes with a disability now have access to a broader range of programs and services, and enjoy a fuller partnership in the mainstream sport system. Mainstream sport organizations are increasingly taking responsibility for and ownership of disability sport. Performances of Canadian athletes with a disability are improving, as well as the depth of the teams.

Notwithstanding the impressive challenges ahead, the future also holds opportunities for the advancement of inclusion. The Sydney Paralympic Games will likely be another turning point in the inclusion process as athletes compete, win medals, and share experiences. National Sport Organizations who have embraced inclusion will have the opportunity to evaluate their programs, and all the partners in the sport system will have a chance to reflect on the strides made since the 1992 Games in Barcelona. While the Paralympics represent only one aspect of the competition for athletes with a disability, the Games can be used as a measuring stick to consider progress made as well as next steps, in view of the size of the event and the degree to which the Paralympic sport community has been involved in the inclusion projects.

The continued development of the Paralympic movement will also have an impact on the progress of inclusion in Canada. While the IPC is working to get world-wide exposure for the Paralympics Games and to promote the event outside of the host city, it becomes increasingly critical for National Paralympic Committees to be able to have the possibility of a global television feed to promote the movement domestically. The increased competition within the sport "market" means that, in order to highlight the achievements of athletes with a disability, telecommunications is essential. And as television coverage is an important tool for attracting sponsorship, this lack of coverage may prove to be a stumbling block to (non-governmental) support of programs and services for athletes with a disability, and future inclusion projects.

The exact structure of the sport system in the future is by no means evident. Thus inclusion should progress, based on the needs of the athletes and sport development, to provide adaptability in changing environments. The Canadian sport system does not exist in isolation; as we move forward we are interested in sharing and learning from common and diverse experiences in the area of inclusion to help ensure a brighter future for (disability) sport.

Appendix: Overviews of Programs Related to the Process of Inclusion

Fitness and Amateur Sport Act of Canada

The Fitness and Amateur Sport Act was passed by Parliament in 1961. The full text can be found on the Sport Canada website at: www.pch.gc.ca/sportcanada

The objects and powers of the Act (section 3) include:

"3. The objects of this Act are to encourage, promote and develop fitness and amateur sport in Canada and, without limiting the generality of the foregoing, the Minister may, in futherance of those objectives,

(a) provide assistance for the promotion and development of Canadian participation in national and international amateur sport;

(b) provide for the training of coaches and such other personnel as may be required for the purposes of this Act;

(c) provide bursaries or fellowships to assist in the training of necessary personnel;

(d) undertake or assist in research or surveys in respect of fitness and amateur sport;

(e) arrange for national and regional conferences designed to promote and further the objects of this Act;

(f) provide for the recognition of achievement in respect of fitness and amateur sport by the grant or issue of certificates, citations or awards of merit;

(g) prepare and distribute information relating to fitness and amateur sport;

(h) assist, cooperate with and enlist the aid of any group interested in furthering the objects of this Act;

(i) coordinate federal activities related to the encouragement, promotion and development of fitness and amateur sport, in cooperation with any other departments or agencies of the Government of Canada carrying on those activities; and

(j)   undertake such other projects or programs, including the provision of services and facilities or of assistance therefor, in respect of fitness and amateur sport as are designed to promote and further the objects of this Act."

National Strategy for the Integration of Persons with Disabilities
(From the evaluation (1995) report prepared by the Corporate Review Branch of Canadian Heritage)

The National Strategy for the Integration of Persons with Disabilities (NSIPD) was developed, in part, as a response to the Second Report of the Standing Committee on Human Rights and the Status of Disabled Persons, **A Consensus for Action: The Economic Integration of Disabled Persons** (June, 1990).

This five year initiative (1991/92-1995-96) had an overall budget of $157.8 million and spanned ten federal departments and two agencies. This interdepartmental, collaborative effort was designed to address barriers to participation in all aspects of society for Canadians with disabilities.

The overall goal of the NSIPD was to enhance the participation of persons with disabilities in the social and economic mainstream of Canada through:

-   equal access

-   economic integration, and

-   effective participation.

The strategy focussed on several priority areas such as:

-   housing

-   employment

-   information sharing

- communication technology

- services for aboriginals with disabilities

- legislation, and

- transportation.

Committee on Integration of Athletes with Disabilities

(From the Mandate for the International Committee on Integration of Athletes with Disabilities)

The mandate of the International Committee on Integration of Athletes with Disabilities is to gain inclusion of events for athletes with disabilities in major international competitions.

The goals of the International Committee on Integration are as follows:

- to develop a lobbying strategy and critical path for the inclusion of selective full medal events for athletes with disabilities initially within the Olympic Games and Commonwealth Games;

- to negotiate, on behalf of the International Paralympic Committee, initially with the International Olympic Committee and the Commonwealth Games Federation, for the inclusion of full medal events for athletes with disabilities in the Olympic and Commonwealth Games;

- to increase the awareness and understanding of the appropriateness of inclusion of full medal events for athletes with disabilities into major international competitions;

- to facilitate the successful conduct of full medal events included into major international competitions;

- to develop a model process for the inclusion of full medal status events for athletes with disabilities into major international competitions;

- to gain interest and financial support for the International Committee on Integration and its objectives;

- to establish formal linkages and effective liaisons with appropriate entities.

Funding and Accountabiltiy Framework for Athletes with Disabilities

The Funding and Accountability Framework for Athletes with Disabilities (FAFAD) concept was introduced in January 1996 for national sport organizations for athletes with disabilities and mainstream national sport organizations. FAFAD is a distinct program from the Sport Funding and Accountability Framework (SFAF) introduced in 1995 but shares the same basic philosophy and operating principles of the SFAF.

Both the SFAF and the FAFAD were introduced in response to the general view that fundamental adjustments had to be made to the federal government's sport funding system. FAFAD was developed following extensive consultation with national sport organizations for athletes with disabilities and mainstream NSOs; it recognizes the unique aspects and diverse needs of sport for athletes with disabilities and attempts to provide more equitable funding for all Canadian athletes supported by the federal government.

In 1995 the FAFAD Working Group, comprising representatives from the sport community and the federal government, developed a discussion paper **Athletes with a Disability and the Sport Funding and Accountability Framework.** In addition to presenting the key issues and challenges facing athletes with disabilities, the paper proposed guidelines and alternate approaches for the development and funding of sport for athletes with disabilities in Canada. The paper also discussed the need to consolidate and reduce administration and duplication within the Canadian sport system. This discussion paper and the SFAF served as key building blocks for the development of the Funding and Accountability Framework for Athletes with Disabilities.

When originally introduced, FAFAD contained three components: disability based, major games, and sport specific components. Indeed the pilot FAFAD assessment questionnaire also contained these three components. Based on the major games questionnaire analysis, and recent funding decisions within the major games area, this component has been removed from the FAFAD. The data gathered from the questionnaire, however, will be incorporated into Sport Canada efforts to develop guidelines for the funding of future major games initiatives.

During the FAFAD analysis, it was discovered that certain areas of the disability based questionnaire duplicated and/or complemented similar areas within the sport specific questionnaire. In order to eliminate the duplication and streamline the Framework, the results of both components were merged into one FAFAD assessment, thereby establishing one overall FAFAD score for each of the 18 organizations that made application and satisfied eligibility prerequisites.

In addition to the change noted above, the FAFAD implementation timetable has also been modified. Initially, Sport Canada planned to pilot the FAFAD by incorporating it into the 1996-97 contributions review process. Unfortunately for a variety of reasons - including the volume of international results which had never before been documented or analyzed, incomplete questionnaires, missing data, and prior delay in the SFAF analysis - Sport Canada was not in a position to use FAFAD as originally planned. Instead FAFAD is being introduced in a pilot format for the 1997-98 contributions review process; it will be modified through ongoing consultation with the sport community during the coming year and fully implemented in April 1998.

Currently, Sport Canada provides funding to four types of sport organizations involving athletes with disabilities:

- disability based

- games organizations

- sport specific organizations for athletes with disabilities

- sport specific organizations for both able-bodied athletes and athletes with disabilities.

The aim of FAFAD is to provide funding to organizations that contribute directly to the achievement of the federal sport objectives and priorities. The premise of FAFAD is to focus on **athletes** with disabilities, not on **organizations** for athletes with disabilities. Although the focus is clearly on athletes with disabilities, the FAFAD recognizes the role that eligible organizations play in delivering programs and services to athletes with disabilities. For organizations which meet the eligibility prerequisite and assessment thresholds, funding will be based on the degree to which they achieve the Framework objectives.

Similar to the SFAF, the FAFAD has two phases to eligibility - prerequisites and an assessment threshold. Organizations meeting the prerequisites are assessed through the questionnaire. To be eligible to be considered for funding, organizations must achieve a score above the assessment threshold. Eligibility for assessment and funding support is determined prior to the beginning of each multi year cycle and is in effect for the entire cycle, conditional on all prerequisites being maintained by the organization. Specific funding levels, however, are determined annually through the federal government budget and Sport Canada's contribution review process.

An organization's funding level is directly related to the points scored on the assessment factors. As noted above, funding is conditional on satisfying prerequisites and an assessment threshold.

As noted in the introduction, the disability based and sport specific components have been merged into a single FAFAD assessment. The major games component was removed from the FAFAD.. The disability based section was designed to measure the role national sport organizations play in serving various disability groups within the Canadian population. It examined leadership and technical knowledge which became part of the FAFAD sport development assessment, as well as general information, lobby, advocacy, and promotion which are now part of the management area of the assessment.

The most significant aspect of the assessment focuses on the sport specific section. This component attempts to reconcile the concepts of **disability, sport, and delivery.** For sports whose athletes are classified under the International Paralympic Committee (IPC) system, applications were accepted from the organization that serves these athletes. However, where inclusion has occurred, for example in the sports of archery, racquetball, shooting, and swimming, applications were only accepted from the mainstream NSOs.

As is the case with the SFAF and as a result of the modifications noted above, assessment is divided into three categories, high performance, sport development, and management. In the high performance category, an organization's score is based on athletes results (major games and world championships) and the high performance sport system. The high performance sport system examines national team program, international representation, officiating, classifiers, and hosting.

The sport development category considers membership, participation in national and provincial championships, inclusion initiatives, technical leadership, athlete, coach, classifier and officiating development. The management category assesses an organization's financial management, official languages, lobby, promotion and advocacy, and women in sport.

In its original format, the FAFAD consisted of three separate components which were designed to address the unique aspects and diverse needs of sport for athletes with disabilities. During the course of the data analysis, the major games component was removed and will be incorporated into the work of the Major Games Unit. The disability based component was merged into the sport specific component creating a single FAFAD assessment score.

Athlete Assistance Program
(For more information, please see the Sport Canada website: www.pch.gc.ca/sportcanada)

The main goal of the AAP is to contribute to improved Canadian performances at major international competition, such as the Olympic Games, Commonwealth Games, Pan Am Games, Paralympic Games, and World Championships. To this end, the AAP identifies and supports athletes already at or having the potential to be in the top 16 in the world.

The AAP has five specific objectives:

-   to identify and support Canadian athletes performing at or having the greatest potential to achieve top 16 results at Olympic/Paralympic Games and World Championships;

-   to help Canada's international-calibre athletes excel at the highest level of competition while enabling them to prepare for a future career or engage in full- or part-time career activities;

-   to facilitate the attainment of athletes' long-range goals of excellence in Olympic/Paralympic or world competition;

- to complement other government and NSO support programs;

- to contribute toward broad Government policy objectives.

The AAP achieves its objectives by:

- providing national standards for the identification and support of high-performance athletes;

- ensuring that appropriate selection standards are in place;

- collaborating with NSOs to provide annual, ongoing, and long-term evaluation of athlete performance and potential;

- helping to offset some of the living and training costs athletes incur as a result of their participation in high-performance sport;

- ensuring the provision of financial support to athletes in a consistent and timely manner;

- providing incentives through the establishment of progressive, increasingly challenging criteria and graduated support;

- recognizing and rewarding Canadian athletes for outstanding performances in major international events such as Olympic/Paralympic Games and World Championships;

- ensuring, in conjunction with the NSO, that appropriate training and competitive opportunities are in place to help athletes reach their full athletic potential;

- providing financial support to allow athletes to attain academic goals and assisting in the preparation for a post-athletic career;

- allowing athletes to maintain a long-term commitment to training and competition to further their athletic goals;

- ensuring that mutual responsibilities are outlined and understood by athletes and NSOs;

- ensuring that athlete/NSO agreements are signed each year;

- linking AAP support to other government and sport-specific initiatives such as National Training Centres or coaching support;

- contributing to the creation of Canadian heroes and to national pride thorugh the accomplishments of Canadian athletes;

- contributing to the creation of role models for Canadian youth;

- contributing to the promotion of national unity through the promotion of the accomplishments of Canadian athletes;

- promoting and ensuring compliance with other government policies, e.g. anti-doping; and

- providing a focal point for government support to high-performance sport and athletes.

Note: The AAP is the only Sport Canada program that provides funding **directly** to athletes.

New Funding for Sport
(From backgrounders distributed at the announcement of the additional funding, January 22, 1998)

- The Government of Canada has approved the allocation of additional resources to assist Canadian high performance athletes achieve the best results possible in international competition.

- Incremental funding of $10 million per annum will be allocated for the 1998-1999 to 2002-2003 fiscal years.

- The objective of the funding is to:

  - increase access to quality training and international competition opportunities for high-performance athletes;

- employ additional full-time high-performance coaches, enhance the salary levels of coaches and support professional development and training opportunities for coaches; and

- directly support additional high-performance athletes.

- Funds will be used to support athletes, coaches, and the training and competition necessary to achieve world-class performances in both the short and long term. The new initiatives will enhance Sport Canada's efforts related to access and equity for traditionally under-represented groups, including women, athletes with a disability, and Aboriginal people as well as the practice of sport through fair and ethical means.

- The federal government supports the achievement of high-performance athletic excellence, advancing the values inherent in sport – excellence, fairness, and teamwork.

- Nearly half of the new funds will be directed toward training and competition opportunities for high-performance athletes.

- Canadian athletes require increased access to training and high-calibre international competitions. An analysis of national team programs reveal that, due to funding conditions over the past several years, there has been a decline in the number and quality of international competition opportunities for Canadian athletes, particularly at the junior and development team levels. In addition, new resources are required to raise the level of training, competition, and coaching support for athletes with a disability.

- Funding will be provided to increase training and competition opportunities for national team and developing high-performance athletes. This includes special initiatives for top performing Aboriginal athletes involved with the North American Indigenous Games.

- About one-third of the new funds will be used to develop and employ the finest Canadian coaches.

- In order for athletes to reach the highest level of international performance, regular access to qualified coaches is essential. The need to increase employment opportunities for Canadian coaches has been highlighted in numerous studies, reports, and consultations with the sport community over the previous decades.

- Currently there are 49 federally supported, full-time national team coaches employed by federally funded National Sport Organizations. To augment the number, quality and remuneration of high performance coaches, funding will be provided to support up to 100 additional full-time high performance coaches. The coach employment program will provide additional funding for coaching salaries from National Sport Organizations and other partners to create additional full-time coaching positions and augment existing coaching positions. These initiatives will help keep our best coaches in Canada.

- Additional support will also be allocated to enhance the salary level of coaches and to support a variety of professional development and training opportunities for coaches. Many part-time coaching positions will be created and professional development opportunities for coaches will be increased. Special mentoring and apprenticeship initiatives will aim at increasing the number of women coaches and Aboriginal coaches.

- About one-fifth of the new funds will be allocated to Sport Canada's Athlete Assistance Program.

- The provision of direct living and training support to athletes through Sport Canada's Athlete Assistance Program enables athletes to remain in high performance sport and maintain the level of training required to reach their full potential. The athlete assistance program provides support to approximately 850 Canadian national team athletes in some 45 sports. These athletes represent Canada at Olympic and Paralympic Games, World Championships, and other international competitions.

- Through this new initiative, the Athlete Assistance Program budget of $7.2 million will be augmented, in order to provide funding to offset living and training expenses and tuition support for an additional 200 developing high performance athletes per year and 100 athletes with a disability. In total, the number of AAP-funded athletes will increase from 837 to approximately 1, 150. This initiative addresses the need to fund more athletes due to increase in the number of events at the Winter and Summer Olympic Games, and to increase the number of Paralympic athletes receiving support.

- This initiative will also deepen the impact of the AAP by providing much needed financial support to an increased number of senior level national team athletes as well as an increased number of junior and developing high performance athletes who represent the feeder system for Canada's future national teams.

Sport Funding and Accountability Framework: Overview

Sport is an essential ingredient in the lives of Canadians and an important and viable component of Canadian identity. It plays a vital role in how we identify ourselves as Canadians.

The Government's over-arching objective in amateur sport is the achievement of high performance excellence through fair and ethical means. In support of this objective, the federal government has set its priorities for sport on athletes, coaches, national sport organizations (NSOs), and increasing access to and participation by under-represented groups.

Several recent reports on sport policy expressed the generally unanimous view that fundamental adjustments had to be made to the sport funding system in Canada. No major changes to the funding system have been made since the federal government first began supporting amateur sport development more than 30 years ago. As a result, the Department of Canadian Heritage (Sport Canada), in consultation with the sport community, has developed the Sport Funding and Accountability Framework (SFAF).

The SFAF is a comprehensive, objective tool to ensure that federal funds are allocated to NSOs that contribute directly to the achievement of federal sport objectives and priorities. It encompasses three main components: eligibility, funding determination, and accountability.

To be eligible to receive funding for the period 1996-2001, NSOs must first meet established prerequisites and, following a detailed assessment by Sport Canada, achieve a score above the eligibility threshold. NSOs provided information to Sport Canada in January 1996 via their responses to a thorough assessment questionnaire. Using a detailed rating guide, Sport Canada then evaluated the responses to determine which NSOs are eligible to receive federal support and to what extent.

The assessment is based on evaluation criteria organized in three key categories: high performance, sport development, and management practices. The 1996 assessment considered data for the period from January 1, 1988, to December 31, 1996. It is largely based on quantitative criteria, with some consideration given to qualitative criteria.

Separate eligibility and funding scores are determined from the questionnaire. This is done to ensure that similarly performing NSOs with the same number of events but involving different numbers of athletes are equally eligible. Thus factors such as national team size and number of events at Olympic Games and World Championships are excluded from the eligibility score calculation.

In the high performance category, an organization's score is based on athlete results and the NSO's high performance system. The score for athlete results is arrived at by weighting World Championships and Olympics results by factors that reflect the competitive profile for each sport. An NSO's score for its high performance system takes into account how an NSO operates its national team and support programs. For example, factors related to coaching, training, athlete monitoring, and athlete involvement in decision-making are used to determine this part of an NSO's score.

Sport development, considers athlete development, coach development and officiating. These in turn are scored according to the NSO's membership, participation in national and provincial championships and the Canada Games, technical resources, and the certification of coaches and officials. Technical resources in this case refers to the extent of leadership provided by the NSO in the development of resource materials and programs for athletes, coaches, and officials.

The management category assessed an NSO's financial operations, service capacity in both official languages, and the opportunities provided for women in sport.

Although athlete participation in decision-making is specifically assessed within the context of the NSO's high performance system, "athlete centredness" is measured in a number of ways, and is rated according to the capacity of an NSO to provide services and programs to athletes at various levels.

As well, while plans and programs designed to improve opportunities for women in sport are assessed in management category, the gender balance and profile for each organization are also considered in other areas such as membership, competitions, coaching, and officiating.

It should be noted that, under the Framework, an NSO can appeal the results of its eligibility prerequisites and assessment based only on incorrect information or misinterpretation of the information provided. An eligible NSO can request a review of the assessment score for any part of the assessment it feels may have been scored incorrectly.

Accountability is an integral component of the SFAF. In an era of tight fiscal restraint, good government not only means spending smarter, but also ensuring that tax dollars are used for intended purposes, and to achieve desired results. All NSOs receiving funding will negotiate an Accountability Agreement with Sport Canada. The agreements will be based on key objectives from the NSO's multi-year plan. The purpose of the accountability agreement is to ensure that public funding contributes to the achievement of federal priorities and policy objectives for sport.

Athletes CAN
(From their website: www.omnilogic.com/athcan/english/default.htm)

The mission of Athletes CAN is to work with others in leadership, advocacy, and education to ensure a fair, responsive, and supportive sport system for athletes. In fulfilling this mission, Athletes CAN is committed to Accountability, Equity, Inclusiveness, and Mutual Respect.

Athletes CAN is an active, proud corporation addressing issues on behalf of athletes in order to ensure their rightful place in the sporting world. As a respected advocacy entity in the Canadian sporting community, Athletes CAN has a significant positive impact on the life of every Canadian athlete.

Membership programs and services

- to improve the awareness of Athletes CAN and the programs and services available to athletes;

- to enhance the well-being of athletes;

- to develop and promote athlete leadership;

- to facilitate communication amongst Canadian athletes and to act as their independent voice.

Paralympic and Olympic Games - separate or together?

Harald von Selzam

Celebration, FL, USA

Introduction

Since Seoul 1988, cities hosting the Olympic Games also have hosted the Paralympic Games. In each case a similar model was adopted: the Paralympic Games took place several weeks after the Olympics, using primarily the same competition sites and non-sport venues for both Games. At the same time, and despite the success of the Paralympics, sports organizations, athletes, and potential organizers of future Games have been discussing other models of staging the Paralympic Games. Possible scenarios range from full inclusion of all Paralympic events into the Olympic program to totally independent Paralympic Games organized in different locations and at a different time. However, in previous discussions, clear criteria have not been established and implications have not been identified. This paper analyzes selected concepts for feasibility and for their potential to maximize the value of the Paralympic Games.

The paper provides a systematic comparison of the following scenarios:

1. Paralympic Games hosted in the same city 2-4 weeks after the Olympics (current model)

2. all Paralympic events held as part of the Olympic program

3. Paralympic Games hosted in the same city but at a different time

4. Paralympic Games hosted as an independent event at a different location.

The comparison includes sports political, operational, and economical aspects, as well as marketing opportunities, spectator attendance, and the "Big Moments" of the Games. Advantages and disadvantages of each model are discussed.

In the first part, basic background information on the scope, operational requirements, and time lines of the Olympic and Paralympic Games will be provided. Secondly, the criteria for the comparison of different scenarios will be listed and the method of comparison and analysis will be explained. Finally, the results will be presented and discussed.

Scope and Operational Requirements of Olympic and Paralympic Games

The Summer Olympic Games are one of the largest sporting events in the world. In Atlanta, about 10.000 athletes from 197 countries participated in 26 sports accompanied by 5.000 staff members including coaches, medical personnel, administrators, and officials. More than 10.000 journalists covered the Games in print and electronic media and almost two million spectators visited the competitions. The Paralympic Games, which were held in the same venues only two weeks after the Olympic Games, represented the second largest sporting event that year. The Paralympic Games are the pinnacle of elite competition for athletes with a disability. In 1996, 3.500 athletes from 106 countries participated in 19 sports supported by 1.500 staff members. (For a side by side comparison of the main figures of Olympic and Paralympic Games, refer to Table 1: Scope of Olympic and Paralympic Games.)

Even though the Paralympics are clearly smaller than the Olympic Games in terms of numbers, they are similarly complex regarding operational preparations and logistics such as venue and competition management, accommodation, transportation, medical services, ceremonies, press and media services, as well as technological support. Consequently, to use the same facilities, equipment, and staff as for the Olympic Games facilitates the hosting of the Paralympic Games and puts the emphasis on re-sizing and re-fitting of installations already used for the Olympics.

However, hosting Paralympic Games includes certain requirements beyond the scope of the Olympic Games. Despite the fact that there are less sports in the Paralympics the number of competitions is actually higher. This is related to the fact that in the Paralympic Games the same event may be staged for several different classes of disabilities, for example the 100m dash event may be staged as several different events for blind athletes, wheelchair athletes, amputee athletes, athletes with cerebral palsy, and athletes with an intellectual disability. As a result, the total numbers of medal events - and thus also the number of medal ceremonies - at the Paralympics may be three times as high as at the Olympics. In addition, participation of athletes with different disabilities requires for many athletes a (re)-classification process prior to competition in order to identify groups with similar degrees of disability to compete against each other. Another challenge for organizers of the Paralympics is presented by the need for a high level of architectural accessibility primarily for sport facilities, accommodation, and transportation. Approximately 1.000 athletes in wheelchairs and 150 fully blind athletes, as well as a high number of spectators, media representatives, and VIPs with a disability require above average means of wheelchair accessibility and guiding systems in all functional areas of the sport venues, the Paralympic Village, hotels, and the bus shuttle system.

One area that - up until now - has not required as much attention for the Paralympics as for the Olympics is the International Broadcast Center. While the media coverage of the Paralympics has steadily grown over the past years, the international "live" coverage still is limited and footage of the Games is usually provided by a local host broadcaster plus a small number of international TV crews served by the main media center.

	Paralympic Games	Olympic Games	Variance PG/OG
Participating Countries	106	197	54%
Athletes	3.500	10.000	35%
Officials	1.500	5.000	30%
Olympic Family	1.000	3.500	29%
Accredited Media[1]	2.500	20.000	13%
Accredited Sponsors	1.000	6.000	17%
Full Time Employees	100	2.000	5%
Temporary Employees[2]	300	1.500	20%
Volunteers	5.000	10.000	50%
Total Accredited Persons	14.800	58.000	26%
Spectators	200.000	2.000.000	10%
Sports	19	26	73%
Venues	15	19	79%
Events	620	256	242%
Expenditures (in 1 million US$)	100	1.500	7%
Revenues (in 1 million US$)	105	1.550	7%

Tab. 1: Scope of Olympic and Paralympic Games (based on the 1996 Atlanta Games)

1: Accredited media personnel: Journalists, photographers, and technical support staff
2: Employed three month and less

Time lines of the Olympic and Paralympic Games

One critical aspect to be considered when looking at the advantages and disadvantages of hosting the Paralympic Games is the time line requirements of each event. The International Olympic Committee (IOC), respectively the International Paralympic Committee (IPC), list detailed requirements of hosting the Games. The IOC requires that the Olympic Games, including the Opening and Closing Ceremonies, are 17 days long and that the Olympic Village must be open for all athletes 14 days prior to the Opening Ceremony and seven days past the Closing Ceremony. Consequently, the time the Olympic Village is open stretches over a total of 38 days. In case of the Paralympics the requirement is to host the Games over 11 days and to have the Paralympic Village open five days prior to the Opening Ceremony and three days after the Closing Ceremony adding up to a total Paralympic Village operation time of 19 days.

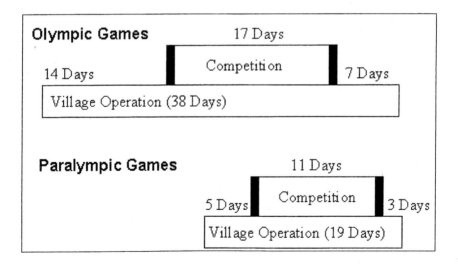

Fig. 1: The Olympic Village is required to be open 14 days prior to the Olympic Games and seven days after. The Paralympic Village is required to be open five days prior of the Paralympic Games and three days after.

Combining the total operation time of both Games adds up to 28 "Game Days" and 57 Village Operation days. The "Game Days" are the days that sport competition venues are in full operation mode for the competition and that spectator services need to be provided. The Village Operation days are the days on which village services and transportation for the athletes to sports venues must be provided. Refitting the villages between both Games requires a minimum of five days if the Paralympics are hosted directly after the Olympics and 12 days if the Paralympics were hosted directly prior to the Olympic Games. Thus, the total Village Operation time would measure 62, respectively 69 days. If more time would be needed for the transition of the village from the Olympic to the Paralympic Games, the total Village Operation time also would have to be further extended.

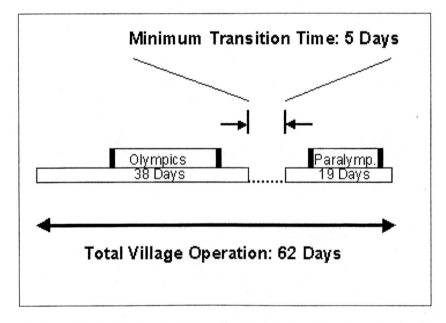

Fig. 2: Hosting the Paralympic Games directly **after** the Olympic Games require a minimum of five transition days between the closing of the Olympic Village and the opening of the Paralympic Village, resulting in a total Village Operation time of 62 days.

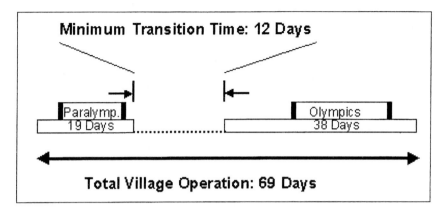

Fig. 3: Hosting the Paralympic Games directly **before** the Olympic Games would require a minimum of 12 transition days between the closing of the Paralympic Village and the opening of the Olympic Village, resulting in a total Village Operation time of 69 days.

Scenarios Selected

For the purpose of this study, four major scenarios were selected. Besides the current model, which is hosting the Paralympic Games 2-4 weeks after the Olympic Games (1), the scenarios included hosting all Paralympic events as part of the Olympic Games (2), hosting the Paralympics by the same city but timely not as closely linked to the Olympic Games (3) and hosting the Paralympic Games at a time and location completely independent from the Olympic Games (4). Two of the scenarios were further broken down into additional alternatives in order to look at fine differences on a smaller scale. In the past, Paralympic Games, even when taking place in the same city, in some cases were hosted by a different Organizing Committee than the Olympic Games. For this reason, it was decided to look at both scenarios separately and to include them in this comparison. In the case of hosting the Paralympics in the same city but at a different time, four different time frames to host the Paralympics were selected because they had been the ones most frequently suggested in previous discussions on this topic. In detail, the following scenarios were included in the comparison:

1. Paralympic Games hosted in the same city 2-4 weeks after the Olympics (current model)
   a) organized by the same committee
   b) organized by two separate committees

2. all Paralympic events held as part of the Olympic program

3. Paralympic Games hosted in the same city and by the same organizing committee but at a different time
   a) one year prior to the Olympic Games
   b) three months prior to the Olympic Games
   c) three months after the Olympic Games
   d) one year after the Olympic Games

4. Paralympic Games hosted as an independent event at a different location.

For the last scenario no specific time or location was identified but it is assumed that in the case that the Paralympic Games would be hosted as an independent event they would also be organized by a separate Organizing Committee and at a different time than the Olympics. While Paralympic Games prior to 1988 may fit one or the other scenario listed above, those have not been included as a reference as they differ significantly in scope and public perception.

In addition, this comparison refers primarily to the Summer Olympic and Paralympic Games. While some scenarios may also apply to the Winter Olympic and Paralympic Games, these have not been considered as part of this study.

Methods and Criteria

In order to compare the different scenarios, five groups with a total of

25 criteria were identified. The five groups are sports political criteria, operational criteria, the "Big Moments" of the Games, marketing and public relation criteria, and economical factors. Sports political criteria include the international sports calendar, the agreements between the IPC and the IOC, the athletes' point of view, perceived independence of Paralympic Games, and the general perception of the Paralympic Games. Operational criteria include the use of permanent and temporary sport facilities, athlete accommodation (villages), transportation systems, staffing, readiness and feasibility. "Big Moment" criteria include the torch run, the lighting of the cauldron, opening and closing ceremonies as well as cultural, scientific, and youth programs. Marketing criteria included corporate sponsorships, government support, philanthropic programs, TV and Media coverage, and spectator attendance. Economic criteria include the expenses for operations, ceremonies and cultural, scientific and youth programs, as well as the revenues from corporate sponsorships, government support, other fundraising programs, and ticket sales.

For each criterion it was defined what aspect would be beneficial or disadvantageous for the Paralympic Games. For example, the international sports calendar refers to the sequence of world championships, world cups, international games, continental, regional, and national competitions. Changing this calendar drastically could result in conflicts with training cycles or with other international competition. Another example would be athletes' accommodation. Most likely, it would be beneficial for the overall success of the Paralympic Games if an Olympic Village with all its functional areas, services and the International Zone could also be used for the Paralympics. If an Olympic Village, on the other hand, was not available to be used for the Paralympic Games, separate facilities would have to be planned and built or otherwise provided, new functional areas and operational plans would have to be designed, staff would have to be trained differently, additional documentation would have to be printed, etc. All these factors would be disadvantageous for the overall success of the Paralympic Games.

If a criterion for a certain scenarios was beneficial, five (5) points were given, if it was neutral and it could not be decided whether it would be beneficial or disadvantageous, three (3) points were given, and if an criterion was disadvantageous one (1) point was given. Since all criteria do not have exactly the same value, the criteria groups were differently weighted. The sports political and the "Big Moments" criteria were given the weight of one, marketing and fundraising as well as economics were given the weight of two, and operational criteria were given the weight of three. Points of weighted groups were multiplied with the factor of their weight. For example, the points assigned to operational criteria were multiplied by factor three (3). In the end, both the non-weighted and weighted results were compared and the scenarios ranked by the total numbers of points.

All criteria and the description of beneficial or disadvantageous aspects for the Paralympics Games are listed in Table 2a and 2b.

Results

The following table (Tab. 3: Results) lists the different scenarios, the total score, and the rank of each scenario. The table also includes the score after the weight factor was applied. Interestingly, the ranking of the scenarios with the regular score and with the weighted score differ in only one case. The scenarios that received the highest score are both representing the current model, hosting the Paralympic Games shortly after the Olympics either by the same or by two different organizing committees. The scenarios that received the lowest score are the ones that are operationally and timely the furthest apart from the Olympic Games. Moving the Olympic and Paralympic Games further apart requires an operational break between both Games, increased installation and dismantling costs, additional need for rental of storage space and equipment, and additional personnel to name only a few. Thus, these scenarios seem to be overall less beneficial for the success of the Paralympic Games.

	Beneficial	**Disadvantageous**
Sports Political		
Sports calendar	Would not have to be changed	Would have to be changed considerably
Independence	Paralympics demonstrate high level of independence	Paralympics are one small piece of a much larger event
IPC / IOC	Current agreements are honored; a good relationship is maintained	Agreements would have to be renegotiated; support by the IOC may be discontinued
Athletes' point of view	Highest possible level of quality, highest possible association with the Olympics, highest possible exposure to media	Low quality of sport facilities and competition management; Para-lympics may be perceived as test event or second class event
Perception	Paralympics are perceived to be very closely associated with the Olympics	Paralympics are not perceived to be closely associated with the Olympics
Independence	Paralympics demonstrate high level of independence	Paralympics are one small piece of a much larger event
Operational		
Permanent facilities	High standard of quality, high likelihood to be used by both Games for the same function	Top level permanent facilities may not be available or may not have a high standard of quality
Temporary facilities	Some competition venues, The International Zone, Dining Area and Media Center have Olympic standard and are used by both events	Temporary facilities would have to be independently constructed or reconstructed.
Athlete accommodation	The Olympic Village can be used for the Paralympics	The Olympic Village cannot be used for the Paralympics
Transportation	Large amounts and high level of trans-portation means are avail-able	Adequate means of transportation may be difficult to be provided
Staffing	Staff and volunteers are well trained and prepared	Recruitment and preparation of adequate staff and volunteers may be difficult
Readiness	Operations have been thoroughly planned, prepared, and tested	Testing of operations is extremely limited
Feasibility	Conditions provide for easy facilitation of high level operations	Conditions prohibit easy facilitation of high level operations

Tab. 2a: Criteria

	Beneficial	**Disadvantageous**
Big Moments		
Torch run	Paralympic and Olympic torch run supplement each other	Paralympic and Olympic torch run conflict with each other
Lighting of cauldron	Olympic cauldron can be used for Paralympics	Olympic cauldron cannot be used
Opening / closing ceremonies	Identical elements can be used for Olympic and Paralympic Cere-monies	Identical elements cannot be used
Marketing / Fundraising		
Sponsorships	Approach of top level sponsors can easily be facilitated	Top sponsors may be inaccessible or would only marginally get involved
Government support	Substantial support is very likely	Government support may be limited
Philanthropic programs	Higher level of independence of the event increases philanthropic funding	Very close association with Olympic Games may reduce philanthropic funding
TV / media coverage	Association with the Olympic Games increases the media interest in Paralympics	Independent disability sport events do not attract a high level of media representatives
Spectator attendance	Close proximity of both events attracts primarily regional spectators, some of whom may or can not attend the Olympics	Inclusion of Paralympic events in the Olympics will not increase total number of spectators; a totally separated event may attract only a limited number of spectators
Economics		
Operations	Close proximity and sharing of resources drastically reduces expenses for operations	As the time frame between both events increases so do the costs for operations
Public relations / marketing	Sharing of resources decreases expenses for public relation and marketing programs	Independent public relations / marketing programs would be extremely expensive
Ceremonies	Using identical elements reduces costs for opening and closing ceremonies	Separate ceremonies would be extremely expensive
Cultural / scientific / youth programs	Sharing of resources decreases costs	Independent programs would be expensive

Tab. 2b: Criteria

	Points	Rank	Weight	Rank
Current model (organized by the same committee)	115	1	224	1
Current model (organized by two separate committees)	105	2	198	2
Paralympics hosted three months after the Olympic Games	93	3	174	3
Paralympic events held as part of the Olympic program	77	4	146	4
Paralympics hosted one year after the Olympic Games	69	5	122	6
Paralympics hosted three months prior to the Olympic Games	65	6	125	5
Paralympics hosted one year prior to the Olympic Games	47	7	84	7
Paralympic Games hosted at different location and time	47	8	76	8

Tab. 3: Results

The data show that the scenario of hosting all Paralympic events as part of the Olympic program ranks fourth and accordingly would be even more favorable than hosting the Paralympics further apart from the Olympics. When looking at the detailed results (see Tab. 4: Detailed results), however, it becomes obvious that even though this model may be beneficial according to some criteria, it would be extremely disadvantageous in others. For example, providing accommodation for all Paralympic athletes and providing sport facilities for all Paralympic sports simultaneously to the Olympic Games and with a similar level of quality would simply not be feasible. Another interesting result is that, in general, it seems to be less favorable to host the Paralympic Games prior to the Olympic Games than after. This may be primarily caused by conflicts related to the IOC - IPC relationship and to the value of the "Big Moments" of both Games. At this point, for example, hosting a Paralympic Opening Ceremony in the Olympic Stadium and using elements of the Olympic Opening Ceremony, including the lighting of the cauldron, prior to the Olympic Games would not be feasible.

( ) = weight factor	One Year Before	Three Months Before	Current Model Separa. Org. Commit.	Same Org. Commit.	Simul- taneous	Three Months After	One Year After	Separa. Location
Sports Political (1)								
Sports calendar	1	3	5	5	5	3	1	3
Independence	3	3	3	1	1	3	3	5
IPC/IOC	1	1	5	5	1	3	3	3
Athletes' point of view	1	3	5	5	3	3	1	1
Perception	3	3	3	5	5	5	3	1
Operational (3)								
Permanent facilities	1	3	5	5	1	3	3	1
Temporary facilities	1	3	5	5	3	3		1
Athlete accommodation	1	1	5	5	1	3	1	1
Transportation	1	3	5	5	3	3	1	1
Staffing	1	1	3	5	5	5	3	1
Readiness	1	1	3	5	5	5	3	1
Feasibility	1	3	3	5	1	3	3	1
Big Moments (1)								
Torch run	1	1	5	5	3	5	5	5
Lighting of cauldron	1	1	5	5	3	5	5	1
Opening / closing ceremonies	1	1	5	5	3	5	5	1
Cultural/scientific/youth	5	5	5	5	3	5	5	5
Marketing (2)								
Sponsorships	3	3	3	5	5	3	3	1
Government support	3	3	5	3	3	5	3	3
Philanthropic programs	5	5	5	1	1	5	5	5
TV / media coverage	3	3	5	5	5	3	3	1
Spectator attendance	3	3	5	5	1	3	3	1
Economics (2)								
Operations	1	3	3	5	1	3	1	1
Public relations / marketing	1	3	3	5	5	3	1	1
Ceremonies	1	3	3	5	5	3	1	1
Cultural/scientific/youth	3	3	3	5	5	3	3	1
Total	47	65	105	115	77	93	69	47
With weight	84	124	198	224	146	174	122	76
Ranking	**7**	**5**	**2**	**1**	**4**	**3**	**6**	**8**

Tab. 4: Detailed results

All detailed scores of each criterion and scenario are listed in Table 4.

Conclusion

Hosting the Paralympics separately from the Olympic Games, while providing the same level of quality, will require considerably more resources without significantly adding value to the perception of the Paralympic Games.

Hosting all Paralympic events at the same time as the Olympics is not feasible unless either the Paralympic program is drastically reduced or the Olympic Games are significantly extended. However, closer proximity of the Paralympic Games to the Olympic Games in terms of time, location, and management structures is more economical and overall guarantees the greater success of the Paralympic Games.

The findings suggest that the Paralympic Games are most successful when organized in very close connection to the Olympic Games. Neither "complete integration" nor "total separation" seem to provide a higher value. Consequently, for the time being, instead of looking at "when" and "where" to host the Paralympics, further developments should rather focus on "fine tuning" the existing model to further enhance the significance of the Paralympic Games as part of the Olympic Festival.

Integration of athletes with a disability – the Alpine skiing model

Jack Benedick

Littleton, Colorado, USA; Chairman, IPC
Alpine Skiing Committee

It is my pleasure to be here today. I had the opportunity to be a presenter at the VISTA '93 Conference in Canada. Now with the VISTA '99 Conference it gives me the chance to see the progress we have made in various aspects of disability sports. My presentation today will discuss the integration of elite disability sports into the "able-bodied" arena. Specifically, I will be talking about the US Disabled Ski Team (USDST) and what we have accomplished in the US. I will also touch on our integration at the international level with the International Ski Federation (FIS).

1. Definitions of integration

1.1 the incorporation as equals into society or an organisation

This is a condensed meaning of integration taken from Webster's New Collegiate Dictionary. For the purpose of my discussion I offer two other definitions of integration.

1.2 the incorporation of a disability sport into the "able-bodied sport federation, either at national or international level

1.3 the incorporation of athletes with a disability into "able-bodied" competitions with some special consideration or an event within an event

In the US we have achieved both of these; however, this has been an ongoing effort since the 1970s and is continuing. I will touch on integration at the international level later.

2. As we discuss integration, we are moving along a continuum from recreation/rehabilitation to top elite.

3. A key ingredient in this process is that both the athletes with disabilities and their organizations along with the "able-bodied" federation must want to move in this direction.

4. An often debated topic is SPORTS SPECIFIC vs. DISABILITY SPECIFIC. From my experience in Alpine skiing this is a major factor and may be the most important. In the past, when disability skiing was getting started and competition began to evolve, someone, either by accident or on purpose, created the FUNCTIONAL CLASSIFICATION SYSTEM. This has allowed disability skiing to be sport specific and thus easily streamlined and aided immeasurably in the integration process.

    Other nations have also integrated at various levels within their national federations and many more are actively studying the feasibility of this incorporation.

    The timeline for what we have done in the US is:

    -   1986: The US Handicapped Ski Team moves from a disability sports organization to the US Ski Federation and is licensed and logoed as the "US Disabled Ski Team".

    -   From 1989 to the present, the USDST has been fully integrated into the US Ski Federation for all operational aspects.

5. The various disability ski programs provide the base and are the main building blocks for the USDST. Almost every ski arena in the US has some type of disability skiing program. These range

from rehabilitation and recreation to elite training centers such as Winter Park, Colorado, and Park City, Utah. As one moves up the competition ladder, the number of participants decreases through a natural process of elimination based directly on performance criteria.

6. As mentioned earlier, we use a functional classification system at all levels of competition. The visually impaired classes allow for only blind racers, but all other IPC classes allow for a multiplicity of disabilities to compete against each other.

7. In the mid 1980s, the US Ski Federation adopted a system that allowed USDST athletes to compete in "able-bodied" races. The Golden Rule, named after Diana Golden, a former USDST member, provides specific start positions for competitors with a disability. After the first 15 starts, the next five start positions are for racers with a disability. This continues throughout the start order. For the second run of a technical event this preferential seeding also applies or racers can use their results from the first run, whichever is to the racer's advantage.

8. During the 1986 World Disabled Ski Championships in Sweden a "HANDICAP FACTOR SYSTEM" was presented to the nations by Nicol Moll, a member of the German Team. This factor system would accomplish several things. It reduces the number of medals won and dispels the SPECIAL OLYMPICS image that the media and general public had. It further levels the playing field and creates a more competitive event. This handicap factor is now in wide use at the national and international level. Using this system you can have an event, the field competes against itself and a single winner is declared. In the US we use it to award the USSA medals at our national championships and further to award cash prize money.

In 1998, the FIS accepted our Disabled Alpine World Cup circuit.

The handicap factor system was a key issue in our discussions with FIS. As with integration at the national level, disability sports must align themselves as close to the "able-bodied" structure as possible. This includes rules, conduct of events, organization, etc. The FIS created a Disabled Alpine Skiing Committee and effective this competition season our world cup circuit is fully under the administration of the FIS. This includes FIS point lists, overall FIS World Cup standings, and appropriate awards at season's end.

9. The handicap factor system enables us to reduce the IPC system down to three categories. Currently this is used only at the World Cups, but will be discussed at the 2000 Disabled Alpine World Championships in Switzerland and may be proposed as a rule change during the Nations' Meeting in Salt Lake during the 2002 Winter Paralympic Games.

While this integration process is dependent on many variables, being mutually beneficial to all parties is also a key issue. Marketing and funding are always important, and in many cases a final decision is based on these. It is everyone's benefit if disability sport or athletes can enhance funding for the national or international federations.

Chevy Trucks are the main sponsor of the US Ski Federation and this includes the USDST. The marketing department of Chevy Trucks has indicated that this commercial is one of the best ever produced and always is discussed at their corporate meetings.

Sport and rehabilitation: Patterns of initial and continuing participation in wheelchair basketball in the United Kingdom and Germany

Trevor Williams † [1], Klaus Schüle[2], Tarja Kolkka[3], Walter Hubach[2]

[1] Department of Physical Education, Sports Science & Recreation Management, Loughborough University, Loughborough, United Kingdom;
[2] Institute for Rehabilitation and Sport for the Disabled, German Sport University, Cologne, Germany;
[3] Finnish Association of Sports for the Disabled, Helsinki, Finland

Introduction

Sport and active leisure are important in the lifelong care and management of many impairments. Research suggests that not only does regular physical exercise help to reduce clinical depression, reduce rehospitalization, and prolong life expectancy (KENNEDY & SMITH 1990) but it can improve physical competence (HEDRICK 1985), self-concept and self-efficacy (AUSTIN 1987), and decrease loneliness (LYONS 1987). Indeed, activity participation has so many positive correlates that it is the most significant contributor to rehabilitation after spinal cord injury (KRAUSE & CREWE 1987). These are well-known arguments, of course, and many successful rehabilitation centers include physical activities such as sport in their programs. However, once individuals leave the supportive, structured environment of the rehabilitation centre, many find it difficult to maintain their active participation.

Much of what is known about post-discharge lifestyles is based on research that has shown dramatic decreases in sport and leisure participation. Studies of individuals with acquired impairments such as spinal cord injury have consistently highlighted sedentary and socially restricted lifestyles in Sweden (LEVI, HULTLING & SEIGER 1996), the United States of America (KLEIBER, BROCK, LEE, DATTILO & CALDWELL 1995), and Australia (KIRKBY, CULL & FOREMAN 1996). Individuals face, among other things, a loss of cultivated skills, a disruption of their social relationships, and an increase in dependency (KLEIBER et al., 1995). These factors are indicators of decreased quality of life, and their effects are a source of frustration for many rehabilitation professionals. Research does well to indicate these difficulties. At the same time, however, we should also draw attention to those individuals who have managed to maintain and develop active post-discharge lifestyles.

Rehabilitation professionals can learn a lot from individuals who are active in disability sport. In particular, it is important to investigate the ways in which individuals become involved in disability sport post-discharge. Information on the problems discharged patients are facing, the solutions patients construct for those problems, and their community experiences is extremely helpful in the development of more effective pre-discharge rehabilitation programs. It would appear, then, that socialization into disability sport is socially and culturally relative. Questions, however, remain and one of the more important is the extent to which socialization into disability sport is socially and culturally relative. Do we observe, for example, similar or different patterns of socialization in the same sport in different countries?

The purpose of this paper is to examine patterns of participation in wheelchair basketball in the United Kingdom and Germany. Specifically, we want to compare howplayers in two of the world's leading wheelchair basketball nations become involved in sport (initial socialization) and how they continue to be involved (continuing socialization). Of particular concern are the links that wheelchair basketball has with rehabilitation medicine, who introduces players to the sport (socialization agents), and in what social contexts they are introduced (socialization contexts).

Methods

A questionnaire was developed in the UK that included variables grouped under the following headings: Personal impairment, health and fitness, socialisation, and participation. The questionnaire was administered and assessed for its content validity in collaboration with the Great Britain Wheelchair Basketball Association (GBWBA). Test-retest reliability was .86.

The questionnaires, together with a stamped and addressed envelope, were mailed to the secretaries of all 30 wheelchair basketball clubs registered with the GBWBA. Instructions for distribution and collection were included and, after using personal contact and telephone follow-up procedures through the GBWBA, 23 clubs (76%) returned a total of 162 completed questionnaires. We were unable to calculate the response rate as a percentage of the number of players in the wheelchair basketball population. The official GBWBA figures for registered players in the UK differed markedly with those of some clubs but the best estimate of the GBWBA was that the sample was highly representative for the UK National League.

The questionnaire was translated into German. German peculiarities as well as special aspects of personal data protection had to be taken in to consideration. Not so many participants were very enthusiastic about filling in this questionnaire because another action in this respect had been finished a short time before. Therefore, we decided to survey the 1st and 2nd national leagues[1]. In total, questionnaires from 22 teams were received (1st national league = 8; 2nd national league = 14). 16 teams (73%) sent us 107 questionnaires for evaluation. This was considered representative for the upper 2 basketball leagues.

The socialisation variables were made operational in similar ways to those found in the literature. For example, Hedrick, Morse, and Figoni

---

[1] Furthermore, we got active support by the intervention of Dr. Horst Strohkendl, the representative of this action. We would like to give our words of thanks to him now.

(1988); Watanabe, Cooper, Vosse, Baldini, and Robertson (1992); and Williams and Taylor (1994) used personal attributes that included gender, age, marital status, employment, impairment, education, and occupation; socialisation agents were those who had introduced the respondent to wheelchair basketball; and socialisation situations were those contexts in which the respondent had been introduced to the sport.

However, starting from the literature, a distinction was made between the introductory element, which was treated as initial socialisation, and the notion of continuing socialisation. Continuing socialisation was made operational as the sources of information on wheelchair basketball during their socialisation in to the sport. Respondents were asked to rate the importance, using a four-point scale from very unimportant to very important, of a number of sources that were identified during the initial development of the questionnaire with the GBWBA.

Results and Discussion

Personal characteristics

A comparison of the personal and biographical characteristics of the British and German wheelchair basketball players was made using the Chi-square test of association. There were no significant differences between the two groups of players with respect to car use/ownership, employment, marital status, pre-impairment participation levels for those with acquired impairments, and gender (see Tab. 1). Both groups exhibited high unemployment rates (compared to the non-disabled rates of 9.6% in the UK and 8.4% in Germany [EUROSTAT, cited in Die Zeit, 1998]) and high car use/ownership which could be seen as an indicator of a mobile and independent lifestyle. The two groups had similar age profiles although there were more British than German players over the age of 40 years and more German than British players in the 30-34 year age group.

	UK %	Germany %		UK %	Germany %
Age			Car use	93.2	96.3
U16 yrs	1.2	0.0	**Employment**		
16-19 yrs	6.8	2.8	Full-time	34.8	43.0
20-24 yrs	19.8	15.0	Part-time	11.8	16.8
25-29 yrs	22.2	23.4	Education	5.0	4.7
30-34 yrs	18.5	27.1	Other	48.4	35.5
35-39 yrs	9.3	14.0	**Marital status**		
40-49 yrs	21.0	11.2	Single	58.4	59.8
50-59 yrs	1.2	4.7	Married	33.5	36.4
60+ yrs		1.9	Other	8.1	3.7
Gender			**Pre impairment**		
Male	89.5	91.6	Active	67.4	55.6
Female	10.5	8.4	Not active	32.6	44.4

Tab. 1: A comparison of the response frequencies (%) of personal characteristics of British and German wheelchair basketball players

Three major differences between the groups were identified using a Chi-square test. First, while more British players were over the age of 40 years, the German players had played wheelchair basketball for a longer time. A significant large proportion (69.1%) of the German players had played wheelchair basketball longer than the majority (56.8%) of the British players (χ^2 = 25.06, df = 5, p < .001). This difference occurred at 6 years (see Tab. 1 and Fig. 1). Second, the frequencies of particular impairments (see Fig. 2) show that German wheelchair basketball players tend to have a spinal cord injury (72.9%), and this contrasts with a spread of spinal cord injury, spina bifida, and a variety of other impairments among the British players (χ^2 = 34.39, df = 4, p < .001). Very few German players have a congenital impairment. This is reflected in, third, the different profiles of the two groups using their ages when impairment occurred (see Fig. 2 and 3).

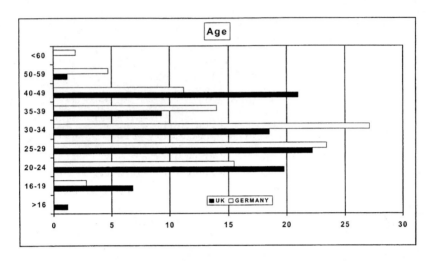

Fig. 1: A comparison of the response frequencies (%) of the age of British and German wheelchair basketball players

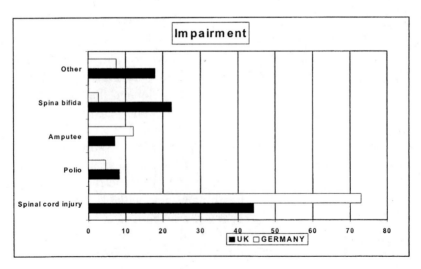

Fig. 2: A comparison of the response frequencies (%) of the impairment of British and German wheelchair basketball players

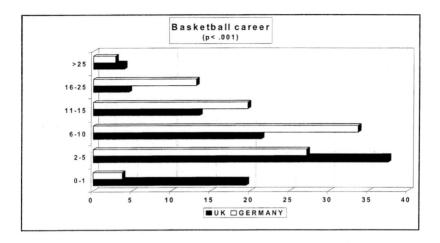

Fig. 3: A comparison of the response frequencies (%) of the basketball career of British and German wheelchair basketball players

Initial participation in wheelchair basketball

The general picture shows that wheelchair basketball clubs in both countries are equally as important in first introducing players to the sport (see Tab. 2).

Introduction Context	UK %	Germany %
Wheelchair basketball club	47.5	41.1
Rehabilitation	13.0	38.3
Education	16.7	6.5
Sport club for people with disabilities	19.1	10.3
Other	3.7	3.7
	100.0	100.0

$\chi^2 = 27.025$, df = 4, p < .001

Tab. 2: A comparison of wheelchair basketball introductory contexts in UK and Germany

A more focussed view, however, shows that the rehabilitation context is much more influential for German players than in the UK and it is almost as important a socialisation context as the wheelchair basketball club in Germany. In the UK, the wheelchair basketball club dominates as an introductory context, with fairly equal, but minor, contributions from rehabilitation, education settings, and sports clubs for people with disabilities. This view is also reflected in the importance of the various introduction agents, with therapists more important in Germany than in the UK. Teachers and a variety of other agents are more important in the UK than in Germany (see Tab. 3).

Introduction Agent	UK %	Germany %
Wheelchair basketball playing friend	48.0	41.1
Non-wheelchair basketball playing friend	5.3	2.8
Another wheelchair basketball player	14.5	11.2
Therapist	11.8	35.5
Teacher	7.2	2.8
Coach	4.6	3.7
Wheelchair basketball development officer	1.3	0.0
Other agent	7.2	2.8
	100.0	100.0

$\chi^2 = 34.396$, df = 4, p < .001

Tab. 3: Comparison of wheelchair basketball introduction agents in the UK and Germany

Further analysis revealed two distinct patterns in the socialisation into wheelchair basketball of the German players. The group of players with a wheelchair basketball career longer than 6 years had been introduced to the sport more in rehabilitation contexts than in the wheelchair basketball clubs. Moreover, much of that introduction had been done by therapists in both contexts. In the rehabilitation context therapists accounted for 64.5% of the introductions while in the wheelchair basketball club they accounted for 20.8%. For those players with careers of less than 6 years, however, the pattern was similar to the British one with a dominance by the wheelchair basketball club and a marked decrease in the contribution of the rehabilitation context (see Tab. 4).

Introduction Context	Wheelchair basketball career	
	Less than 6 years %	6 or more years %
Wheelchair basketball club	55.6	34.3
Rehabilitation	25.0	44.3
Education	5.6	7.1
Sport club for people with disabilities	5.6	12.9
Other	8.3	1.4
	100.0	100.0

$\chi^2 = 9.25$, df = 4, p < .05

Tab. 4: A comparison of wheelchair basketball introductory contexts for German players with careers of more and less than six years

When it came to initial difficulties taking up wheelchair basketball, UK players experienced more problems getting their basketball wheelchair ($\chi^2 = 20.696$, df = 1, p < .001), getting information ($\chi^2 = 4.393$, df = 1, p < .05), obtaining money to support their participation ($\chi^2 = 11.709$, df = 1, p < .001), learning the skills ($\chi^2 = 5.143$, df = 1, p < .05), and training ($\chi^2 = 4.730$, df = 1, p < .05) than their German peers. There were no significant differences between the players with respect to difficulties with travel and coaching; this reflects the high car use/ownership and the dominance of the wheelchair basketball clubs as initial socialisation contexts in both countries (see Fig. 4).

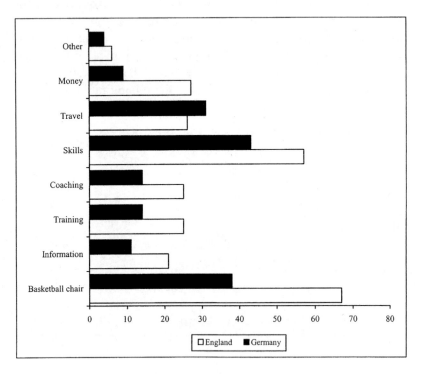

Fig. 4: Initial introduction difficulties among wheelchair basketball players in the UK and Germany as percentage of players experiencing problems in each country

Continuing socialisation

While therapists are less influential in initial socialisation in the UK this situation is reversed in the process of continuing socialisation. Here, the UK therapists are much more important sources of information for players than they are in Germany. This could be because, in many UK wheelchair basketball clubs, therapists play a "basketball" rather than a therapeutic role in the game. They act as volunteers in the organisation and management of teams. This was the case in Germany (see above) but it no longer occurs; hence the influence of German therapists during continuing socialisation decreased. Other players, coaches, coaching manuals, and the wheelchair basketball organisation (via newsletter) were significant more important sources of information for UK players. An additional resource, "Rollstuhlsport Magazine" (published by Deutsche Rollstuhl-Sport-Verband) was important for information among German players in the absence of a German wheelchair basketball newsletter.

Conclusion

1. There are clearly different socialisation patterns that are produced by German and UK historical and structural conditions.

2. The structure of German sport clubs and UK wheelchair basketball clubs accounts for differences in continuing socialisation information sources.

3. Germany and the UK have moved to wheelchair basketball as a sport, rather than a rehabilitation activity.

4. If rehabilitation centres are going to be more effective in socialisation into sports, then the sports knowledge and involvement in sport of therapists are important.

5. The co-operation between rehabilitation centres and clubs must be reinforced. It is recommended to have a contact person.

References

AUSTIN, D.A.: Recreation and persons with physical disabilities: A literature review. In: Therapeutic Recreation Journal 21 (1987), 1, p. 36-44

EUROSTAT. Arbeitslosigkeit in der EU. Die Zeit, 26.2.1998

HEDRICK, B.N.: The effect of wheelchair tennis participation and mainstreaming upon the perceptions of competence of physically disabled adolescents. In: Therapeutic Recreation Journal 19 (1985), 2, p. 34-46

HEDRICK, B.N., MORSE, M.I., & FIGONI, S.F.: Training practices of elite wheelchair road racers. In: Adapted Physical Activity Quarterly 5 (1988), 2, p. 140-153

KLEIBER, D.A., BROCK, S., LEE, Y., DATTILO, J. & CALDWELL, L.: The relevance of leisure in an illness experience: Realities of spinal cord injury. In: Journal of Leisure Research 27 (1995), 3, p. 283-299

KRAUSE, J.S. & CREWE, M.M.: Prediction of long-term survival of persons with spinal cord injury. In: Rehabilitation Psychology 32 (1987), 4, p. 205-213

KENNEDY, D.W. & SMITH, R.W.: A comparison of past and future leisure activity participation between spinal cord injured and non-disabled persons. In: Paraplegia 28 (1990), p. 130-136

KIRBY, R.J., CULL, J. & FOREMAN, P.: Association of prelesion sports participation and involvement in wheelchair sports following spinal cord injury. In: Perceptual and Motor Skills 82 (1996), 2, p. 481-482

LEVI, R., HULTLING, C. & SEIGER, A.: The Stockholm spinal cord injury study: 4. Psychosocial and financial issues of the Swedish annual level-of-living survey in SCI subjects and controls. In: Paraplegia 34 (1996), p. 52-157

LYONS, R.F.: Leisure adjustment to chronic illness and disability. In: Journal of Leisurability 14 (1987), 2, p. 4-10

SHERRILL, C., POPE, C. & ARNHOLD, R.: Sport socialisation of blind athletes: An exploratory study. In: Visual Impairment & Blindness 80 (1986), 5, p. 740-744

SHERRILL, C., RAINBOLT, W., MONTELIONE, T. & POPE, C.: Sport socialisation of blind and of cerebral palsied elite athletes. In: SHERRILL, C. (ed.), Sport and disabled athletes. Champaign, Ill., USA 1986, p. 189-195

WATANABE, K.T., COOPER, R.A., VOSSE, A.J., BALDINI, F.D. & ROBERTSON, R.N.: Training practices of athletes who participated in the National Wheelchair Athletic Association training camps. In: Adapted Physical Activity Quarterly 9 (1992), 3, p. 249-260

WILLIAMS, T. & TAYLOR, D.: Socialisation, subculture, and wheelchair sport: The influence of peers in wheelchair racing. In: Adapted Physical Activity Quarterly 11 (1994), 4, p. 417-428

WILLIAMS, T. & KOLKKA, T.: Socialization into wheelchair basketball in the UK: A structural functionalism perspective. In: Adapted Physical Activity Quarterly 15 (1998), p. 351-369

High adventure outdoor recreation – the right to risk

Anne Morash Johnson

Casa Colina Centers for Rehabilitation, Pomona, CA, USA

Participation in high adventure outdoor pursuits and accessing of personal choice is the right and desire of people of all abilities. Often times persons with disabilities are excluded from these experiences based on a preconceived perception of inability and/or liability.

The Casa Colina Outdoor Adventure program in Pomona, California, USA, focuses on empowering persons with disabilities to experience both physical and emotional success through high adventure outdoor experiences. Building self-confidence, promoting personal growth, increasing independence, and enhancing health and wellness are the program goals. Activities include adaptive snow and water skiing, sailing, kayaking, backpacking, rock climbing, horse packing, Minnesota dog sledding, adaptive scuba certification, deep sea fishing, white water rafting, spring and fall camps, and conservation work on Catalina Island.

Utilization of a comprehensive risk management plan eliminates the danger and promotes the value and benefit of high risk activities. Utilizing professional outfitters, staffing trips with rehabilitation professionals and trained volunteers, careful screening of clients prior to participation assists in ensuring safety and success of activities.

Since 1985 the Outdoor Adventure Program of Casa Colina Centers for Rehabilitation has successfully and safely provided high adventure experiences to thousands of persons with disabilities. During those years only three medical emergencies were experienced, all of which were seizure related. Attention to safety, careful planning, and comprehensive supervision have been key to the successful implementation of these high adventure outdoor experiences.

Outdoor adventure programs of this kind are a necessity not a liability. Outdoor adventure recreation in participation is a personal right, and it is our responsibility to provide these activities which encourage personal choice for people of all abilities.

Equity issues in disability sport

Washington State University, Pullman, Washington, USA;
President, International Federation of Adapted Physical Activity

Introduction

In discussions of equity issues in sport, it is important to note that the experiences of athletes with a disability in sport are complicated by the intersection of gender and disability as well as by type of impairment (e.g. spinal cord injury or cerebral palsy) and severity of impairment (e.g. paraplegic or quadriplegia, visual impairment or blind) and sport. In the fight for rights as athletes, much of the struggle for, and within, disability sport has been focused on disability rather than gender or race/ethnicity (DEPAUW & GAVRON 1995). Female athletes with disabilities, in fewer numbers than their male counterparts, have been present in disability sport since the early 1920s but have yet to gain the visibility afforded male athletes with disabilities.

Historical Perspective

Similar to many able-bodied women who have participated in sport and who have sought competitive opportunities throughout history, females with disabilities have also sought competitive opportunities. Although history primarily records the experiences of men including more recently men with disabilities, women with disabilities have participated in a variety of sport events spanning the 20th century. Significant milestones and many of the early "firsts" for female athletes with a disability are presented in Table 1.

Women with disabilities have competed in the Olympic Games as early as 1952. Since then, two females (1984 archer from New Zealand,

1996 archer from Italy) have competed in the Olympic Games (DEPAUW & GAVRON 1995, MASCAGNI 1996).

1924 First International Silent Games (Paris, France); women among competitors

1952 Liz Hartel (post-polio, Denmark) won silver medal in dressage at Summer Olympic Games

1957 First U.S. National Wheelchair Games (New York) to include women

1960 First International Games for Disabled (Paralympics) in Rome, Italy; women included among the competitors

1968 International Special Olympics founded by Eunice Kennedy Shriver; first competition held in Chicago, IL; girls and women among competitors

1974 Six teams participated in the first United States National Women's Wheelchair Basketball tournament

1976 UNESCO conference established right of individuals with disabilities to participate in physical education and sport; rights secured for females as well as males

1977 Sharon Rahn (Hedrick) became the first woman to win the women's wheelchair division of the Boston Marathon with a winning time of   3:48:51.

1982 Karen Farmer (a single leg amputee) became one of the first to earn an athletic scholarship and to compete on the track team for Eastern Washington University. Karen was also the first winner of the U.S. Women's Sports Foundation Up & Coming Award in the Physically Challenged division.
Blind women compete for the first time in the World Goal Ball Championships at Butler University.

1983 The first international Women's Wheelchair Basketball Tournament was held in France separately from the Paralympics.

1984 Neroli Fairhall (NZ) first wheelchair athlete to meet eligibility and compete in Summer Olympic Games; competed in women's archery
First wheelchair races as exhibition events for 1984 Olympics (1500m won by Paul Van Winkle [Belgium] in 3:58.50; 800m is won by Sharon Rahn Hedrick [U.S.] in 2:15.50)
The October 1984 issue of Runner's World ran the first commercial magazine to run a full length article on a disabled athlete. The article was about Linda Down, a Class 5 cerebral palsied athlete, who completed the 1982 New York Marathon in 11 hours, 15 minutes.

1988 Candace Cable-Brooks won the women's wheelchair division of the Boston Marathon for the sixth time; her winning time was 2:10:44.
After her gold medal performance in the disabled skiing Exhibition event during the 1988 Winter Olympics in Calgary, Diana Golden became an official spokesperson for ChapStick Challenge for Disabled Skiing and signed a corporate sponsorship agreement with Subaru, the official car of the U.S. Disabled Ski Team.
Winter Olympics in Calgary include exhibition events (3 track Alpine, Blind Nordic) for males and females.

	Summer Olympics (S. Korea) include wheelchair races as exhibition events (1500m for men; 800m for females); Sharon Hedrick wins second Gold Medal in Olympic Wheelchair 800m (2:11.49).
1989	Seven women (and seven men) became the first winners of the United States Disabled Athletes of the Year Award.
1990	Dr. Donalda Ammons appointed the first deaf female Director of the World Games for the Deaf U.S. Team
1991	Jean Driscoll (USA) becomes the first athlete with a disability to win the Sudafed Female Athlete of the Year.
	Sue Moucha (USA) attends as the first athlete with a disability at the International Olympic Academy (IOA) in Greece.
	Jan Wilson named the first Coordinator, Disabled Sport Programs, United States Olympic Committee (USOC).
1992	Connie Hansen (Denmark) and Candace Cable (USA) become the only two women to compete in all Summer Olympic Exhibition events.
	Tanni Grey (Great Britain) named the "Sunday Times" Sportswoman of the Year by Her Majesty The Queen
	Tricia Zorn (USA) won 12 gold medals (10 gold, 2 silver) at the 1992 Paralympic Games in Barcelona (also won 12 in 1988 in Seoul, Korea Paralympics).
1994	Monique Kalkman (the Netherlands) earned the title of Amsterdam's Sportswomen of the Year.
1996	Jean Driscoll (USA) became the first person to win the Boston Marathon for the seventh time.

Tab. 1: Selected "Firsts" and significant milestones for women with disabilities in sport (adapted from DEPAUW, K. P. & GAVRON, J., 1995)

In addition to these women who participated in full medal Olympic events, male and female athletes with disabilities competed in Exhibition Events at Olympics Games beginning with the 1984 Winter Olympics in Sarajevo and the 1984 Summer Olympics in Los Angeles and continued since then.

Female athletes with a disability have also been found in elite national and international competitions beyond the Olympic Games, specifically the Paralympic Games. The Paralympics represent the largest single event in which female athletes with disabilities compete in a variety of sporting events. Although female athletes with disabilities have been competitors since the inception of the Paralympic

Games, they are still underrepresented in the Paralympic Games (DEPAUW 1994; SHERRILL 1997). According to Sherrill (1997), the gender ratio for the Barcelona Paralympic Games was 3:1 (male to female) and decreased to 4:1 at the 1996 Atlanta Paralympic Games. In Atlanta, 49 of the 104 participating countries (47%) brought no female athletes and most countries brought fewer than 9 female athletes (SHERRILL 1997). Given this trend and growing concern, the International Paralympic Committee (IPC) Sports Council established a Women's Initiative to address the issue of female representation and participation in future Paralympic Games.

In addition to the Paralympic Games, a large contingent of women participate in the World Games for the Deaf. Women were among the first competitors in the 1924 World Games for the Deaf (Paris) and continue to participate in the summer and winter competitions every four years (in the year following the Olympic Games). International Special Olympics also includes girls and women with mental retardation among the competitors.

The Boston Marathon also stands as an additional example of competitive opportunities for athletes with disabilities. Wheelchair athletes were among its entrants as early as 1974. The first female wheelchair competitor, Sharon Rahn (Hedrick), won the 1977 Women's Wheelchair Division with a time of 3:48:51. Since then, not only have the times decreased dramatically but the gap between the winning times for women and for men has narrowed as well. Currently, wheelchair men regularly finish under 1:30 and wheelchair women finish under 1:45.

Sport as Contested Terrain

Sport has been viewed as a reflection of society. Recently, sport has been examined for its role in the production and reproduction of social inequality in sport (Donnelly 1996). That is, sport has served to produce and reinforces dominant societal values which are often rooted in power and oppression. On the other hand, sport can also be a site for resistance to those same dominant cultural values and for the production of social equality. Although much of current disability sport reflects the able-bodied sport model and has therefore contributed to reproduction of dominant cultural values, the mere presence of athletes with disabilities in sport can be considered an act of resistance and contributes to the transformative power of sport to effect change in sport and society (DEPAUW 1997).

Recently, sport has been examined from three theoretical perspectives: sport as a reflection of society, as a site for the reproduction of dominant societal values, and as a site for resistance (DONNELLY 1996). Research on social inequality in sport has been conducted on three levels of analyses linked to the three theoretical perspectives of sport articulated above (DONNELLY 1996; HALL 1995). Categoric, distributive, and relational analyses have been used to examine sport as a cultural representation of social relations (e.g., gender, race, class) (HALL 1995) and emanated from research on gender issues in sport (DEWAR 1993) and on women of color in sport (SMITH 1992). Although these levels of analyses have been used to examine issues of race, class, and gender in sport, they have yet to be utilized in studies of disability and sport (DEPAUW 1997).

Categoric research focuses on differences in characteristics or behavior (e.g. athletic participation, performance, skills) among categories of individuals. Distributive analysis refers to research that examines the distribution of resources and opportunities across categories of individuals (e.g. race, class, gender). Relational analysis moves beyond the study of categories as discrete entities to analysis of social relationships among and across categories of individuals in their cultural contexts.

In addition to the interconnection between the theoretical perspectives and levels of analyses briefly described above, the stages of inclusion of marginalized group members (access, accommodation, and transformation) contribute to a framework for studying sport

(DEPAUW 1997).

Access refers to gaining access to and entrance into the sporting arena. Today, women, persons of color, and individuals with disabilities have gained access to sport.

Accommodation implies that modifications or adaptations are made to more easily integrate individuals into the existing structure of sport. Examples of accommodation include modifying rules to allow individuals with sensory and physical impairments to compete with able-bodied individuals (e.g. two bounce rule in wheelchair tennis, visual start for hearing impaired athletes, touch start in wrestling for blind persons). Accommodation has the effect of "allowing" individuals with disabilities to participate in sport but does not necessarily alter sport.

Moving beyond accommodation to transformation requires that sport, as a social institution, undergo fundamental change. It is indeed difficult to envision such a fundamental shift in sport because such a change requires reconceptualization of basic and underlying tenets of sport and especially our socially constructed views of body, ability, athletic performance and sport (DEPAUW 1997).

Our understanding of sport has been enhanced through the inclusion of marginalized groups into sport because as these individuals increasingly gain access to sport, sport can no longer simply "reflect" dominant societal values nor reproduce the "prevailing hegemonic versions of social reality" (SAGE 1993, p. 161). "If we become more active in the construction of our social world, we become active agents rather than merely the objects of sociohistorical processes; we make our own history by transforming social structures instead of being dominated by them" (SAGE 1993).

Sport and Disability

Analyzing sport through a lens of disability challenges our basic notions of movement and helps us redefine the meaning of movement and sport on a continuum (DEPAUW 1997). Dunn and Sherrill (1996) have argued that "individuals with disabilities contribute much to our general understanding of movement and its meaning" (p. 387) through helping others appreciate and value activity and its contributions as a worthy end in it itself. Although this argument is valid, it is important to extend the dialogue to challenging our notions about sport and physical activity. It is important to acknowledge that sport is socially constructed **by** able-bodied individuals and primarily **for** able-bodied individuals but that sport can also serve as a site for resistance to dominant societal values (DEPAUW 1997; DONNELLY 1996).

The disability rights movement has challenged us to view disability in the context of social relationships (CHAPPELL 1992; GOFFMAN 1968; HANKS & POPLIN 1981; SHAPIRO 1993). The disability rights movement has also challenged us to recognize the ways in which we have continually used (and have privileged) able-bodied paradigms in our definitions of healthy bodies and efficient physical activity including sport. To date, the primary participants in the dialogue about gender and disability are females with disabilities. These women (e.g., BROWNE, CONNORS & STERN 1985; FINE & ASCH 1981; MORRIS 1989, 1991, 1992; WILLMUTH & HOLCOMB 1993) have explored issues facing (mostly white) females with disabilities and have just begun to examine the complexity of gender and ability/disability issues. Extensive analysis of females with a disability in sport has yet to occur.

In the area of sport, the first principle of the Brighton Declaration on Women and Sport (1994) calls for equity and equality in society and sport. Specifically, it states that:

"equal opportunity to participate in sport whether for the purpose of leisure and recreation, health promotion or high performance, is the right of every women, regardless of race, color, language, religion, creed, sexual orientation,

age, marital status, disability, political belief or affiliation, national or social origin" (p. 3).

A similar stance was reiterated in the Windhoek Call to Action.

Toward Transformation of Sport

By their presence in sport, athletes with a disability have changed sport and our images of sport and the sporting body. Today, there are numerous images of individuals with disabilities that portray our changing views of sport and simultaneously reflect changes in the broader cultural context as well.

Most of the images of athletes with a disability are those in which the athlete is portrayed competing or performing in sport (e.g. dramatic visual images of athletes with a disability climbing mountains, skiing, the highly competitive "final four" of wheelchair basketball [men's and women's], and wheelchair dance competitions for individuals with disabilities). Recent images have also portrayed athletes with disabilities as part of sport; images of athletes with a disability alongside able-body athletes at sporting events, on covers of books and magazines, and announcements designed for the general public or able-body sporting world.

In addition, there are visual images that invite us to reconceptualize sport and athletes with a disability (DEPAUW 1997). In these images, the focus is on the sport or the ability; the disability is minimized or discreetly visible. Examples include announcements or advertisements for the Grand Prix Circuit (i.e. only one indicator that the event is for wheelchair tennis), a new magazine (i.e. golfer lining up his putt), and a disability sport book (i.e. we see the long jump first, prosthesis second). One of the advertisements for the 1996 Paralympic Games dramatically demonstrated the athletic ability required to be successful in the high jump (the shoes and high jump records of Olympic medalists Bruce Jenner & Dan O'Brien; the one shoe and high jump record for Paralympic medalist Arnie Boldt).

The lens of disability allows us to make problematic the socially constructed nature of sport. As we move toward the transformation of sport, we can change our view of a sprint event and gold medal performance. We are able to view the images of Tony Volpentest, Jean Driscoll, visually impaired runners, and other athletes with a disability with images of Linford Christie, Gail Devers, FloJo, Michael Johnson, Donovan Bailey, and other Olympians and interpret the performances as differences in style but not substance. This transformation of sport means that we are able to "see" sport and athletes with a disability without seeing any contradiction, without assuming a physical liability, stigma, or deformity, and without assuming an impaired athletic performance. That is, we will see an athlete, an athletic peformance, and a 'sporting body'.

References

Brighton Declaration on Women and Sport. In: Women sport and the challenge of change. Brighton, England 1994

BROWN, H. & SMITH, H.: Whose 'ordinary life' is it anyway? In: Disability, Handicap and Society 4 (1989), 2, p. 105-119

BROWNE, S.E., CONNORS, D. & STERN, N.: With the power of each breath. A disabled women's anthology. San Francisco, CA, USA 1985

CHAPPELL, A.L.: Towards a sociological critique of the normalization principle. In: Disability, Handicap and Society 7 (1992), 1, p. 35-50

CONNORS, D.: Disability, sexism, and the social order. In: BROWNE, S.E., CONNORS, D. & STERN, N. (eds.), With the power of each breath: A disabled women's anthology. Pittsburgh, PA, USA 1985, p. 92-107

DEPAUW, K.P.: A feminist perspective on sport and sports organizations for persons with disabilities. In: STEADWARD, R.D., NELSON, E.R. & WHEELER, G.D. (eds.), VISTA '93 - The outlook. Edmonton, Alberta,

Canada 1994

DEPAUW, K.P.: The (in)visibility of disability: Cultural contexts and 'sporting bodies'. In: Quest 49 (1997)

DEPAUW, K.P. & GAVRON, S.J.: Disability and sport. Champaign, IL, USA 1995

DEWAR, A.: Sexual oppression in sport: Past, present, and future alternatives. In: INGHAM A.G. & LOY J.W. (eds.), Sport in social development: Traditions, transitions, and transformations. Champaign, IL, USA 1993, p. 147-165

DONNELLY, P.: Approaches to social inequality in the sociology of sport. In: Quest 48 (1996), p. 221-242

DUNN, J. & SHERRILL, C.: Movement and its implications for individuals with disabilities. In: Quest 48 (1996), p. 378-391

FINE, M. & ASCH, A.: Disabled women: Sexism without the pedestal. In: Journal of Sociology and Social Welfare (1981), p. 233-248

GOFFMAN, E.: Stigma: Notes on the management of spoiled identity. Englewood Cliffs 1968

HALL, M. A.: Feminism and sport bodies. Champaign, IL, USA 1996

HANKS, M. & POPLIN, D.E.: The sociology of physical disability: A review of literature and some conceptual perspectives. In: Deviant Behavior. An Interdisciplinary Journal 2 (1981), p. 309-328

MARTIN, D.: Disability culture: Eager to bite the hands that would feed them. In: Week in Review, New York Times (June 1, 1997)

MASCAGNI, K.: Paola Fantato: Sports as a means of social integration. In: Olympic Review 75 (1996)

MORRIS, J. (ed.): Able lives: Women's experience of paralysis. London 1989

MORRIS, J.: Personal and political: A feminist perspective on researching physical disability. In: Disability, Handicap and Society 7 (1992), p. 157-166

MORRIS, J.: Pride against prejudice: Transforming attitudes to disability. Philadelphia, PA, USA 1991

SAGE, G. H.: Sport and physical education and the new world order: Dare we be agents of social change? In: Quest 45 (1993), p. 151-164

SHAPIRO, J.: No pity: People with disabilities forging a new civil rights movement. New York, NY, USA 1993

SHERRILL, C.: Paralympic Games 1996: Feminist and other concerns - what's your excuse? In: Palaestra 13 (1997), p. 32 - 38

SMITH, Y.: Women of color in society and sport. In: Quest 44 (1992), p. 228-250

WILLMUTH, M.E. & HOLCOMB, L. (eds.): Women with disabilities: Found voices. Binghampton, NY, USA 1993

Gender concerns in integration, development and recruitment of female athletes with a disability

Claudine Sherrill

Texas Woman's University, Denton, TX, USA

Proportionately fewer females than males engage in sport at all levels: Paralympic, competitive, and recreational (DEPAUW 1994; OLENIK, MATTHEWS & STEADWARD 1995; SHERRILL 1993; 1997). This is true in both disability and non-disability sport and challenges us to consider ways to increase opportunities and decrease barriers for females. According to Coakley (1998), "gender and gender relations has become the most popular topic in sociology of sport since 1990" (p. 211). Coakley, author of the sociology of sport textbook that most universities in the US require, continues: "Sociologists now realize it is important to explain why sports traditionally have been defined as men's activities, why half the world's population traditionally has been excluded or discouraged from participating in many sports, how sports influence people's ideas about masculinity and femininity, and why the topic of sexual orientation and sports is so controversial" (p. 211).

Attitudes and practices regarding girls and women in sport are changing, but very slowly. World class events like the recent Women's Soccer World Cup Championships (football) have inspired a phenomenal amount of interest. Over 90,000 fans, including President Clinton, attended this event and millions watched it on television. The media finally are giving women's sport considerable attention (e.g., "Time Magazine" cover, July 19, 1999; "Sports 'N Spokes" cover, May 19, 1999). In addition, a variety of cartoons have been published in newspapers all over the world (e.g., "Remember when 'You play like a girl' was an insult?"). Sport magazines exclusively for girls and women are now being published in the United States. Little girls now have role models they see on television and in magazines; they hear parents and others talking about women's sports; they know opportunity exists! This same sense of excitement about elite female competitors, however, does not seem to exist in disability sport.

Women in the Paralympics

In 1996, when asked to write an article on Paralympics for "Palaestra", I chose to focus on feminist and other concerns (SHERRILL 1997a). Atlanta was my fourth Paralympics, and I was genuinely distressed about the small number of females participating as athletes, coaches, and administrators. Table 1 shows the percentage of women participating in each of the 19 Paralympic sports in Atlanta. With the exception of equestrian sports (75%), basketball (42%), swimming (40%), and lawn bowls (41%), fewer than 33% of the participants in each sport were females. Five (26%) of the sports had no women participating.

Archery	26%
Athletics	22%
Basketball	42%
Boccia	19%
Cycling	13%
Equestrian	75%
Fencing	31%
Football/soccer	0%
Goalball	40%
Judo	0%
Lawn bowls	41%
Powerlifting	0%
Rugby	0%
Shooting	27%
Swimming	40%
Table tennis	27%
Tennis	33%
Volleyball	0%
Yachting	5%

Table 1: Percentages of women in each
of the 19 Paralympic sports in Atlanta

Overall, the percentage of women competing in the Atlanta Paralympics was about 24% compared to 33% in Barcelona. Of the 104 countries participating in the Atlanta Paralympics, 49 (47%) brought no female athletes. This is almost 50%!!! In most cases, countries bringing no women had athlete delegations of 8 or less. I suspect that these figures reflect economic limitations. When money is limited, tradition seems to dictate that it be spent on men. But these figures also indicate an overall lack of interest and opportunity for women in sport in these countries. The reasons for lack of interest are complex. It may be that, because of tradition or religion, females are not exposed to sport and truly have no interest. If one has no knowledge of something, no concept of the possibilities, then one will not be interested. In sociological terms, such women have no socializing agents and thus are not likely to change.

Socialization into Sport

Much research, including that of the late Trevor Williams, shows that athletes with disabilities have been socialized into sport primarily by themselves or by peers who are athletes (RUCKERT 1980; SHERRILL 1986; WILLIAMS 1994; WILLIAMS & KOLKKA 1998). As early as 1980, Ruckert reported findings of a poll of international athletes with disabilities from 18 countries. Responses to the question, "Who stimulated you to become involved in sports?" were as follows: themselves, 29%; friends with disabilities, 27%; able-bodied friends, 27%; family, 9%; and physicians, 8%. The implication is that women with disabilities must take initiative and get themselves involved in sport or must have access to friends who are in sports. Given the fact that far more males than females participate in sport in most countries, it is likely that these friends will be males. So how do we interest male athletes in helping females train and compete? In countries where females are not perceived as potential athletes, how do we change perceptions and athletes?

Research Concerns

A critique of research on gender and disability indicates that little attention has been given to how gender structures influence the experiences of disability sport participation (HUTZLER & FELIS 1999; KOLKKA & WILLIAMS 1997). Hutzler & Felis (1999) reported that only 2% of the 253 research articles on disability sport from 1983 through 1997 specifically addressed female samples. Additionally, a few articles combined a small number of female participants with male participants, but findings offered no insight into female performance. Recently "Adapted Physical Activity Quarterly" adopted a policy that males and females should not be combined for statistical treatment because the information on females is lost when this practice is followed. Means and standard deviations always represent the majority group (males), and the minority group (females) tends to decrease the validity of the findings. Research is needed specifically on women because genders differ significantly on most body composition, performance, and other variables.

Research Needs

Research on women is especially needed in the areas of development, recruitment, and integration. Specifically, "there is a need for a more sophisticated theoretical foundation, different theoretical perspectives, and different approaches, and for alternative research designs to increase our knowledge about gender, disability, and sport participation" (KOLKKA & WILLIAMS 1997, p. 8). The lack of female role models for women with disabilities and the failure of professionals to be aware of the few women with disabilities who do excel in sports means that girls and women who aspire to become involved in sports are almost totally dependent upon strong personal motivation and goals and their ingenuity in obtaining support from men. Sport sociologists Williams and Taylor (1994) emphasize that, when women do participate in disability sport, "they tend to do so in ways defined by men and because their influencing peers are male"

(KOLKKA & WILLIAMS 1997, p. 14). Research indicates that able-bodied women are socialized into sport in ways that are different from able-bodied men (COAKLEY 1998). We simply do not know how women with a disability are socialized into sport but many factors, including the sport itself, affect lifespan sport socialization. Most research to date is qualitative (e.g. OLENIK et al. 1995; SHERRILL 1997b) and based on interview data from a relatively small number of women. Olenik et al. (1995) reported that elite women athletes with a disability had mostly become involved in sport in adulthood rather than childhood and that their involvement was encouraged by a significant other who knew about disability sport. Sherrill (1997b), using data from interviews of elite women wheelchair racers in 1995 and Paralympic athletes in Atlanta in 1996, reported diverse, complex sport socialization patterns. A central theme was a significant other in either childhood or adulthood who told them they were good at sports and the availability of opportunities for practice and support from significant others so that feelings of perceived sport competence could develop.

Link Between Adapted Physical Activity and Disability Sport

Research indicates also that the onset of the disability (congenital vs. acquired) and the severity of the disability affect the way one becomes involved in sport. These factors interact with gender in complex ways, reflecting societal attitudes and traditions toward women's roles. In some countries today, schools provide adapted physical activity instruction to children with disabilities at an early age (SHERRILL 1998), with emphasis on learning sports that will enable them to participate with individuals of their choice (able-bodied or disabled) in settings of their choice (GOODWIN & WATKINSON 2000; SHERRILL & WILLIAMS 1996). Adapted physical activity services, depending upon needs, may be delivered in either mainstream settings (often called inclusive or integrated) or separate settings. Research indicates that in the US 37% of adapted physical activity specialists employed to teach in the public schools report coaching some form of disability sport after school and on weekends (KELLY &

GANSNEDER 1998). Likewise, increasing numbers of regular education coaches are accepting students with disabilities into their afterschool training and competition programs (KOZUB & PORRETTA 1998).

Promotion of Sport for All

The International Federation of Adapted Physical Activity (IFAPA) is the major organization that promotes physical activity and sport for individuals with disabilities of all ages throughout the lifespan. Its official journal, "Adapted Physical Activity Quarterly", regularly publishes research on disability sport (e.g. see July 1999 issue devoted exclusively to disability sports). Presidents of IFAPA (e.g. Gudrun Doll-Tepper, Karen DePauw, Greg Reid) and board members have all been very involved in and supportive of disability sport, particularly Paralympic sport. Likewise the president of IPC, Robert Steadward, and many leaders in the Paralympic Movement are members and advocates of IFAPA and adapted physical activity. There are many benefits to IPC and IFAPA working together to achieve the common goals of sport for all Paralympic sport for the truly elite.

Advocacy for the adapted physical activity profession and for IFAPA appears to be one way to assure that children and adolescents will be socialized into all forms of sport at early ages. Strong links should be formed between adapted physical education teachers and adult disability sport groups in the community; promoting sport for children should be a collaborative effort. Such cooperation should also promote involvement of athletes with disabilities in the coaching of children and adolescents and in employment in various forms of sport.

Individuals with congenital disabilities are likely to be socialized into disability sport in different ways and at different ages than persons with acquired conditions. Still, the socialization process requires that both male and female teachers, as well as family members, be aware of the appropriateness and desirability of sport for boys **and girls** with a disability. Resources must be made available, and men control these resources in many societies. Girls' and women's participation in sport should not be a female concern, but one that is shared by both genders.

Strategies for Promoting Women's Sport

Clearly, one way to approach development of girls' and women's sports in locations where females are underrepresented in sport is to conduct awareness sessions for male athletes, coaches, and administrators at the Paralympics and other times when they leave their countries and can be exposed to new ideas. A second strategy might be to offer monetary and other kinds of incentives to countries that increase the number of women athletes that they bring to sporting events. A third approach might be to establish policy and/or a requirement that all countries must bring a certain percentage of female athletes. Gender equity in disability sport cannot occur without the leadership of males and the strong initiative of the International Paralympic Committee. Males hold most of the power in the IPC just as they do in the International Olympic Committee (IOC). What they do with that power largely determines the future of women's Paralympic sport! Now is the time to address this issue before the number of women involved falls lower.

The IPC, by virtue of being founded in modern times, is far ahead of the IOC. However, numbers of women participating in the Olympics are increasing whereas numbers of women participating in the Paralympics have been decreasing. Let's examine these increases for the Olympics:

1984	Los Angeles	1,620 females	22.8%
1988	Seoul	2,476 females	25.8%
1992	Barcelona	3,008 females	28.5%
1996	Atlanta	3,684 females	34.0%

The Sydney Olympic Organizers project a record 3,906 female

competitors for 2000. To achieve this, however, they have cut back on the number of male competitors from 7,061 in Atlanta to 6,416 in Sydney. Equity cannot be achieved without sacrifice. I was unable to obtain the projected number of females for the Sydney Paralympics.

Let's look also at the number of Summer Olympic events open to women and men (see Fig. 1).

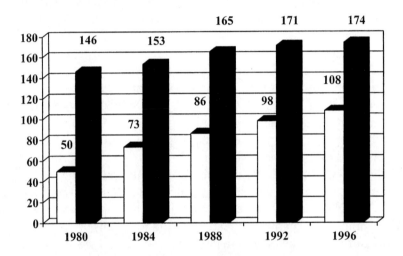

Fig. 1: Number of Summer Olympic events open to women and men. (Eleven events in 1996 were mixed, or open to both men and women. These eleven have been added to both totals for men and women. This procedure was also used for each of the other Olympics in this graph.)

Note, in 1996, that 174 events were open to men, but only 108 events were open to women. Again, we do not seem to be able to access such data for Paralympic women. We know the percentage of women entered in each sport, but not the numbers entered in events. All of us can remember, however, the disappointment of the many female athletes whose events were deleted in Seoul, Barcelona, and Atlanta because insufficient numbers of women came to the Paralympics. Moreover, we are aware of the many women who were forced to compete with athletes in different sport classifications and thus had little opportunity for a fair chance to win.

A first step in resolving inequities is to collect information and maintain a data base that is accessible to eligible researchers and/or the general public. The Olympic data concerning gender is an open record for everyone to view; why not the Paralympic data? We should all know the www access address on the web and be able to inform ourselves and others with regard to equity. Athletes and coaches all over the world should have the power to access information, discuss statistics, compare their country with others, and create local, national, and international strategies for change. I strongly believe that maintaining and disseminating information about gender (and racial) equity should be an essential requirement in the Paralympic bid package as well as various official reports. Without facts, we do not know what kind of negligence or discrimination is occurring. In addition to access to information, the IPC should consider establishing an official policy and ways to monitor and enforce the policy.

The IPC, as the chief policy making body, can help in many ways. Publications, films, and other forms of media should also be monitored for fair and equitable coverage of gender (SCHELL & DUNCAN 1999). The IPC and related sports bodies might commission and/or simply encourage research on this issue. The IPC might conduct a series of workshops on gender equity and/or gender awareness at the Sydney Paralympics and subsequent world sport events. Computer networks for women athletes with and without disabilities might be established to enable women to maintain contact with each other and empower themselves as a viable force in international sport. More emphasis should be placed on the recruitment and training of women coaches and administrators. Individuals like Colin Higgs who have grants for sport work in underdeveloped countries can give special attention to promoting sports for girls and women. Finally, all of us can commit ourselves to supporting girls' and women's sports in our local communities and working from the grassroots up.

References

COAKLEY, J.J.: Sport in society: Issues and controversies. 6th ed. Boston, MA, USA 1998

DEPAUW, K.: A feminist perspective on sports and sport organizations for persons with disabilities.. In: STEADWARD, R.D., NELSON, E.R. & WHEELER, G.D. (eds.), Vista '93 - The outlook. Edmonton, AB. 1994, p. 467-477

GOODWIN, D.L. & WATKINSON, E.J.: Inclusive physical education from the perspective of students with physical disabilities. In: Adapted Physical Activity Quarterly 17 (2000), 2

HUTZLER, Y. & FELIS, O.: Computerized search of scientific literature on sport for disabled persons. In: Perceptual and Motor Skills 88 (1999), p. 1189-1192

KELLY, L.E. & GANSNEDER, B.: Preparation and job demographics of adapted physical educators in the United States. In: Adapted Physical Activity Quarterly 15 (1998), 2, p. 141-154

KOLKKA, T. & WILLIAMS, T.: Gender and disability sport participation: Setting a sociological research agenda. In: Adapted Physical Activity Quarterly 14 (1997), 1, p. 8-23

KOZUB, F.M. & PORRETTA, D.L.: Interscholastic coaches' attitudes toward integration of adolescents with disabilities. In: Adapted Physical Activity Quarterly 15 (1998), 4, p. 328-344

OLENIK, L.M., MATTHEWS, J.M. & STEADWARD, R.D.: Women, disability, and sport - unheard voices. In: Canadian Women Studies 15 (1995), 4, p. 54-57

RUCKERT, H.: Olympics for the disabled: Holland 1980 commemorative book. Haarlem, The Netherlands 1980

SCHELL, L.A. & DUNCAN, M.C.: A content analysis of CBS's coverage of the

1996 Paralympic Games. In: Adapted Physical Activity Quarterly 16 (1999), 1, p. 27-47

SHERRILL, C.: Disability sport and classification theory: A new era for research. In: Adapted Physical Activity Quarterly 16 (1999), 3, p. 206-215

SHERRILL, C.: Adapted physical activity, recreation, and sport: Crossdisciplinary and lifespan. 5th ed. Dubuque, IA. 1998

SHERRILL, C.: Paralympic Games 1996: Feminist and other concerns: What's your excuse? In: Palaestra 13 (1997), 1, p. 32-38

SHERRILL, C.: Interviews with elite female athletes with disabilities. Unpublished report, Texas Woman's University, Denton, USA 1997

SHERRILL, C.: Women with disability, Paralympics, and reasoned action contact theory. In: Women in Sport and Physical Activity Journal 2 (1993), 2, p. 51-60

SHERRILL, C. Social and psychological dimensions of sports for disabled athletes. In: SHERRILL, C. (ed.), Sport and disabled athletes. Champaign, Ill. USA 1986, p. 21-40

SHERRILL, C. & WILLIAMS, T.: Disability and sport: Psychosocial perspectives on inclusion, integration, and participation. In: Sport Science Review 5 (1996), 1, p. 42-64

WILLIAMS, T.: Disability sport socialization and identity construction. In: Adapted Physical Activity Quarterly 11 (1994), p. 14-31

WILLIAMS, T. & TAYLOR, D.: Socialization, subculture, and wheelchair sports: The influence of peers in wheelchair racing. In: Adapted Physical Activity Quarterly 11 (1994), 4, p. 416-428

WILLIAMS, T. & KOLKKA, T.: Socialization into wheelchair basketball in the United Kingdom: A structural functional perspective. In: Adapted Physical Activity Quarterly 15 (1998), 4, p. 357-369

Exploring the sporting lives of women with a physical disability

Heike Tiemann

Institute of Elementary Education, Free University Berlin, Germany

> *"Disabled people throughout the world are increasingly naming and confronting the prejudice which we daily experience, expressing our anger at the discrimination we face, and insisting that our lives are value."* (MORRIS 1991, 1)

This statement from a feminist with a disability is not only directed towards individuals with a disability in general. It can be seen as an important description of the present situation of women with a disability in particular.

Recent publications concerning the experiences of women with a disability show that they do encounter prejudice and discrimination (e. g. EHRIG 1996). Nevertheless, it should be noted that there has been little scientific work or systematic study of the circumstances and needs of women with a disability.

In recent years the situation slowly began to change but it is still common for many studies to ignore the way gender might affect the experience of disability and hence disability identity. Thus, society is still remarkably unaware of the unique issues surrounding women with a disability, who as a minority group are experiencing many sources and forms of discrimination. Cultural values existent in the Western European and North American society lead to specific opinions and attitudes towards women with a disability, which then often culminate in discrimination. In a society where people are systematically taught to hate and fear old age and disability and to equate them with "ugliness", often one strives after "prettiness" and youth. In this society it is especially difficult and stressful for women with a physical disability to meet these demands. They are perceived in Western European and North American society as being inadequate, unable to totally fulfill culturally defined norms and role expectations, especially concerning physical attractiveness, physical activity, motherhood, employment and sexual partnership. They often feel that they are considered to be asexual or "neutered sexual beings" (MORRIS 1989). This is also reflected in the common genderless language. The public in general refer to "the disabled population", - paras and tetras, the blind and the deaf - as to a minority group, which is identified primarily as being disabled, gender is seldom differentiated.

The effects of discrimination can be illustrated by examining the socio-economical system. Women with a disability for instance are at a serious disadvantage compared to the rest of the population in the labour market (LONSDALE 1990). Similar findings are shown by research done in the United States relating to education (HANNA & ROGOVSKY 1991). It can be seen from the above that women with a disability have to face restrictions and disadvantages in different areas of everyday life.

One such area is that of sport. Thus it is necessary to question how women with a physical disability experience sport. How are certain role expectations and attitudes transferred from other spheres of society into the sports world? What can be projected from sport experiences to certain values and beliefs women with a disability have to face in society? Why are there significantly fewer women with a physical disability participating in sport in comparison with men with a disability (GRIMES & FRENCH 1987)?

These are only a few of the questions that are important to examine in this context. For if the general subject of women with a disability has received scant attention, it follows that the specific issue of women with a disability in sport has been largely neglected in research. It is only in the last few years that more attention has been drawn towards gender-specific issues related to female athletes with a disability. Even so, a lot of research still has to be done.

Therefore, the purpose of this research is to identify the issues and experiences that are particular to women with a physical disability in sport: that is to say, the gender-specific sporting experiences of these women. This study will especially focus on socialisation into and via sport and the perceived role of female athletes with a physical disability.

Methodology

A qualitative paradigm applying qualitative methods was used as the basis for this research. The primary method was an open-ended "less-structured"[1] interview (an interview schedule was used). The interviews were conducted with physically impaired female athletes during the Paraplegic National Games (1992) in Stoke Mandeville. The eight women interviewed were all basketball players and members of the Great Britain women's wheelchair basketball team. Five of them played for the only predominantly female wheelchair basketball team in England. The other three played for different teams that included male basketball players.

Before each interview started, specific facts were established: background information concerning current personal data, disability and current activity patterns were recorded on a prepared form. With the help of a Personal Leisure History Chart (NEWMANN 1990), life events and their participation in sport were graphically represented over a certain time span. By showing respondents how various aspects of their lives could be plotted across a number of years they were able to clarify their thoughts with respect to associated events or conditions, which were essential for the second part of the interview. Based upon the Personal Leisure Life History Chart, the following topics determined the framework for the interviews:

---

[1] The term "less structured" interview refers to Kidder & Judd (1986). The term "un-structured" interview (Lofland 1971; Burgess 1989) can be used identically.

- socialising agents towards initiating sport participation
- first experience in disability sport
- reactions, behaviour, attitudes etc. of the different socialising agents outside the disability sports world towards sport participation
- reactions, behaviour, attitudes etc. of the different socialising agents inside the disability sports world towards sport participation
- perceived effects of sport participation (psychological/physical)
- experiences of discrimination inside and outside the disability sports world
- perceived role expectations as a female athlete with a physical disability
- expectations of future developments.

The material collected by interviewing the athletes was transcribed and interpreted. The analysis was based on the "Qualitative Inhaltsanalyse" (MAYRING 1995). Pseudonyms were used in the interview extracts. One of the important tasks in this study was to give voice to the female athletes themselves.

Besides general problems and limitations associated with the applied qualitative methods, which are widely discussed in the literature (LOFLAND 1971; JONES 1985; BARNES 1992) it has to be mentioned that the limited numbers of interviews in this research restricted the range of possible interpretations. However, these limitations were not crucial for the outcome of this study since its aim was to initiate an examination of the experiences of female athletes with a disability.

Results and Discussion

In examining the socialisation into disability sport the results confirmed the necessity to look separately at women with congenital and at women with acquired disabilities. With regard to the interviewed women with congenital disabilities who were socialised into sport during their school years, the interviews suggest that the importance of the school setting must be highly valued. Experiences in special schools differ from the social situations experienced in inclusive mainstream schools. In the latter, living and learning with able-bodied class mates may influence the pupil with a disability to accept able-bodied athletes as role models as well, who initially motivate the pupil with a disability to participate in sport. In segregated settings such as special schools, able-bodied role models do not exist and are therefore rarely seen as role models for physical activity. Consequently, the importance of peers with disabilities as socialising agents must be considered. A significant event in the process of socialisation into sport is the first time the women experienced disability sport. These experiences were described as memorable and positive events and induced them to continue participating.

The process of socialisation into sport of women with acquired physical disabilities is influenced by their sport experiences before they acquired their physical disability. Most of the interviewed women participated in various kinds of able-bodied sport through which they acquired attitudes and beliefs associated with their participation in sport. However, most of them did not participate in top-level sport prior to acquiring the disability but now belong to the female elite athletes in Great Britain's wheelchair basketball.

Due to the onset of impairment, women with acquired disabilities most often experience the process of socialisation into disability sport much later in life and in a different phase of their life than the women with congenital disabilities. Therefore, the interviews highlighted different aspects of this process. After their significant life event, the impairment, the interviewees were strongly influenced by peers and other people with disabilities, physiotherapists and role models. These people were the most important socialising agents who introduced the women to disability sport and supported their socialisation into sport. Concerning the importance of peers with disabilities and other people with disabilities this result corresponds with Goffman (1963) who emphasises their significance while explaining general patterns of socialisation of stigmatised people. In contrast, able-bodied peers were not influential, nor were family members or medical staff. Another important group with regard to socialising agents are physiotherapists. They introduced the women to disability sport or passed on information about sport opportunities. Most of the women acquired their disability after they left school; therefore, school as a socialising situation is not relevant.

For most of the women asked, role models were very influential. It is interesting that some of the role models belonged to the peer group. In addition it is necessary to mention that most of the women did not point out a certain person as "the role model". Rather, they expressed that they felt impressed and motivated by watching the performances and the abilities of a certain team of athletes with disabilities. Usually they came in personal contact with their role models. Role models presented by the media were less important.

In contrast to the interviewees with congenital disabilities, the athletes with acquired physical disabilities expressed very contradictory feelings toward their first participation in sport. It could be suggested that because of the sporting experiences before the onset of impairment some women had certain expectations of themselves and of this "new" sport that influenced their first emotions.

The interviews also highlighted aspects in the process of socialisation into disability sport that could be found in both groups. The women themselves, both with acquired and congenital disabilities played an important part in this process. Especially getting and staying involved in their sport of choice - wheelchair basketball, the women expressed their self-initiative, their active and self-determined role.

It was also clear in both subgroups that the socialisation process into disability sport was clearly male dominated. Most of the influential peers and other influential people with disabilities were male, as were the role models. All women interviewed were initially socialised into wheelchair basketball teams that were all-male or consisted mostly of male athletes. The teams were also coached by men. That is to say they were socialised into a male dominated disability sport environment. These circumstances were not satisfying for some of the women and they then moved to a female dominated team coached by a woman.

Suggestions with regard to certain social and psychological influencing factors during that period of socialisation - for example which experiences influenced the decisions of the latter mentioned women - could be given while researching the socialisation via disability sport. Again it was necessary to distinguish between congenital disability and an acquired disability perspective in that those with congenital impairments internalise cultural norms and beliefs toward people with disabilities from birth on. People with acquired impairments develop an able-bodied identity before disability changes their perspective. Even though people with acquired disabilities experience values and norms toward people with disabilities, it was assumed that they still carry beliefs concerning this group from their former able-bodied identity.

Nevertheless, only two differences between the subgroups could be established. The interviewed women with congenital disabilities never addressed weight problems while speaking about physical effects of sport. They grew up experiencing the functions of their body and accepting and coming to terms with their shape and the weight of their body. In contrast, some of the interviewees with acquired physical disabilities highlighted sport as significant factor for getting rid of excess weight to get back in shape after the onset of impairment when they suddenly experienced being overweight. This change was connected with a gain of self-confidence. Some women with acquired disabilities also emphasised that they did not want to become too "big" as a sport related physical change. Considering that being overweight or being "too muscular" contradicts the normative ideal of female beauty in our society, the desire to lose weight by participating in sport emphasises a societal norm that seems to be closer to women with acquired disabilities.

Another difference between the subgroups was revealed when the significance of sport in the socialisation of the women was investigated.

After acquiring a disability, most of the interviewed women lost contact with many important people in their social surrounding, friends, a husband, a fiancée or members of the family. Participating in sport they built up a new social network which was especially meaningful for them in this phase of life. The social network of the interviewees with congenital disabilities developed more continuously. Therefore, sport participation can be seen rather as the broadening of an existing network.

Studying the perception of societal attitudes, beliefs and values in the context of the participation of women in disability sport findings concerning women with acquired disabilities agree with those concerning women with congenital disabilities. This is not surprising considering that people act and react to athletes with physical disabilities without knowing if they are acquired or congenital.

The interviews clearly reveal that society outside the disability sports world very often sees female athletes as helpless and pitied victims of some tragic happening. Sport is primarily viewed as occupation, rehabilitation or therapy. This aspect again stresses the dominance of the medical model of disability in our society. The wheelchair can be seen as a symbol for the functional "deficiencies" which gets more attention than the individual. The focus is therefore on the disability and a differentiation between male and female athletes with disabilities is seldom made by people outside the disability sport world.

Inside the disability sport world another approach must be used. Gender is then the main category that dominates the experiences of female athletes with a disability. This can be verified by gender-specific discrimination all interviewed women experienced in different ways connected to their participation in wheelchair basketball. They reported unequal treatment from officials, players and coaches. They also experienced gender-specific abusive language directed toward them mainly from male players. Comments and behaviour of certain men inside the disability sport world (in this case inside the wheelchair basketball world) gave the female athletes the impression that they are not taken seriously as athletes.

Being included in a male dominated sports world where a comparatively small number of women are playing in and against clearly male dominated teams, where coaches are usually male and the responsible association is almost exclusively male, the female athletes were seen as weaker. It is becoming obvious that inside the disability sports world the view of women with physical disabilities corresponds with the view of able-bodied women in society.

Another aspect clearly pointed out through the interviews were the psychological effects of the participation in sport, which were without exception seen as very positive. The athletes related their self-esteem to their involvement in wheelchair basketball. In this context, it seems to be of importance that very often they have to strive for equal treatment. It is also important that participating in disability sport means having to socialise with people who are sharing similar experiences. Depending on whether or not there are other women in the basketball team that the woman belongs to, gender-specific aspects do or do not belong to the shared experiences. However, the women expressed that meeting with and being physically active with other people with disabilities - a differentiation between female and male athletes was not made - on a regular base helps to increase their self-esteem.

Looking at the different experiences of female athletes with physical disabilities, the results of this research stress the necessity of differentiating the two main systems of influence, which structure the experiences of the women. The system inside the disability sports world transfers different norms, values and beliefs towards the female athletes. Gender is valued differently in this context than in the system outside the disability sport world.

Inside these two systems, the female athletes are influenced by different social role expectations that bear different role conflicts. Outside the disability sport world, where the women have to face opposing expectations concerning the "disability role", the "female role" and demands arising from the intersection of both role expectations, the dominant societal focus is on the disability. Inside the disability sport world, the women are confronted again with opposing role expectations concerning being an athlete, and being an athlete with a disability. However, here the disability seems to be an irrelevant factor - the expectations are centred around being an athlete. When playing wheelchair basketball, where female athletes are in competition with male athletes, they experience gender-specific discrimination related to traditional societal role expectations of women. These expectations are obviously transferred into the disability sports world. Consequently, when the women participate in wheelchair basketball, they experience that they are primarily seen as women. Thereby they experience discrimination because they are women.

Although the female athletes are supposed to be subordinated, the fact that being and staying involved in this competitive elite sport illustrates that the female athletes are putting up resistance to the different existing prejudiced role expectations. This resistance is also evident in the way the interviewees expressed their self-determination and self-confidence acting and reacting in this sports world. Thereby many of the interviewed women developed an even stronger personality which also influenced their life outside the disability sports community. Sport participation then provides a stimulus for liberation from certain role expectations. A role reorganisation mastering new roles outside the disability sports world can be seen as an important effect.

Conclusions

This study exploring the sporting lives of women with physical disabilities offered some facts which could be used as a base for further examination. The study must, however, be viewed as being only a beginning in this field of research which still leaves certain research approaches ignored, questions unasked, certain perspectives not considered and interpretations neglected. More work in this area of research is certainly required.

Considering a qualitative paradigm as a basis, different qualitative methods are needed in the future. Different forms of personal interviews, such as "depth-interviews" (JONES 1985) as well as "life story interviews" (TAGG 1985) should help to improve the insight into the sporting lives of women with physical disabilities. Information should be gathered not only from a small number of female elite athletes with physical disabilities, but also from women who participate in disability sport on a lower level of performance. Findings of this research would then reflect a broader spectrum of experiences.

An important aspect which should be more closely examined in the future is the significance and the effects of female role models presented in the media - a factor which some of the interviewed women also pointed out. Taking into account that over the last few years media coverage of disability elite sport has slowly increased, a corresponding effect on women with disabilities in context with their sport participation could be expected. The type of female role models presented in the media should also be examined, as well as the social values and norms that are encouraged. Additionally, it should be asked how women with physical disabilities feel and react on this coverage. Considering that our society is steadily moving towards an age where the media has an increasing degree of power, these types of questions must be seen as a challenge for the future - particularly in the context of women and disability sport.

However, it should always be the objective of this type of research to give a voice to the women themselves and - to come back to the quotation at the beginning of this study - thus to identify prejudiced norms and beliefs which the women increasingly confront.

References

BARNES, C.: Qualitative research: Valuable or irrelevant. In: Disability, Handicap and Society, 7 (1992), 2, p.115-124

BURGESS, R. G.: The unstructured interview as a conversation. In: BURGESS, R.

G. (ed.), Field research: A source-book and field manual. London 1989, p.107-110

EHRIG, H.: Verminderte Heiratschancen oder Perspektivgewinn? Lebens-entwürfe und Lebenswirklichkeiten körperbehinderter Frauen. Bielefeld 1996

GOFFMAN, E.: Stigma. Notes on the management of spoiled identity. Harmondsworth 1963

GRIMES, P. S. & FRENCH, L.: Barriers to disabled women's participation in sports. In: Journal of Physical Education, Recreation and Dance 58 (1987), 3, p. 24-27

HANNA, W. J. & ROGOVSKY, B.: Women with disabilities: Two handicaps plus. In: Disability, Handicap and Society 6 (1985), 1, p. 49-63

JONES, S.: Depth interviewing. In: WALKER, R. (ed.), Applied qualitative research. Vermont 1985, p. 45-55

KIDDER, L. H. & JUDD, C. M.: Research methods in social relations. New York 1986

LOFLAND, J.: Analyzing social settings. Belmont, CA, USA 1971

LONSDALE, S.: Women and disability. The experience of physical disability among women. London 1990

MAYRING, P.: Qualitative Inhaltsanalyse. Weinheim 1995

MORRIS, J.: Able lives. Women's experience of paralysis. London 1989

MORRIS, J.: Pride against prejudice. London 1991

NEWMANN, I.: Countryside recreation and people with disabilities. Unpublished doctoral dissertation. Sunderland Polytechnic 1990

TAGG, S. K.: Life story interviews and their interpretation. In: BRENNER, M., BROWN, J. & CANTER, D. (eds.), The research interview: Uses and approaches. London 1985, p. 163.-199

Women working in sport for people with disabilities: Career paths and challenges

Mary A. Hums, Anita M. Moorman

University of Louisville, Louisville, KY, USA

The sport industry has been traditionally dominated by able-bodied men on the playing fields in terms of participation, media coverage, salaries, and other resources. However, women world-wide are beginning to enter the sport arena in increasing numbers, not just as athletes but also as sport managers. For example, professional leagues and teams, national governing bodies, and sport facilities now employ female sport managers at all levels. Just like managers in non-sport organizations, sport managers must plan, organize, staff, direct, and evaluate their employees and organizations. Sport managers are people who serve in management positions in any segment of the sport industry. They can represent a broad range of positions and titles such as ticket manager, event coordinator, vice president for marketing, community relations director, or Paralympics manager. Sport managers also hold these positions in a number of settings. The sport industry is made up of a number of different segments, including professional sport, intercollegiate sport, health and fitness, recreational sport, sporting goods, event management and facility management (MASTERALEXIS, BARR & HUMS 1998; PARKS, ZANGER & QUARTERMAN 1998). Another less widely recognized aspect of the sport industry is sport for people with disabilities. This segment, also known as disability sport, refers to sport that has been designed for or specifically practiced by athletes with disabilities (DEPAUW & GAVRON 1995).

In the United States, sport organizations working with people with disabilities include Disabled Sports USA; Dwarf Athletic Association of America; Special Olympics, Inc.; United States Association for

Blind Athletes; United States Cerebral Palsy Athletic Association; United States Deaf Sports Federation; and Wheelchair Sports, USA. Internationally some of these organizations include Cerebral Palsy International Sport and Recreation Association; Disabled People's International; International Association for Sport for Persons with Mental Handicap; International Blind Sport Association; International Committee of Sport for the Deaf; International Federation for Adapted Physical Activity; International Paralympic Committee; International Sport Organization for the Disabled; and International Stoke Mandeville Wheelchair Sports Federation. Sport managers are involved with the operations of these organizations.

From physiological, economic, and social standpoints, athletes and participants (primarily male) in this segment have been extensively researched for decades. However, within this realm very little scholarly work has been done critically analyzing management or organizational policy issues (WOLFF 1998). An area of research which is just now being explored is the place of women working in management capacities in sport for people with disabilities (DEPAUW & GAVRON 1995; HUMS & MOORMAN 1999; OLENIK 1998). This paper examines involvement by women sport managers who work with sport for people with disabilities.

Little scholarly information is available about women working as sport managers in able-bodied sport, and even less is known about the careers of women working in the management of sport for people with disabilities. The impetus for this study came as a direct result of a subcommittee of women who met at the Second European Conference on Adapted Physical Activity and Sports, held in Leuven, Belgium, in December 1995. At that conference, a number of subcommittees met and discussed issues of importance to sport for people with disabilities. One of these groups dealt with women in sport for people with disabilities. The charge to the subcommittee was to gather information about women in different aspects of sport for people with disabilities. One of these aspects was women in management. A literature review of major sport management journals for the last seven years found no scholarly research articles examining women working in the management of sport for people with disabilities.

Given this dearth of information, this study attempted to establish some baseline information about women in this area. This study focuses exclusively on women in the **management** of sport for people with disabilities. The study at hand is part of a larger, more comprehensive research agenda examining the involvement of women in management positions throughout the sport industry. For instance women in the management of professional baseball have been studied (HUMS & SUTTON 1999) as well as women in the management of professional basketball (HUMS & SUTTON 2000). Just as the careers of women in the management of professional baseball or professional basketball had never been studied, the same is true for women in the management of sport for people with disabilities.

Purpose of the Study

This study will provide baseline information about women working in sport for people with disabilities, and will provide the researchers the ability to compare responses between the women working in sport for people with disabilities and those working in professional baseball and professional basketball. The purposes of this descriptive study are as follows:

1. describe women working in management of sport for people with disabilities (demographics);

2. examine the career paths of women working in the management of sport for people with disabilities;

3. determine the most enjoyable and least enjoyable aspects, and the greatest challenges of being a woman working in management of sport for people with disabilities;

4. determine career advice women working in management of sport for people with disabilities would offer to women wanting to enter this profession;

5. Determine short-term and long-term career aspirations of women working in the management of sport for people with disabilities.

Method

Participants

Participants were women holding management level positions in disability sport organizations in the United States. Their names were generated in three ways: 1. contacting disability sports organizations directly and requesting a list of women working in management positions; 2. searching the organizations' internet sites for lists of staff members; 3. asking women in management positions if they knew other women working with disability sport organizations. All the women surveyed worked at national level sport organizations and represented a cross-section of different disability sports organizations. For purposes of this study, women sport managers are defined as women working as paid full-time staff members with managerial responsibilities. This is consistent with the previous work by Hums & Sutton (1999, 2000). Therefore women on boards of directors or women in clerical positions, for example, were not included.

Participation in this study was totally voluntary. Subjects indicated their informed consent by returning the completed survey in an enclosed self-addressed stamped envelope. Subjects who did not wish to participate did not return the survey. Subjects were identified by a number used for mailing purposes only. No names were written on the survey and responses were not individually identifiable.

The staffs of the disability sports organizations tend to be rather small, and therefore the population of women holding management positions numbers a select few. Twelve women were contacted and nine returned survey instruments. While this number of respondents is small, it does represent a cross section of disability sports organizations, and provides interesting qualitative data about these women and their careers. The responses to the open-ended questions produced many interesting observations.

Instrument

The survey instrument was developed and then examined by a panel of outside experts. After incorporating their suggestions the instrument was finalized. The instrument is based on the instrument used by Hums & Sutton (1999, 2000) in their previous studies of women sport managers. The survey instrument was divided in several parts. First participants were asked their present position in sport for people with disabilities. Next participants were asked about their work experience in the past 10 years in three areas: 1. in sport for people with disabilities, 2. in the sport industry outside of sport for people with disabilities, and 3. outside the sport industry. Participants were specifically asked to provide the following information about their previous 10-year job history: 1. their job titles; 2. the type of organization for which they worked; and 3. the number of years they worked at each position.

Next participants were given a list of the most common methods of finding employment in sport for people with disabilities. They were asked to indicate from this list how they got their first job in sport for people with disabilities. These questions were followed by a question on compensation package, asking the participants if they thought their compensation package was higher, lower, or equal to their male counterparts. The next section included the following open-ended questions: 1. What is the best part about being a woman working in the management of sport for people with disabilities? 2. What is the worst part about being a woman working in the management of sport for people with disabilities? 3. What are the biggest challenges faced as women working in the management of sport for people with disabilities? 4. What advice would they offer to women wanting to make a career in the management of sport for people with disabilities? 5. What are their career goals in five years? 6. What are their long-term career goals? And 7. What are their thoughts on the interaction of gender and disability status for women working in sport for people with disabilities? Finally, participants were asked to provide demographic data, including age, income, education, and major in school.

Results

Overall, the responses tended to be relatively gender neutral. This is in direct contrast to the women working in the management of professional sport. This will be elaborated on in the discussion section. Sample responses to the open-ended questions are presented next.

Enjoy most/least about the job

In both of these areas the responses were gender neutral. Working with athletes was mentioned most often as the best aspect of the job. One respondent wrote "working directly with athletes," while another said "the contact I have with athletes, " and a third said "working with the athletes – they show us what it's really about." Forwarding the cause of sport organizations for people with disabilities was mentioned, as evidenced by these comments: "making a difference in the disability sport movement," "pursuing opportunities for athletes in competition and fund-raising," and "bringing in money to make the programs possible."

Respondents' comments about the least liked part of their job varied greatly. One respondent said "none", while another said "really there is not one. I enjoy my job. The only limitations are self-imposed." Disability status came into play as one person felt "judged as 'inferior' because I am not disabled myself," and another wrote that "disabled athletes are thought of as 'less' than able-bodied athletes." Other responses related more to managerial aspects of their job, such as "fund-raising," "overseeing the day to day operations of the organization and staff," and "working for a social board of directors who are stagnant in their thinking." Only one respondent directly mentioned gender, saying "men sometimes take advantage of you (because you're a woman)."

Biggest challenges

The biggest challenges respondents mentioned centered around respect in the workplace. For example, comments included "being respected as an equal by my male counterparts," "proving my ability to organize a national event," "earning the respect of my co-workers, male and female," and "earning the respect and trust of the athletes this organizations serves." One respondent said "gender makes no difference," while another felt a challenge was "overcoming the stereotypes that exist for younger women." Another challenge dealt with communicating information about sport for people with disabilities, as evidenced by these comments: "communicating the difference between Paralympics and Special Olympics," and "communicating the importance of sports and recreation for persons with physical disabilities."

Career advice

The advice for women wanting to work in sport for people with disabilities was decidedly gender neutral and focused on basic career advice for someone in the sport industry. Getting to know people in the field was represented by comments such as "network, network, network," "volunteer with community organizations and events (network)," and "look for experience where you can – volunteering, internships." The need to work hard was noted by comments like "be aggressive and toot your own horn," "be assertive," and "always work hard and never give up." Some words suggested the importance of knowledge of the organization and its clients, including "never lose sight of the goals of your organization," "have a clear idea of your goals and whether the organization will help you move in that direction", and "respect the customer/athlete you work for." One respondent summed up her advice this way "on the sport side – open your eyes – the possibilities are endless!"

Career goals

Interestingly the career goals mentioned were more cause directed than self directed, that is, the comments dealt with career goals related to promoting sport for people with disabilities in general, rather than aspiring to a certain job title. Comments which illustrated this included "see my sport organization reach self-sufficiency," "to raise funds so that athletes don't have to pay to represent their country in international competition," "begin grassroots programming in track & field and cycling", "grow donor base," and "be a consultant to future Olympic/Paralympic Committees to improve each Games and further the Paralympic Movement." Only two comments mentioned personal career goals, with one respondent wanting to "work as a CFO" and another desiring to "own my own event management/consulting company."

Does having a disability or not make a difference in the job?

The overwhelming response to this question was no. Here are some sample responses. "I am able-bodied and do not feel I would conduct my job any differently if I had a disability. I might have a different perspective if I were in a wheelchair, but my responsibilities and execution would stay the same. I do think a former elite disabled athlete with management background would be an ideal combination and role model." "I think people with disabilities should be a major part of the decision-making processes of any organization for people with disabilities. However, I don't believe it should exclude others (non-disabled)." "This isn't a job requiring empathy. It requires the usual list of good employee skills, management and customer service, and a general willingness to keep an open mind and work for a greater cause." "The importance is in the skill set you bring to the job and the sensitivity of the person in the job."

Discussion

Although small, the respondents offered a rich set of qualitative data to examine. They also represent an interesting contrast with women working in professional baseball and professional basketball (HUMS & SUTTON 1999, 2000) and from women working in national sport organizations in Australia, New Zealand, and Canada (MCKAY 1997).

First of all, the women working in sport for people with disabilities gave responses which were relatively gender neutral, and which often focused on the business of working in sport for people with disabilities. This is in direct contrast from women sport managers who indicated gender was an important factor. For example, subjects in Hums & Sutton's (1999, 2000) and McKay's (1997) studies used language like being left out of the old boys network, working in a male-dominated environment, limited access because of being a woman, and misperceptions of why women work in professional sport. These were absent in the responses of the women in the present study when respondents discussed the most challenging and least enjoyable aspects of the job.

As far as career advice is concerned, in the present study the respondents mentioned only job related advice and not any advice related to being a woman, as the previous studies did. Also, women in this study, when asked about career goals, discussed goals that were more altruistic in nature and dealt with furthering the disability sport movement. This is in direct contrast to the other studies (HUMS & SUTTON 1999, 2000; MCKAY 1996) where the subjects talked only in terms of potential future job titles such as Vice President or General Manager, and did not mention any altruistic goals about the betterment of professional sport.

Subjects resoundingly answered "no" when asked if having or not having a disability made a difference since they worked in sport for people with disabilities. It is interesting to note that none of the respondents had a disability themselves. However, the respondents did recognize the importance of input from people with disabilities in the governance of these sport organizations. The question of the place of able-bodied people managing sport for people with disabilities is complex, and is sometimes a "hot button" with people expressing strong opinions. In this case, these particular individuals did not see one's ability status as a prerequisite for working in sport for people with disabilities.

The differences in responses between the women working in professional baseball and women working in sport for people with disabilities are interesting, albeit not totally surprising. Baseball is a traditionally male sport, managed mostly by men, and played exclusively by men on the professional level. This would tend to produce an environment which could result in barriers for women. Women working in traditionally male environments often feel they need to work harder, need to establish credibility, feel isolated without other female peers, and face difficulty moving to higher management positions (sometimes referred to as the "Glass Ceiling"). Women working in professional baseball experienced similar feelings to those experienced by women working in traditionally male environments. Organizational differences between disability sport organizations and professional baseball may explain the differences in attitudes. For example, sport organizations for people with disabilities on the other hand, sponsor activities for both genders on various levels. One may speculate that the different organizational climates contributed to the respondents' answers. It would be interesting to see how the respondents' answers would compare perhaps with women working in the management of non-professional sport or even not-for-profit agencies in general, which are areas where there are already more female clients and executives.

As mentioned earlier, this study is part of an on-going line of research examining women working in sport management in various industry segments. More research needs to be done with this particular group of women sport managers. First, the study needs to be replicated on an international level. Respondents in this study were from the United States. An international sample may also include women with disabilities, which could allow a comparison of their responses with able-bodied respondents working in the management of sport for people with disabilities. Also, are women sport managers with disabilities treated differently than their male counterparts with disabilities who may work in similar capacities? The fact that none of the respondents had disabilities also suggests further research could be done on why so few women are represented in these jobs. Since women are under-represented in sport management in general, does this study reflect this under-representation, or is something else operating in the environment effecting women with disabilities.

Little published research exists examining these complex issues which circle around the intersection of gender and disability. Truly this is an area ripe with questions which need to be addressed.

References

DEPAUW, K. & GAVRON, S.: Disability and sport. Champaign, Ill., USA 1995

HUMS, M.A. & MOORMAN, A.M.: Women working in the management of sport for people with disabilities: Complex issues. Presented at the 50th Anniversary Conference of the International Association of Physical Education & Sport for Girls and Women, Northampton, MA, USA July 1999

HUMS, M.A. & SUTTON W.A.: Women working in the management of professional baseball: Getting to first base? In: Journal of Career Development 26 (1999), 3, p. 147-158

HUMS, M.A. & SUTTON, W.A.: Women working in the management of professional sport: Comparison of careers in professional baseball and basketball. Presented at the Annual Conference of the North American Society for Sport Management, Colorado Springs, CO, USA June 2000

MASTERALEXIS, L.P., BARR, C.A. & HUMS, M.A.: Principles and practice of sport management. Gaithersberg, MD, USA 1998

MCKAY, J.: Managing gender: Affirmative action and organizational power in Australian, Canadian, and New Zealand sport. Albany, NY, USA 1997

OLENIK, L. M.: Women and disability sport: Perceptions and approaches of women working in the Paralympic Movement. Unpublished doctoral dissertation, University of Alberta, Edmonton 1998

PARKS, J.B., ZANGER, B.R.K. & QUARTERMAN, J.: Contemporary sport management. Champaign, Ill., USA 1998

WOLFF, E.: Status of seven disabled sports organizations and recommendations for the future. Unpublished manuscript, Brown University 1998

Organization / Administration

The (dis-?)organised chaos of sports for persons with disabilities

Hans Lindström

Swedish Federation for the Disabled, Farsta, Sweden;
President, EUROPC

"In many ways we have spent a lot of time resisting change and dwelling on the past and while this is a natural reaction to change, it is now time for all organisations including the IPC to seriously address the issue as to how we can best serve people with a disability in the world of sport." (Development Plan adopted by the 1998 General Assembly of the International Stoke Mandeville Wheelchair Sports Federation).

Introduction

The title of this paper may imply that it deals with the whole movement of sports for persons with disabilities. It is, however, limited to what is commonly called the "Paralympic Movement", namely the International Paralympic Committee (IPC) and those of the International Organizations of Sports for Disabled (IOSD) which are members of the IPC, leaving out "Deaf Sports" and the Special Olympics movements. It should be recognized that many civil servants and politicians of national governments and of the European Union tend to perceive all of those groups as being part of one movement, often expecting a united approach from all of the sports for persons with a disability including also these three main parts. It is hard enough for just the Paralympic Movement to appear united. Let us not, however, give up the hope that we some day will stand united in all-important matters.

The organisational structure of the Paralympic Movement consists of a mixture of different international bodies in the form of either autonomous federations for disabilities, or federations for sports, or sub-committees for sports. Some of these bodies seem to have contradicting or interfering aims and objectives. And when these are applied they can give the impression that there is a competition going on for "market shares" of the international sports competition calendar. The roles of the international bodies in general appear to be unclear or confused. In some cases interference is also verified by constitutions and in agreements between organisations. The international organisational structure of sports in the IPC sphere does not reflect the realities of how it is organized nationally. There are many national variations between the two extremes of organisational concepts: 1. one national body for all disabilities, or 2. one national body for each disability. In both concepts integration into national federations for the able-bodied is practised. Without claiming to be exhaustive, this paper is an attempt to sort out and describe anomalies, and to identify what perceived problems need serious attention, focused on IPC needs. My guiding principle is that it must be possible to accommodate all real needs.

The core of the complications and confusion seems to be the interference between the IPC and the IOSD on the so-called multi-disability sports. This is certainly one of the most significant causes, but there are also others. In this context I think it is important to understand the needs that led to the creation of the IPC. It was an action started by national sports organizations for persons with disabilities because they wanted changes to the international structures and competition programmes so it would correspond better to the prevalent national realities (motions to ISOD and ICC in 1984 from, among others, Canada and Sweden). The needs expressed are well summarised by the International Sports Organisation for the Disabled (ISOD) in its position paper to the ICC "Arnheim Seminar" in 1987:

"-to make Paralympics more compact, controlled by one

strong body;
- to make a World Championships programme in the main
sports for the Paralympic disabilities, also compact, and
controlled by one strong body;
- to co-ordinate the single disability games for the
Paralympic disabilities accordingly, so that they can be a
complement to the joint World Championships programme."

In addition there was a strong requirement for national influence on the international competition programmes. These points along with the above ISOD statement were in essence the basis for the creation of the IPC.

Is it still like that, or are the needs different today?

The IPC's Main Aims and Objectives

The main aims and objectives of the IPC as worded in the constitution are:

- to form and be the international representative organisation of sports for athletes with disabilities at Paralympic standards

- to award, supervise and co-ordinate the Summer and Winter Paralympic Games

- to award, sanction and where appropriate assist in the co-ordination and supervising of World and Regional multi-disability Games and Championships as the sole international multi-disability organisation with the right to do so" (Article IV.2 of the IPC constitution also says that the "international organisations of sports for athletes with disabilities shall continue to have the right to conduct their own affairs and to assist the IPC in multi-disability events)

- to co-ordinate the Sports Competition Schedule of international and regional competitions for athletes with disabilities whilst guaranteeing to respect the sports technical needs of each individual disability group.

The International Representative Organisation

One strong cause for the IPC objective to be **the** international representative organisation of sports for athletes with disabilities is that it is certainly the wish of the International Olympic Committee (IOC) to communicate with one single representative body for sports for athletes with disabilities. When this stipulation came up in the 1980s it was meant to also include Deaf Sports.

Many national federations for sports for persons with disabilities consider the IPC to be the highest controlling body for all sports for athletes with disabilities, or at least for all sports within the Paralympic Movement. Although that may have been a dream or a hope at the time of the first conference in 1987, it was never the case. The IPC is the controlling body for the Paralympic Games on one hand, and the international umbrella organisation for the IPC multi-disability sports on the other. All IOSD are autonomous and free to do what their assemblies of nations decide. As the IPC has a constitution of its own it too is autonomous, but its constitution and bylaws provide the IOSD with influence not only over the Paralympic Games, but also over the IPCs non-Paralympic championships programme for the multi-disability sports.

The fact that the IPC claims to be "the international representative" has not stopped the IOSD to take their own initiatives both with the IOC and with International Sports Federations (IF). This tells us that the claimed objective either is wrong or not adequately specified. None of the IOSD claim to be "the international representative", but the International Sports Organization for Disabled (ISOD) refers in a general way throughout its constitution to "sports for the disabled" as its target activity. In the first article of ISOD's constitution, however, amputees and locomotor disabilities are specified as ISOD's target groups.

Helena Hankova, Slovakian Paralympic Committee, wrote in EUROPC News 4/1999 that "there are unclear competencies of the IPC as the top organ of our sport and unclear relations with IOSD." From studying the constitutions of the IPC and the IOSD one can easily reach the conclusion that she is right regarding the question of who is responsible for what.

The IPC main objective to "be the international representative organisation of sports for athletes with disabilities at Paralympic standards" is unprecise and allows a wide range of interpretations.

What does it comprise in practical terms?

The IPC national member organisations should be invited to send in their views and to agree on formulations of main objectives that describe the IPC's role precisely.

Competing for Market Shares of Championships in Multi-Disability Sports (Co-ordinating the Sports Competition Schedule)

IOSD claims

The constitutional task for the IPC to co-ordinate the calendar is met by articles in four of the five IOSD constitutions mentioning co-ordination or co-operation on calendars with other sports organisations for athletes with disabilities. The ISMWSF does not have this requirement in its constitution, but recognises the need just the same.

The ISMWSF 1998 General Assembly recognised in a Development Plan of July 1998 the IPC development of elite sport for athletes with disabilities and decided to re-examine the ISMWSF's role. In the document it is said that the ISMWSF has changed the emphasis of the annual Stoke Mandeville Games from elite to developmental.

All five of the IOSD have in their constitutions as an objective to organise or promote (ISOD) or conduct (ISMWSF) competitions for their respective disability groups. CP-ISRA, IBSA and INAS-FID specify regional/continental and world levels for their programmes whereas ISMWSF and ISOD do not. CP-ISRA and IBSA do not refer to their competition programmes as "championships" but as "sporting events" (CP-ISRA) and "competitions and sporting events" (IBSA). Both CP-ISRA and IBSA organise championships anyway.

The five IOSD further signed a joint agreement in March 1998, the "IOSD Agreement in Principal". In this it is among other things stated that they agree in principle to identify and reaffirm their role within the IPC: "To be responsible for the development of competition programmes and world championships in their respective disabilities and where possible to have collective competitions." The formulation of the IOSD agreement in such a way that it might be interpreted as intended to duplicate the IPC multi-disability programme was brought up at the 1998 General Assemblies of CP-ISRA and ISMWSF and of INAS-FMH in 1999. CP-ISRA and ISMWSF passed motions that the agreement should be re-negotiated to ensure that duplicated programmes with the IPC are avoided. A formal motion was not put forward to INAS-FMH, but in the discussion its President ensured he would act accordingly.

Thus there are six international organisations with possible championship programmes in multi-disability sports like athletics and swimming for the Paralympic disabilities. There can also theoretically be five different championship programmes in table tennis, four in archery and so on - all of them organised according to current constitutions with the formal exception of CP-ISRA and IBSA, but all in accordance with the IOSD agreement.

The IPC Swimming and Table Tennis Assembly Executive

Committees promote the use of the functional classification system in events organised by IOSD in order to increase the number of competition opportunities for the athletes. If two of three possible IOSD use this classification in their swimming or table tennis championships, it makes it theoretically possible for one athlete with a certain locomotor disability to compete in her/his specialist event for four different championship titles, just like in today's professional boxing. Athletes with visual impairment and intellectual disability are so far limited to two titles. The difference between these titles is the name of the international organisation that hands it out. The athletes that are eligible to compete for the titles are the same, provided that their national organisation is affiliated with the relevant international organisations, and that the event to be competed is the same in each organisation.

It is important to observe here that there can be two types of Championships organised by the IOSD. The one reserved for the own specific disability only, and the one that might be open to other disabilities within functional classification. The latter is so far possible only for locomotor disabilities.

The fight for shares of the championships market is more evident in some sports than in others. The most exposed sports are swimming, cycling, and athletics of the summer sports and alpine and nordic skiing of the winter sports. There seem to be no guarantee, though, that the fight might not spread to other sports.

Athletes Committee view

The IPC Athletes Committee recognises the inflation of championships titles in this system, or perhaps rather in the lacking of a system, and addresses it in a policy statement to the 1997 EUROPC Conference. It is stated that "European Championships are top level events... when all elite level athletes from the various disability groups in the respective sports take part." And that " other events, where athletes from one disability group may take part... are very welcome as additional competitive options... but such events cannot use the brand European Championship!" I believe it can be assumed that these statements by the IPC Athletes Committee also are valid for World and Continental Championships other than European.

IBSA made a survey among visually impaired athletes in connection to its World Championships in Madrid 1998. Among the conclusions are that "there is an outstanding preference for championships especially for blind", and a "general preference for IBSA to organise world championships as well as regional ones", and "that the IPC organises Paralympic Games as well as the world championships". I think there is no doubt that all athletes want many competition opportunities. The question remains whether it must be competitions for championship titles more than once in the same championships cycle.

Co-ordination of championships

In 1997 and 1998 collisions occurred between the IPC multi-disability European and World Championships and the IBSA Championships in the same sports. The IPC was required by IBSA to delete visually impaired athletes from their championship competitions. As a consequence of this unfortunate situation the IPC General Assembly in November 1997 agreed that: "The sports programme is the responsibility of each sport; the sport should ensure that as many events as possible are organised, and that the same events title is not used in the same year" (Minutes of the IPC General Assembly in Sydney 1997). Both the IPC Handbook and some of the IOSD rules specify general cycles for world and regional/continental championships.

It must be considered to be a reasonable requirement that fixed championships cycles be established so NPC, athletes, and interested organisers know what to expect. Due to the differences between the sports, general cycles including all sports are no longer practical. The cycles should be determined sport by sport. The 1997 IPC General Assembly commission to the sports has not yet resulted in required administrative efforts to publish a fixed cycle of championship competition in the multi-disability sports. In 1999 there was a four months advance notice of ISOD's World Championship in athletics. It is not known whether the event was co-ordinated with the IPC Athletics Sports Assembly Executive Committee (SAEC) or not. In the case of the 1999 World Championships in swimming for intellectually disabled, IPC Swimming reports that the Swim SAEC never was contacted by INAS-FID for co-ordination.

The EUROPC has received information from IBSA that the European Swimming Championships 2003 for visually impaired are planned to be held on a long course (50-m pool). IPC Swimming has informed EUROPC that a long course 2003 EUROPC European Championship is desirable as one of the most important qualification opportunities for the 2004 Paralympic Games. Both IBSA and the IPC Swimming SAEC want to have long course European Championships in 2003 but they are of different opinions as to whether 2003 is co-ordinated between them or not. This issue was raised at a meeting with the team managers at the EUROPC European Swimming Championships in August 1999, and preference was given to long course championships for the EUROPC the year before the Paralympic Games. A majority of the participating swimming teams does not want to separate their teams in two different championships.

Championships programme problems

The real and the theoretical IOSD multi-disability World Championships in some sports and the "collective competitions" of the IOSD contradicts the IPC constitution statement that the IPC is the sole international multi-disability organisation with the right to award and sanction world and regional multi-disability Games and Championships.

Fixed cycles for the IPC multi-disability sports are not agreed or not published. Co-ordination year by year is insufficient for the users.

If the same title shall not be competed twice the same year, the three years between Paralympic Games are not enough to accommodate the number of theoretically possible World and Regional Championships in the multi-disability sports.

To find solutions for the IPC multi-disability sports some questions need to be answered:

- Is it desirable to provide opportunities for athletes with disabilities to win World and Continental Championship titles in the same event and against the same competitors in more than one international federation?

- If it is found that there is a need for single-disability World and Continental level competitions for a given disability group in a multi-disability sport, can it be titled Games, Cup, Grand Prix, or Invitational?

- If IPC and IOSD Championship cycles for some reason should collide, can the national organisations and their athletes be trusted with their own choice of which competition to participate in if not in both?

The needs to provide opportunities for championships titles in the multi-disability sports should be assessed and determined by the national member organisations that raise the money for the athletes of their countries to participate.

In view of the fact that the sports in question are Paralympic sports, it seems logical that the multi-disability championships of the IPC should be given preference before single disability championships of the IOSD in the same sports.

The Rule-Making Powers for Multi-Disability Sports

Constitutions and bylaws

The IPC Sports Assemblies (SA) and Sports Assembly Executive Committees (SAEC) are responsible for the multi-disability sports. The IPC bylaws for Sports Assemblies require them to "act to further the development of its sport, in particular with regards to Paralympic Games, including the establishment of rules, classifications, programmes and calendar" (IPC bylaw 2.4 article 3.5.1). The SAEC shall "prepare and submit amendments to the rules as appropriate for its sport or as decided by its SA" (bylaw 2.4 article 4.4.8).

Some of the IOSD constitutions speak another language on this issue. CP-ISRA states in its first sentence after the article with the name in its constitution that it is the ultimate international authority on sports matters for persons with Cerebral Palsy and related neurological conditions. IBSA has as its first paragraph under purpose and territorial scope that "it constitutes the supreme international authority on sports matters for the blind and visually impaired, and therefore has the broadest authority and functions that could correspond to any international federation". ISMWSF's Memorandum of Association declares that ISMWSF has the power to draw up universal rules for sports in which the Association may be involved.

Co-operation and co-ordination between the IPC and the IOSD is referred to in some form in most of the relevant constitutions.

"International Federations"

In February 1997 an agreement was signed between the IPC and IBSA in Lausanne, witnessed by President Samaranch. This "Lausanne Agreement" says three things. It confirms the right of IBSA to organise its own sports competitions as actually stated in the IPC Constitution, article IV.2, already before the time of the signing of the agreement.

Secondly IBSA agrees to co-operate with the IPC in such a way that qualification and classification systems are appropriately implemented. Thirdly it gives IBSA the opportunity to have representatives as an integral part of the IPC SAEC. The IPC bylaws at the time held a note that persons with experience from the relevant disability categories should be represented on the SAEC. This was strengthened in the June 1997 version of the bylaws. Already in March 1994 the IPC Executive Committee had agreed that "where it appears appropriate to the IOSD, technical representatives from the IOSD have the right to be included in a SAEC" (Minutes E.C. VI/11/12). In practice therefore, the three points in the agreement were confirmations of long existing rulings and decisions.

As a basis for the "Lausanne Agreement" it is stated that the IPC is the supreme authority as it relates to the Paralympic Games, and is responsible for the co-ordination of multi-disability World Championships in co-operation with the International Federations, and that IBSA is the International Federation of sport for the visually impaired.

The "IOSD Agreement in Principal" from March 1998 (page 4 above) states that the IOSD want to be recognised by the IOC and the IPC as the International Federations in the same manner "as International Sporting Organisations are recognised by the IOC", as "agreed by IOC and IPC, for IBSA". The "Lausanne Agreement" however, has no reference to any comparison between an IF for a disability group and an IF for a sport. There does not seem to be any doubt though that the IOSD are recognised as the International Federations for their respective disabilities.

It seems to be unclear whether the IPC SAEC in turn are recognised by the IOSD as the bodies in the IPC structure, which in the sports technical meaning for Paralympic Games and multi-disability championships are equivalent to an IF. It may complicate the matter further in suggesting that the IPC has the IF role in the administrative sense for the multi-disability championships programme.

It is the IF in the able-bodied sports world that control their sport in full, including the rule making. The able-bodied sports world, however, does not have organisations for different disabilities. It is therefore not self-evident that direct comparison is possible in this matter.

All organisations claim responsibility

A brief summary of the facts on who determines what on the IPC multi-disability sports programme tells us,

- that the IPC Sports Assemblies of member nations and the SAEC are responsible for the multi-disability sports including rules, classification, programmes, and calendar,

- that the IOSD are the ultimate international authorities on sports matters for their specific disability,

- that the IOSD representatives have the right to be included in the IPC SAEC where they consider it appropriate,

- that the IOSD are the IF of their disability groups.

I think one can draw the conclusion that this is a good example of confusion of roles and responsibilities in the Paralympic Movement.

Multi-disability sports control problem

- There are contradicting statements on where the jurisdiction lines should be drawn in connection to the establishing of rules, classifications, programmes and calendar for the IPC multi-disability championship sports.

- There is a lack of understanding that a multi-disability IPC sport because of its multi-disability character may not for a given disability in all aspects be identical to what the IOSD for that disability group might offer in its own competition programme.

I think that we here have the fundamental difference within the movement in interpreting who is responsible for what. Initiative must be taken to sort out the responsibilities for the multi-disability IPC sports.

In many of the multi-disability sports this is evidently no problem, in others again it either is or may be. In these sports there are up to five interest groups defending each their own territory. Historically it was the nations that wanted a multi-disability world competition programme, as a majority of them had national multi-disability sports programmes. The IOSD neither had the knowledge or the interest in it, so the structure for it was not only created in the IPC, it was one of the incitements for its founding. It was created in order to get **one** controlling body for each multi-disability sport instead of the four, later **five,** bodies having control over each one part of these sports.

No one would deny that a certain disability group should have the right to a sports competition programme suitable for the disability in question, but if we shall uphold a multi-disability competition programme, then there are some questions in need of clarification:

- Where lies the best competence to determine rules, classifications and programmes for a multi-disability sport?
    - with the assembly of nations whose members have an interest in a multi-disability sports environment?
    - with single-disability assemblies and organisations?

- Would one clear authority for the multi-disability sports be better than five?

These are admittedly somewhat leading questions, but I think they may illustrate a problem that is a reality for the Paralympic Movement. I think it needs to be either reaffirmed or rejected that the IPC shall "organise according to sport and not disability".

The national member organisations of the IPC, representing their athletes, need to agree on what the needs are. Whatever those needs prove to be, clear and distinct mandates should be given each concerned international body.

National Structure and Organisation

Overview of structures

To my knowledge there is today no complete overview on how the nations have organised sports for persons with disabilities in the countries. A couple of things are certain though. Whether there is one national sports organisation for all disabilities that is structured by sport, or a number of disability organisations, they are all umbrella organisations for a number of different sports committees. Also, in almost all member countries that have a structure by disability, there is an umbrella organisation acting as the National Paralympic Committee (NPC). There have been surveys made on how the nations are organised for sports for persons with disabilities. The responses to these surveys were few at every known occasion.

ISMWSF tells about a survey in its Development Plan of 1998 that received only 9 replies. Of a list with 9 points, the following are relevant to the national structure:

- Most nations operate on a sports specific approach and cover all three physical disabilities.

- Structure and organisations of each country vary depending on population, geographic dispersion etc, but essential elements of administration, marketing/fundraising, sports administration and sports science are common.

- Most countries cater for a wide range of sports.

Through research and discussions with other nations ISMWSF says the listed points are common to virtually every nation with the exception of war-torn countries or countries with poor social economic standing or underdeveloped countries.

In 1998, the European Non-Governmental Sports Organistions (ENGSO) made a survey on sports for persons with disabilities among its member organisations, National Sports Confederations or National Olympic Committees. They had replies from 19 countries. Among the conclusions are:

- Only one country had a structure of sports for persons with disabilities similar to international organisations.

- The NPC is the most important organisation for sport for persons with disabilities in 13 of the countries.

- Among national federations there is a great differentiation in the organisation of sport for persons with disabilities.

The EUROPC made a survey on the structure of its member nations in 1996. Eight countries responded. Some of the results were:

- The number of organisations per country ranged from two to five, deaf sports included.

- Organisations for persons with an intellectual disability were listed in 5 countries and were included in the national sports federation for persons with disabilities in two countries.

- Separate organisations for the visually impaired were listed in 6 countries.

- Wheelchair and CP sports had separate organisations in one country each while the rest had locomotor disabilities in one organisation.

- All countries have an umbrella organisation in the form of a "Sports Organisation for Persons with Disabilities" or an NPC.

In the 1970s and 1980s a common national model was to have one organisation for locomotor disabilities and visually impaired together. With very few exceptions sports for persons with an intellectual disability were organised outside of the traditional national sports organisations for persons with disabilities. Available information suggests that this is still the case in many countries otherwise organised with one body for the other disabilities.

Factors influencing national structures

For countries with a relatively small population or limited financial resources for sports for persons with disabilities it is neither practical nor financially justified to have a structure and organisation for each disability. It is also rather common for governments and national sports authorities to advocate a unified model for sports for persons with disabilities. Despite these incentives many nations have disability organisations. IBSA is promoting separate national organisations for visually impaired. The IBSA constitution requires that a national member organisation in its statutes must clearly state "that its principle purpose is the promotion of sports for the blind and visually impaired". The international structure with 5 IOSD does influence new member countries to copy that nationally.

National membership requirements

The IPC constitution does not give a very clear picture of what a national member organisation should be and do. The preamble of the membership article is over 200 words long. In a rather confusing way it seems to explain that a national member organisation can be a National Paralympic Committee or "a national co-ordinating or umbrella organisation" which represents all or some of the disability groups, and those other organisations that represent a single-disability group. A National Paralympic Committee is described as "comprising all national organisations for the disability groups covered by the IPC".

Apart from being somewhat confusing, the IPC membership article on national member organisations does not properly cover for example a country where persons with disabilities are integrated in national sports federations.

Confusion in national administration of international participation

The complicated national (and international) structure causes administrative confusion both for national member organisations, for organising committees of international championships, and for IPC sports committees. Here are some examples from just the past year. In all fairness it should be said that it is not only the complicated structure that causes the problems, but also that the responsibilities of an NPC are not well understood.

- An organising committee for an IPC World Championship finds one country having two different national teams appearing at the event. One of the teams was entered by an organisation that is not a member of IPC.

- The Organising Committee of the EUROPC 1999 European Championships in Swimming reports that about 60% of the entered swimmers were not originally entered through their NPC. One country had as many as four different national disability organisations sending in entries.

- Entries to a European Open Championship in a team sport are not made through the responsible NPCs, and unacceptably late withdrawal spoils the tournament.

- A country wanting to organise multi-disability European Championships in a particular sport approaches both one of the IOSD and the EUROPC for sanctioning and suggests that the IPC should be the contracting international organisation.

- Invitations to international invitational events are being distributed without references either to international or national sanctioning.

- The EUROPC is approached with requests to take action on what is reported to be badly organised championships by two different IOSD.

This tells us that many NPC do not have appropriate national rules and procedures in place to ensure that their responsibility towards the IPC and Organising Committees for entries from their country is fulfilled. Some NPC do not have control over or appropriate co-operation with all entities in their country organising athletes eligible for multi-disability IPC competition. Appropriate IPC procedures for control of entries at multi-disability championships is either missing or not enforced.

An organising committee for an official IPC championship competition, world or continental, must send in their bids through their NPC. Both the organising committee and the NPC in the country have a right to expect that the NPC in the participating countries take responsibility for the entries and the participation. In countries where a particular IPC sport is integrated in a National Sports Federation, or where there is a specific national organisation for the sport, it is still only through the NPC membership in the IPC that participation is possible. This requires that appropriate agreements between concerned national organisations and the NPC be in place.

It may seem that most of the different anomalies brought forward here are matters that only require some common sense and logic thinking to be corrected. A simple education package may be all that is needed. The IPC has identified this problem and started to prepare a list of the responsibilities for publication to its national member organisations.

Problems related to national structures

- National members of the IPC do not live up to their role as supreme national representatives for the IPC and its programmes, including the IPC championship sports.

- The membership article in the IPC constitution does not properly describe a national member organisation of the IPC.

- The national structures are not homogenous. Is the variation in national structures a problem area?

I think the variation in national structure indeed is a problem area. The IPC's multi-disability competition programme requires that its national member organisations be able to represent all concerned disabilities. IBSA's constitution on the other hand requires separate national organisations for "blind sports". Can all those national organisations agree on a joint policy for the IPC multi-disability sports and for a less confusing international administration than there is today? In an article in EUROPC News n° 4/99, I elaborated on the possibilities and powers of the national members to determine the international organisational structure. It must be the responsibility of the nations at the Assemblies to identify the roles of the numerous international organisations in such a way that they provide the nations with the sports programme the nations want, preferably avoiding that those programmes are in conflict with each other. A large number of different national disability organisations in one country may make it difficult to reach a common policy on how to act internationally, because each may wish to guard its own identity nationally and internationally. I have heard, for example, that in some countries NPC, which are based on a disability groups structure, have refused to act internationally to argue against separate championships for separate disability groups when asked to do so by their national team in a sport.

Some of the problems surfacing in some nations' administration of their international participation could possibly be avoided by a simplified and more distinct formulation of the membership article in IPC's constitution.

It is important that the NPC negotiate written agreements with sports organisations that for one reason or another are not a part of the NPC. That would include, for example, integrated national sports federations, national sports-specific federations for persons with disabilities, and any concerned disability group. In this way circulation of invitations and making of entries can be regulated through the proper IPC member.

Organisational Dilemmas for the IPC Multi-Disability Sports

Administrative capacity

The IPC SAEC have no paid employees, only volunteers, mostly with regular full time jobs. The tremendous efforts and accomplishments we see in many of the sports must be seen against that background.

The SAEC are comparable to the sports committees of an IF for the able-bodied with many disciplines. As for instance FINA has Technical Committees for swimming, diving, waterpolo, synchronized swimming, and open water swimming, the IPC has the SAEC for the multi-disability sports for which the IPC is the IF. The committees of the IF for able-bodied have their IF as the administrative roof, which provide them with the required administrative services. This also serves to secure that there are tight bonds between the sports committees and the IF. The very young IPC, however, has not had the financial means available to provide an efficient administrative roof for its committees. There has not been staff available to take care of the administrative needs for the SAEC, and according to the IPC Technical Officer's report of August 1999 to the Executive Committee that has not changed. The IPC has not published an updated rulebook for its sports since 1994. As a consequence the SAEC have in many aspects been forced to act as IF for their sports themselves. This may quite understandably sometimes have caused gaps between some SAEC leaderships and the IPC Executive and Assemblies.

It is also important to have in mind that in other IF, the committees may have more in common than the entirely different sports of the IPC may have. Each sport has its own unique needs and particularities. What is good for one sport may not necessarily be true for another.

Sports structures

There are a few things that are, or should be, common for the IPC multi-disability sports. The IPC bylaws require that the Sports Assemblies and the SAEC function within the aims and policies of the IPC. Based on discussions at General Assemblies, Sports Assemblies, and European regional assemblies (other Regional assemblies opinions have not been studied) it can be assumed that some of these aims and policies are:

- to organise sport according to each sport, and not each disability,
- to provide functional classification in the sport,
- to provide a joint rule package for the sport,
- to provide a system for world and regional championships in the sport.

The IPC Handbook, Section II, Chapter 2, covers the joint rules requirement, Chapter 3 the championships programme, and Chapter 5 the functional classification part. The Handbook is more clearly formulated in these areas than the IPC constitution.

In their effort to fulfil the responsibilities of establishing joint rules, functional classifications, and championship programmes, the IPC Sports Assemblies and their elected SAEC have chosen different organisational solutions. Some have taken the IOSD's constitutional claims to be the ultimate international authorities on sports for their disabilities as the key ruling, while others more closely followed the IPC bylaws and Handbook.

Thus, for instance, IPC Powerlifting, Swimming, Table Tennis, and Alpine and Nordic Skiing have been organised entirely as sports by themselves, while Athletics and Cycling organise more or less as it was before the founding of the IPC, with in essence one department for each disability group. This is also reflected in the rules for these sports. The former have IPC rules while the latter refer to the respective IOSD rules. Functional classification is not implemented in athletics and cycling. This variation in certain fundamental principles of IPC multi-disability sports adds to the confusion of organising committees and NPC.

Sanctioning

Decisions on sanctioning of sports events are in essence taken by the respective sports committees, in the IPC by the SAEC and in the IOSD by the Sports Sections/Committees/Co-ordinators. Although the IPC constitution declares that the IPC is the sole organisation with the right to sanction multi-disability championships, a look in the July 1999 Newsletter of the Southern Cross Multi-Disability Championships in October 1999 tells us that

- athletics is sanctioned by 4 IOSD,
- swimming by 2 IOSD and the IPC,
- powerlifting by 3 IOSD,
- table tennis by 2 IOSD and the IPC SAEC Table Tennis,
- cycling by 3 IOSD.

The IPC constitution claims that the IPC is the only international organisation with the right to sanction multi-disability games and championships. The intention is to spare the organisers the trouble to communicate with up to six international organisations for one event. There is obviously no system in place to ensure that this is avoided.

In the measurable sports most IOSD have an interest to keep world records and ranking lists for their own disability which may explain why they are eager to sanction also multi-disability sports events. The question arises why not an IPC sanction alone would be sufficient to ensure that all requirements for approval of results are followed.

For the ratification of world records in athletics by amputees and les autres, ISOD Athletics requires that an ISOD Technical Delegate (TD) be present. In his article "Missing the gate" in EUROPC News 4/99, the EUROPC Athletes Representative, Mr. Wilfried Mätzler, reports that only one person in the world has this authorisation and that he lives in Canada. He pointed out that European organisers of national championships in order to secure ratification of a possible world record must pay for the travel and accommodation for this person. The failure to do so due to the costs involved resulted at one occasion in a new record not being ratified, and the athlete involved lost out on a reward by a sponsoring prosthesis manufacturer.

Also, the IPC multi-disability sports have difficulties providing a reasonable number of authorised Technical Delegates and classifiers available on all continents/regions. In IPC Swimming, for instance, the only one authorised TD in the world lives in Australia. That means that each Region for its Swimming Championships must fly in the TD from Australia. In swimming there is however, no need to have any specific international official from disability sports to ratify a record, even if set at nationals. The signature of the Chief of Competition suffices provided that he/she is an authorised Federation International de Natation (FINA) official.

Sports "going independent" require an understanding of national structures

The constituencies of the SAEC are the Sports Assemblies (SA) of nations, which elect the SAEC. The agendas for the SA deals with sports technical and classification issues plus the administration of the SAEC. The national delegates selected to represent their NPC to the SA are therefore sports people like national sports committee chairmen, coaches, trainers, classifiers, and athletes. The IPC Sports Technical structure is built on the principle of umbrella organisations for sports, where the IPC is the umbrella organisation for its subcommittees for sports, the SAEC, and the NPC as the members of the IPC are the national umbrella organisations for its national subcommittees for sports. That means that the SAEC constituencies do not consist of independent national organisations, but of subcommittees that must answer to its national umbrella organisations. This has sometimes proved to be difficult to understand by some within the sports technical domain.

As an example an IPC Sport Assembly Executive Committee (SAEC) made in 1998 far going plans with a national sports committee for the sport in question to organise European Championships in1999 without contacting the responsible NPC. The NPC had already made commitments for European Championships in another sport plus large National Games close in time for the intended event. The NPC had some difficulties making the SAEC understand that it held the supreme responsibility for the competition programme in its own country, and could not allow competing fundraising for three major events close by in time.

For many years leaders in various SAEC have spoken about "going independent", meaning that a sport for athletes with disabilities should form an international sports federation. I think that is a natural reaction by the sports committee leaders in view of the unclear and confused situation on the responsibilities and roles of the IPC and the IOSD.

Independent sports federations control their own championships programme without interference from any other organisation. Also some leaders in the movement, not directly engaged in the SAEC, promote the thought. The idea has been discussed at two EUROPC Conferences, the latest in 1996. It was found that it does not fit in with the realities of the nations who participate in the sports (Lindström, IPC Magazine, spring 1996). The 1996 IPC Extraordinary General Assembly dealt with the question as a proposal from the Task Force appointed in 1995 to review the structure. The Assembly voted it down, which is logical due to the national realities. An international federation must have a constituency of national federations. For an international specific sports federation limited to persons with disabilities, there are three possible types of national organisations that could be members:

- the NPC as the national umbrella organisation for the sport,
- a national sport federation exclusively for disabled in the sport,
- the respective NSF for able-bodied if the sport is integrated in the country.

If the first option were the case, the NPC would then have to expect to become member in about two dozen further international federations, to pay membership fees and general assembly participation, in addition to the 6 it already has to deal with. If the national structure were by disability groups they would either have to come together to form national committees for the different sports or leave it to the NPC.

The second solution would require forming of independent specific sports federations in the nations. For any national sports federation to be officially recognised as such by the National Sports Confederation or NOC, it would have to be of a certain size and have a certain quantity level of clubs, members, and activities. It does not take a very small country to get in trouble in trying to get recognition for a national specific sports federation for persons with disabilities. There are simply too few persons with disabilities active in one given sport in most of the countries. You do not form clubs for two to three members, or a national federation for three four clubs with 20-50 athletes in total. There is also a financial aspect to consider. The smaller the country, the larger the problem.

The integrated national federation in the third option would be a practical solution if integration were easily accepted by the able-bodied national sports world. It is accepted and promoted in some countries, but according to what representatives from many countries tell, this is not a world-wide situation.

The responsible administrators in the IPC member countries with lower population or with limited economy are aware of these problems, which is why they are reluctant to accept international independent sports specific federations.

A solution where the sports seek integration in the International Sports Federations (IF) would probably enhance willingness to integrate in the nations, and would satisfy the independence goal as well.

Organisational shortages for the IPC SAEC

- The administrative support for the SAEC is insufficient.

- Some SAEC are organised by disability and not by sport.

- There are too few persons in the world authorised as Technical Delegates and classifiers in the IPC sports.

- There is interference from the IOSD in sanctioning of competitions in multi-disability sports.

- Is there a lack of understanding of national realities among the SAEC in discussions on sports "going independent"?

As the sports are different, so are their needs for administrative support. The larger sports would probably need a full-time administrator each, while the smaller sports very well might be able to share a staff person. Such a link with the Headquarter secretariat would certainly also help to close possible gaps between the sports and the IPC administration. I think this should be a priority for the IPC.

Concerning the IPC sports that still are organised more according to disability than according to the sports I think that they should take a discussion about possibilities for development of the sport with a sports oriented structure. It is recommendable that the leadership of the SAEC prioritises education programmes for TDs and classifiers. On the question concerning understanding of national realities, I can just hope that this paper might have been of some assistance.

Conclusions - Questions

Control of the multi-disability programmes

The core of the complications and confusion of roles is the question about who really controls the multi-disability sports programme. Different constitutions, bylaws, rule books, and agreements give contradicting messages. It is very much a matter of establishing clearer than presently the role of the IPC. If the IPC really is an autonomous organisation, its constitutional objectives must reflect that in clearer language than presently.

There are a number of questions that should be answered:

- What organisation shall have the supreme control over the multi-disability sports? If it is the IPC, why does not the IPC constitution just say that instead of talking about assisting in the co-ordination and supervising at the same time as it says that the IPC awards and sanctions as the sole organisation with the right to do so?

- What does the IPC's main objective to "be the international representative organisation of sports for athletes with disabilities at Paralympic standards" mean in practice?

- Do the athletes need opportunities to win world and continental championship titles in the same event and against the same competitors in more than one international federation? If not, can the IOSD call their competitions Games, Cups, Grand Prix, and invitationals?

- If IPC and IOSD championships for some reason should be held in the same year, can the national organisations and their athletes be trusted with their own choice of which competition to participate in?

If the IPC shall have the role to control the multi-disability sports, then the IOSD role in providing disability specific programmes in these sports should be adapted accordingly.

The national member organisations of the IPC

I can not resist offering a humble suggestion for an amendment of the IPC membership paragraph. It would perhaps be made clearer by a text describing an IPC member as **"a National Paralympic Committee or equivalent organisation, being the nationally recognised representative in matters pertaining to the IPC, the Paralympic Games, and the IPC multi-disability competition programme"**. Then both preamble and all text about other national organisations can be deleted. An NPC may then be organised and structured as it suits the national situation and culture.

The sports

The IPC should create strong administrative support to the SAEC and strengthen the ties between the SAEC and the central deciding bodies and the secretariat.

If any SAEC wants to try to "go independent", the most logical way seems to be to integrate in the respective IF. Whichever way, a constituency of nationally recognised organisations is required.

How can we do it?

I think it is time to organise another "Arnhem Conference" to give the nations again an opportunity to make a number of statements on how they want the international sports programmes to be organised and to draw clearer lines for the different responsibilities which are unclear today. The National Paralympic Committees should agree internally on a national policy so that different persons from the same country give the same message in the IPC as well as in the IOSD.

All of us who are engaged in international sports for athletes with disabilities have a responsibility to work for an attractive and dignified elite sports programme. I hope we can do so in the spirit of the words commencing this paper: **"It is now time for all organisations including the IPC to seriously address the issue as to how we can best serve people with a disability in the world of sport."**

The international organisation and structure for disability sport and the need to accelerate the development of the regions

Bob McCullough

Forest Lake, Queensland, Australia; President, ISMWSF

Introduction

The subject of the organisation and structure of sport for people with a disability has been addressed and reviewed many times over the past forty-five years, and I am quite sure many people who have been involved will say 'not another examination of the international organisations and their structure!' It is certainly an attitude that is understandable because past proposals for change have resulted in a lot of discussion and arguments, and invariably in the majority of cases proposed changes in organisation and structure have failed. Many of the proposals for change have been sound in reasoning and for the benefit of sport for people with a disability, but their rejection was the result of power play amongst the key people and the tendency not to recognise the need for **change**.

In the modern world of sport, and with the acceleration in the development of sport for people with a disability, it is very apparent that in order to bring our organisation and structure into an effective and efficient business operation at national, regional, and international levels we must make the approach on a sound businesslike footing. If we fail to do so, we will continue to struggle in the overall development for both sports and the support services required. More importantly, we will not pass the scrutiny of governments, the corporate sector, and funding organisations in ensuring that funding is used and applied in the most effective manner. Evidence of this is available in Australia, where the Federal Government Sports Minister has declared it was time to end the 'amateur hour' approach to the running of sports across the nation and treat it as a major industry. It is being projected as the biggest shake-up in 25 years and involves an inquiry into sports administration, participation, and sponsorship. No doubt it will have its effect on sport for people with a disability!

We may ask 'what has changed so much that we need to address how we go about managing the business of sport for people with a disability?' There are a number of significant factors which have driven the need for change and they are:

1. the advent of the successful parallel games in 1988 in Seoul, Korea, and the acceptance that the Paralympic Games would immediately follow the Olympic Games:

    The 1988 Paralympic Games were the first Games held under the International Co-ordinating Committee and marked the acceptance of the ICC into the Olympic Family (SCRUTON 1998).

2. the success of the 1992 Paralympic Games in Barcelona:

    The 1992 Barcelona Paralympic Games are described by many as the ultimate in the organisation of Paralympic Games with the remarkable feature of tremendous public response with over two million people coming to watch the overall program of events (SCRUTON 1998).

3. the formation of the International Paralympic Committee (IPC) and its role and successful impact at the elite level and its potential for the future:

    Since the formation of the International Paralympic Committee there has been considerable progress in the development of elite sports and of the IPC Sports Sections. However the next steps in the overall development of the organisation are crucial, as the transition from a volunteer management system to a permanent professional staff at the new headquarters in Bonn needs firm handling.

The management of the sports is another area that needs attention. While the development has been quite remarkable when you consider that they are being guided and administered by a small number of volunteers. Certainly the sports of athletics, swimming and powerlifting are at the stage where full-time administration is essential and we need to look at the International Federations to play a greater role in Paralympic sports administration, just like what has been achieved by the International Tennis Federation.

4. the introduction and development of the Functional Classification system in a number of sports:

The area of changes to the 'classification' system, through the introduction of a functional system, for the physically disabled together with the sports being responsible for the control and development of their respective classification systems, is one which has made a significant improvement in competition for the athletes and in the organisation of more viable competition for the sports involved. However, it has left a void in the responsibilities of the relevant International Organisations for the Disabled, particularly ISMWSF, ISOD and CP-ISRA, and these organisations have since been faced with the need to readdress their areas of responsibility. In the case of ISMWSF (which prior to 1992 had a large responsibility for all wheelchair sports, technically and in administration), the advent of the functional classification system has reduced this responsibility to wheelchair athletics, fencing, and wheelchair rugby.

While the functional classification system has resulted in a positive move forward there is still a lot to be accomplished to streamline the process of classifying athletes for competition. There are too few classifiers throughout the world, and until such time as we can move into a situation of having trained national classifiers in each country and a number of international qualified classifiers in each geographical region, we will have difficulties. Proper classification of athletes at the time of entry into a competition is essential and the need for athletes having to arrive at competitions for classification several days beforehand should not be required. Such an achievement would go a long way in validating our sports with the general public, reduce costs to the athletes, and assist organisers of competitions .

5. the development of the IPC World Championship program:

Who should organise World Championships has been a controversial subject within the IPC membership since the decision was made some time ago for the IPC to be responsible for international multidisability competitions and world championships. Nevertheless a system is now in place and while not perfect, all sports in the present period have successfully conducted world championships, and there is a developing calendar.

The need to ensure that World Championships are organised in a professional manner needs urgent attention as it is only through creating a strong image of our sports that we will succeed.

There have been a number of very well organised World Championships organised by the International Organisations for the Disabled in this present quadrennial. These include the IBSA World Championships held in Madrid, and the INAS-FMH World Cup Soccer held in Leicester, England in August 98.

Irrespective of the debate of who organises championships and competitions it is very important that the events are professionally run and that we have an overall competition program throughout the world which provides athletes with the opportunity to structure their competition program.

6. the need to develop regional and worldwide competition programs to enable athletes and teams to access regular competition:

The development of the regions as defined by the IOC and IPC is very important, yet the only region which is moving ahead is Europe. Europe has developed a strong competition program including regional championships, and is addressing many of the issues raised in this paper. Admittedly Europe has certain advantages over other regions in terms of the close geographical proximity of the countries which makes travel to competitions inexpensive in comparison to other regions. Nevertheless, the development of all regions is very important in providing opportunities for people with a disability to participate in sport and to provide strong competition to aid the development of athletes and the respective sports.

The establishment of the FESPIC Federation in 1975 has provided the region with the basis for development. The 7th FESPIC Games (FESPIC Bangkok 99) was a tremendous success and there is little doubt that it has left Thailand with a legacy for the recognition of people with a disability and the future development of sport for the disabled. However we need to capatialise on the success of these games, not just in Thailand but throughout the Asia Pacific region. Maybe I am a dreamer but looking at the excellent facilities specially built for the Asian Games and the FESPIC Games and the link with the University I believe it provides an excellent opportunity to create an international 'Centre of Excellence' for sport for people with a disability. Such a centre could include the training of people in coaching and in the technical areas as well as providing the facilities for coaching elite athletes in the region. I would see such an initiative as being prestigious, a business for the Thammasat University, and an asset to Thailand and the Asia Pacific region athletes with a disability.

The FESPIC Games are certainly a sound basis on which to build, but we need to help the development of the Games by establishing regular regional championships and providing training for coaches and technical personnel to service the sports.

While the above addresses the Asia Pacific region the need to fast track the development of all regions into viable effective organisations in order to widen the participation in our sports and to provide regular viable competition is vital. This is most important both in providing opportunities to people with a disability and gaining recognition by governments and the community of the social and economic benefits that can be derived.

7. the need for professional event management:

The days of national disability organisations taking on the responsibility and funding of major events such as regional and world championships are disappearing, as city and regional government administrations are recognising the economic benefits in bringing major sporting events to their areas. Good examples of this are the World Track & Field Championships hosted by the Birmingham (UK) City Council, the World Swimming Championships hosted by the Christchurch City Council (NZ), and now the World Wheelchair Games in October 1999. The Wheelchair Basketball Gold Cup held in Sydney, Australia, in 1998 is yet another example of commercial enterprise forming a partnership (Company) between Wheelchair Sports, the Australian Paralympic Committee, the Australian Government, State Government, the corporate sector, and the Sydney Paralympic Organising Committee. The event had a financial budget well in excess of $A 1m and it attracted large commercial sponsorships.

It is important that we do lift the overall image of our sports through sound event management by those who have the necessary qualifications and expertise.

8. the need to address development of athletes and sports from grass roots through to the elite at national and regional level:

Sport for people with a disability has come a long way from its beginnings as rehabilitation therapy for spinal injury, and it is now at a point where people with a disability expect and want to play sport. Furthermore many want to learn and develop the necessary skills and fitness levels to achieve a competitive level, and to achieve excellence at national and international level. Unfortunately we are lagging behind in delivering the necessary training for coaches, classifiers and officials, and it is an area to which we must address.

Just as a matter of interest, let me illustrate the number of sports being practiced by people with a disability in many countries (Table 1). Add to this twin basketball, wheelchair dancing, cue sports (snooker, 9 ball), handcycling, lawn bowls and the possibility of curling as a ice sport, and it provides a wide range of choice.

9. the need to turn our sports, games, championships and services into commercially viable products:

The great concern and challenge that we face in the future is finding the financial resources to support the development of our sports. We have all tried very hard to find that magic formula which encourages the commercial business sector to provide sponsorship funding. It all seems so simple but unfortunately we have not developed the product we are offering to the point of attracting sponsors. It is an area in which we need to work very hard to develop our products to a point where they offer sound benefits to the sponsor, and we must deliver whatever benefits we offer. We must avoid promising the impossible, like large data bases of membership, exposure to large numbers of spectators and signage at the venue etc.

Alpine Skiing	Flag Football	Roller Skating
Aquatics	Floor Hockey	Shooting
Archery	Goal Ball	Slalom
Athletics (Track & Field)	Golf	Soccer
Badminton	Gymnastics	Softball
Basketball	Handball	Speed Skating
Boccia	Handcycling	Table Tennis
Canoeing Cross Country	Ice Hockey	Team Handball
Cue Sports (Snooker & 9 Ball)	Judo	Tennis
Curling	Lawn Bowling	Twin Basketball
Cycling	Nordic Skiing	Volleyball
Diving	Poly Hockey	Weightlifting
Equestrian	Powerlifting	Wheelchair Dancing
Fencing	Racquetball	Wheelchair Rugby
Figure Skating	Road Racing	Wrestling

Tab. 1:   Sports for people with a disability (Reference: JEFFREY A. JONES & MICHAEL J. PACIOREK: "Sport & recreation for disabled" 2nd ed.)

10. the need to gain support from governments, international aid organisations and trusts:

There is no doubt that more and more governments throughout the world are realising the benefits of ensuring that people with a disability are part of society and that there is no discrimination. The objectives of the 1999 Bangkok FESPIC Games state it clearly.

There is strong evidence that governments will provide financial and other resources provided there is a sound professional and unified approach. I say unified, because governments do not wish to receive submissions from every disability, but they will respond to proposals which assist in bringing people with a disability into mainstream society and helping to achieve those objectives illustrated in Figure 1.

Equality in One World

- to promote the sport talent and equality of opportunity of the disabled in the FESPIC region

- to elevate social recognition and understanding of the disabled's abilities and opportunities

- to promote the FESPIC Federation's goals of equal participation of the disabled in a great variety of sport events, acitivities, and sports competition

Fig. 1: Objectives of the 1999 Bangkok FESPIC Games

I have listened to the International Paralympic Committee President, Dr. Steadward, on a number of occasions when he states that in his contacts with governments and top level officials during his extensive travels, the reception for support is most encouraging but they await that professional approach. The problem is that we do not have the organisation and structure to follow through and take advantage of doors being opened to governments by people like the IPC President.

11. the need to provide worldwide services to sports in terms of coaching and technical management:

In the past fifty years there have been significant achievements by a number of countries in developing services to sport including coaching, sports science, education programs and the classification system. The development includes the production of systems and manuals in many of these areas. However little attempt has been made over the years to share this knowledge and information on a worldwide basis. There are in place attempts to address this issue. ISMWSF has, in the last twelve months, adopted the Australian program of "Coaching Athletes with a Disability" (CAD), and initiated the formation of an International Coaching Council to start delivery of the program and to develop coaching courses from basic principles through to high performance. The ISMWSF recognises the need to do the same with classification and technical officials. These aspects presently under consideration.

The benefits of having a universal system in the areas of coaching and classification are significant for the development of our sports and such a scheme as that being put in place for coaching will ensure that all countries, particularly the many under developed countries, will have access to coaching and technical programs, as well as information. If we can succeed in this area we will have made a great step forward in the overall development of sport for people with a disability.

Having covered the eleven points which indicate the progress of our sports and what needs to be done to enhance the international organisation and structure for sport for people with a disability. Let us summarise the points in Table 2.

1.	the advent of the Parallel Games
2.	the success of the 1992 Barcelona Paralympic Games
3.	the formation of the IPC and its success
4.	the introduction and development of the Functional Classification system
5.	the development of the world championship program
6.	the need to develop regional and world-wide competition
7.	the need for professional event management
8.	the development of athletes from grass roots through to elite
9.	the need to develop our marketing products
10.	the need to gain support from governments and international funding organisations
11.	the need to provide technical and other services

Tab. 2: Points driving the need for change

This paper is not just another review of our organisation and structure but rather an awakening call to put sport for people with a disability on a path that will clearly demonstrate a sound professional approach in management at national, regional and international levels. It is most important that irrespective of whether a person or organisation is operating at club, national or regional level that we recognise that we are all playing a part in the development of our sports. There is really no room for power play and 'them and us' attitudes.

Observations on Present Organisational Structures

The following observations and comments on the IPC and the IOSD members are the personal observations of the writer and should not be considered as any more than that.

International Paralympic Committee (IPC)

The IPC is the authority for Summer and Winter Paralympic Games, World Championships and multidisability events including regional games.

The organisation is governed by an Executive Committee consisting of a President, three Vice Presidents, Technical Officer, Treasurer, Medical Officer, Winter and Summer Sports Representatives, Secretary General six regional representatives and the five IOSD Presidents. The day to day decisions are handled by a Management Committee consisting of President, Vice Presidents, Technical Officer, Medical Officer and Secretary General.

The IPC has entered a transitional management change from what has been until now a very heavy dependence on voluntary positions, to the engagement of professional employed staff at the new IPC Headquarters in Bonn. This transition means that the IPC must look at its structure and change from an operational type management Executive Board, to one of making policy decisions, implementing policy, and dealing with the political aspects of the organisation.

While the author must be cautious in commenting on the future organisational structure, the modern trend leans heavily toward Executive Boards being small, and consisting of a mix of elected people along with recognised commercial experts to make management decisions. Advice to the Executive Board on sports technical matters, sports programs, media and public relations, sports science and medical matters should, in effect, be through sub committees or commissions consisting of the necessary professional expertise. Perhaps the Executive Management Board is no more than six people plus the President who needs to have considerable time available to attend to meeting with governments and other high level people who have influence in policy and decision making in relation to sport for people with a disability. It may well be that the demands of this position are such that it in fact needs to become an executive President with salary.

The area of individual sports management needs attention as with the exception of wheelchair basketball and wheelchair tennis, which are governed by International Federations, all other sports are managed by volunteers, many of whom are saturated with the administration demands and needs. It is an area which needs to be addressed to ensure that there is continuity in development and the day to day matters. One aspect that must be understood is that the range of sports that are currently being practiced in various parts of the world cannot all be in the Paralympic Games. As our sports develop, we will get to the same situation as the Olympics where sports are selected to be part of a Paralympic Games. In the longer term it is quite likely that a number of sports will become International Federations in their own right, and a number of smaller sports will become affiliated with their mainstream counterparts. The ISMWSF is encouraging this trend.

International Stoke Mandeville Wheelchair Sports Federation (ISMWSF)

The International Stoke Mandeville Wheelchair Sports Federation (ISMWSF) conducted a review of its operations in 1998, which culminated in the production of the current 1999-2001 Development Plan. This plan is very much alive and it takes into consideration the need to:

- move into effective management through a small Management Board

- adopt the same geographical regions as the IPC in order to maximise collaboration within the regions

- establish a foundation (Wheelchair Sports Worldwide Foundation) as the funding arm of ISMWSF

- encourage ISMWSF sports to become international organisations in their own right where possible and others to become affiliated with their mainstream counterparts

- adopt the Australian 'Coaching Athletes with a Disability' (CAD) program, and to establish an International Coaching Council as the co-ordinating body. The first CAD coaching course is to be held at Stoke Mandeville on 7 & 8 August this year followed by one in Singapore in September and one in Christchurch in October at the time of the World Wheelchair Games

- amalgamate the International Sports Organisation for the Disabled (ISOD) with ISMWSF, through the formation of a new organisation for the physically disabled

- develop the annual World Wheelchair Games into a major world event, to be at a different location each year; and

- develop the Stoke Mandeville Sports facilities as a 'Centre of Excellence' for the development of sports and the conduct of international seminars and workshops.

International Blind Sports Association (IBSA)

IBSA is a strong viable organisation supported by the ONCE Foundation, with its headquarters in Spain. It is currently implementing its overall development plan which was passed by the IBSA Assembly of Nations in 1997, at Casablanca. One notable feature of the plan is to reduce the number of geographical regions from seven to five: namely Asia, Oceania, Americas, Europe and Africa. Considerable work is being done in these regions, as detailed in a recent report produced by IBSA including the establishment of formal agreements with governments and authorities.

Strong aspects which point to the reasons for the success of IBSA are:

-   good levels of funding from within IBSA and through ONCE

-   effective management system at IBSA Executive level and at regional level

-   the ability to fund regional programs

-   good communications with member nations and regions through periodic magazine and Web site which is available in large print with graphics and large print without graphics to facilitate use. IBSA is a strong supporter of information technology

-   a williness to develop new and innovative marketing and fundraising techniques

-   a proven record in event management.

International Sports Organisation for the Disabled (ISOD)

ISOD is the authority for amputee, les autres and dwarf sports and the provider of technical and other services. The organisation is managed by a small Executive Committee consisting of the President, First Vice President, Vice President, Medical Officer, Technical Officer, Secretary General and three Members at Large. The organisation at this time does not have any employed personnel. The organisation is working to a development plan which gives high priority to:

-   the appointment of a full time professional staff person

-   development of a comprehensive sports calendar and bid process

-   development at grass roots level with a junior competitive component

-   development of new sports e.g. soccer, badminton and golf

-   investigation of foreign funding sources.

The plan also addresses the need for amalgamation with ISMWSF.

International Sports Federation for Persons with Mental Handicap (INAS-FMH)

This young organisation has, beyond a doubt, the largest task of all the disability organisations just in terms of pure numbers of people with an intellectual disability throughout the world. Nevertheless the organisation is growing fast and is having a significant impact in providing sport and services for persons with a mental handicap.

The organisation, in a very short space of time, has organised many World Championships and has clearly demonstrated an ability in event management. The work in the regional areas of Europe, Asia, South Pacific, South Africa, Middle East and America is forging ahead with committees established. The outward and visible signs of the organisation, in terms of publicity and the distribution of information through the high quality periodic magazine, are impressive. The financial support of the ANDE Foundation is apparently of great assistance in the work of the organisation.

Cerebral Palsy International Sport & Recreation Association (CP-ISRA)

CP-ISRA is a young organisation and it does not have the financial resources to meet its heavy demand in an area which encompasses a large world population of cerebral palsy sufferers from a mild state through to the severely affected. The organisation has developed rapidly since its inception and it conducts a number of major events on a regular basis around the world including the Nottingham Games, European Championships, and the World Boccia Championships. The organisation is governed by a similar Executive as the other IOSDs. Sports include boccia for the more severely disabled along with athletics, archery, cycling, powerlifting, swimming, soccer, shooting and table tennis. The organisation places a strong emphasis on educational programs including classification workshops.

Summary

The above observations indicate to me that IBSA is delivering a well balanced program from elite competition through to development of the regions in a sustainable manner. The approach in management in the development of the regions will pay dividends in the future for blind sports.

For INAS-FMH, although not as advanced as IBSA in their overall structure and technical development, there is little doubt that given the numbers of people with a mental disability throughout the world, and the value of sport as a means of social integration , the organisation will become a major international sporting organisation. The evidence is already present with the large number of successful World Championships conducted in 1998.

The future of the range of sports for the physically disabled is assured, and the participating numbers in all three groups (ISOD, ISMWSF & CP-ISRA), together with the number of common sports, indicates that a common administration at both the international and regional level would be beneficial for the sports and the athletes. There are no sound reasons as to why ISMWSF and ISOD cannot be combined, and reasons given are mostly those of resistance to change. For CP-ISRA there are plausible reasons because of the nature of the physical condition of sufferers that CP athletes could be disadvantaged in any amalgamation of the physically disabled, and there is certainly a need to protect and to ensure that there will always be provision for the more severely disabled. It is for these reasons that amalgamation of the physically disabled should in the first instance be considered for ISMWSF and ISOD.

I have deliberately left the IPC to the last as I am confident that this organisation will meet the challenge of the transition to full time professional staff, and will continue to be very successful in the delivery of Summer and Winter Paralympic Games, and World Championships. The organisation will need strong collaboration with the IOSDs and the individual nations in developing the regions and ensuring that services are delivered to all athletes throughout the world. It is in fact an exciting time, as it marks the start of a new era in the promotion of the Paralympic Games, and the development of the regions and sports.

Conclusions

In this paper I have scratched the surface in addressing the needs for change in the organisation and structure for sport for people with a disability, and the areas which need addressing. Some of the areas are further explained in the ISMWSF Development Plan 1999-2001, and in a paper on the timing and amalgamation of ISMWSF and ISOD, which are available on request. On reflecting on the areas which could be changed to the benefit of sport for people with a disability the important and pressing areas are:

- streamlining of organisations and management

- sports management

- integration with mainstream sports

- establishing universal formal training programs to deliver courses for classifiers, coaches and technical expertise

- regional development and regional competition programs

- further development of FESPIC

- professional event management

- grass roots development

- establishing government and other support through a professional collective approach

- creating 'Centres of Excellence' in regions throughout the world.

Finally, I would hope that some of this presentation would have an impact on your deliberations over the next few days. It would indeed be a significant step if this conference can be the start of accelerating the development of this region for the benefit of all athletes.

References

ISMWSF Development Plan 1999-2001

ISMWSF Paper on amalgamation of ISMWSF & ISOD

SCRUTON, J.: Stoke Mandeville - road to Paralympics 1998

CP – ISRA. Decades of development

Margret Kellner

Kirchseelte, Germany; Secretary General, CP-ISRA

Introduction

CP-ISRA was founded in 1978 following the successful International Games for Athletes with Cerebral Palsy held in Edinburgh, Scotland. Before that, sport activities for athletes with cerebral palsy were organised by the Sport and Leisure Group of the International Cerebral Palsy Society (ICPS). This subcommittee became independent in order to give people with cerebral palsy their own sports organisation. The newly founded organisation "Cerebral Palsy - International Sports and Recreation Association" (CP-ISRA), still maintains a relationship with ICPS. Among the international organisations for sports for persons with a disability, CP-ISRA is the youngest one.

First Decade: 1978-1987

To facilitate its functionality the organisation was structured into three committees:

1. the Executive Committee which managed the affairs of the Association,

2. the Medical/ Technical Committee which was responsible for rules for competition, the classification of athletes, the format of competitive events and all other medical and technical matters,

3. the Recreation and Leisure Committee which promoted recreative and leisure activities according to the requirements of the different countries by organising workshops and seminars, publishing

journals and distributing information (set up in 1982).

The aims and objectives of CP-ISRA were:

1. development - assisting member nations in developing programmes, organising seminars, workshops, coaching sessions etc.,

2. competitive sport - providing opportunities for all functional classes to take part in all events, the very severely disabled included,

3. recreation - holding seminars and workshops to inform about recreational sport and other forms of recreation that can be enjoyed by everyone,

4. training - arranging courses for the training of leaders in all forms of sport and recreation,

5. publications and visual material - producing and publishing visual material on technical issues etc.

Between 1978 and 1982 much work and effort was involved in preparing the Classification and Sport Rules Manual. This is revised at the end of each Paralympic cycle. The 5th International Games for Athletes with Cerebral Palsy held in Greve, Denmark, in 1982, were based for the first time on the new CP-ISRA classification system.

In order to improve its operations the Executive Committee of CP-ISRA decided at its meeting held in Vienna in 1985 to replace the "Medical / Technical Committee" by the Sports Advisory Group (SAG). The reason for this decision was to move away from the purely medical diagnosis towards a stronger emphasis on sports function. Members included were sports technicians, physiotherapists and medical doctors. The main aims of the group were to advise the Executive Committee on matters relating to sport for people with cerebral palsy mainly on a competitive level and to promote sports for these people. Sports coordinators for each sport already nominated at that time worked together in close cooperation with the Sports Advisory Group, reported and held regular meetings with this committee.

The 6th International Games for Athletes with Cerebral Palsy held in Gits, Belgium in 1986, was one of the first tasks of that newly established group.

CP-ISRA is the only international sports association with the "R" for Recreation in its name. The need for involvement of CP-ISRA in recreational activities was always seen. It was also in Vienna that the organisation decided to replace the former Recreation and Leisure Committee by the Recreation Advisory Group. The aims of this group were to advise the Executive Committee on matters relating to recreation and to promote recreational activities in both segregated and integrated situations.

A first pilot workshop on recreation was held in Portugal. A second one (organised by the newly formed group) followed in 1986 in Yugoslavia, a third in Greece in 1987.

In March 1982, the four international sports organisations for the disabled, namely ISOD, IBSA, ISMGF and CP-ISRA, met. The reason for their meeting was "to establish a cooperative committee". At the following meeting in July of the same year the committee was given a name: the International Coordinating Committee (ICC). For the next eleven years, up until 1993, it was now the ICC that was responsible for the Paralympics which at this time were still called the International Games for the Disabled. In one of their meetings in 1984 it was agreed that the full title of the committee would be "International Coordinating Committee (ICC) of World Sports Organisations for the Disabled".

From the beginning, CP-ISRA has been an active member of this committee. CP-ISRA has had representatives on the Executive as well as on the Technical and Medical Committee.

Within this first decade of its existence CP-ISRA built up a strong organisation in order to give athletes with cerebral palsy and related conditions the opportunity to take part in sports events on both levels: competitive and recreational. In 1980, for the first time athletes with cerebral palsy (only the less disabled) took part in Paralympic Games. In 1984 all functional classes took part in the International Games in New York.

At the end of this decade a strong Sports Advisory Group worked in an effective way. A number of sports coordinators and classifiers helped to develop the association.

Second Decade: 1988-1997

The second decade can be called the "Decade of Development". During this period, CP-ISRA organised an enormous number of classification and coaching workshops and seminars. Workshop participants from all over the world took part and were introduced into the CP-ISRA classification system as well as in the existing functional integrated systems. At the same time workshop participants were offered sessions on coaching techniques in different sports.

The major workshops and seminars CP-ISRA organised were: 1989, 1993, 1997 at the World Championships/ Robin Hood Games in Nottingham. Two further seminars were organised in Nottingham in 1991 and 1996 at the International School of Sport, an event carried out every year at Easter time. Other major workshops were organised in 1995 in Australia, Hong Kong, Argentina, in 1996 in New Zealand, and in 1997 in the Czech Republic. Besides, CP-ISRA received workshop requests from Russia, Lithuania, Jordan and Taiwan. Furthermore, many CP-ISRA technicians took part in development workshops organised by the ICC and held in five different regions of the world.

While the number of workshops and seminars increased, new sports were developed which were introduced at these events. To be mentioned is the Petra event. Another one is polybat, a table top game.

In order to deal with all these requests and demands, CP-ISRA decided to give the Sports Advisory Group a slight change in structure. The Sports Advisory Group was divided into two sections: a Development Section and a Competition Section. Both sections appointed a coordinator. I became the coordinator of the Development Section. Both sections formed the Sports Advisory Group which has its chairperson and sports technical secretary. The responsibility of the Development Section was to look after classification, new sports, sport for women, sport for athletes with a severe disability, research etc. The responsibility of the Competition Section was to provide competition at all levels, to review rules and regulations. Over a period of 3 years CP-ISRA was fortunate to have a paid Development Officer.

As a result of the workshops and seminars being held, the number of international classifiers increased to 22 at the end of 1996.

This development was good and necessary because together with the development side of CP-ISRA the number of competitions increased as well. And to each international competition it was necessary to send a classification panel. Such a panel consists of three members: a sports technician, a therapist and a medical doctor. For special events it was agreed to send just a sports technician and a paramedical expert. The reason for this agreement was also that we still did not have enough classifiers for the steadily growing amount of sports events.

Some of the CP-ISRA sports developed in an unforeseen way. To be mentioned is mainly boccia which expanded in a way that was never anticipated. But soccer and cycling also developed very well. The number of teams and athletes were growing. Boccia has founded the

International Boccia Committee (IBC) but has stayed within CP-ISRA. At the last World Championships in 1998 held in the USA, 21 nations took part.

CP-ISRA has been involved in making improvements in the functional classification system in swimming and has supported and given all its experience to establish new functional systems. An example is table tennis. First steps to establish a system for wheelchair athletes in track and field were made as well. Our winter sports coordinator has been part of the discussions to review the present systems.

During the second decade from 1988 until 1997, CP-ISRA athletes took part in three summer Paralympics. While at the Paralympics held in Seoul CP-ISRA athletes were well represented in all functional classes - classes 1 and 2 included - the number of more severely disabled athletes decreased more and more at each following Paralympics. A similar development has occurred with women athletes. It is interesting to mention that during the same period CP-ISRA has organised three International Games for athletes with cerebral palsy, the so-called Robin Hood Games. Interesting and worth noting is that at these Games the number of CP athletes always increased. Compared with the summer Paralympics an opposite development could be observed.

Another observation we made was that athletes moved from one sport to another sport. It was quite obvious that with the official introduction of the functional classification system in swimming the more severely disabled athletes moved from swimming to boccia. This movement was reinforced by the deletion of field events from the Paralympic programme. On national level it was observed that some of the less disabled athletes moved to track and field.

Another sport which suffered during that period is slalom. After the summer Paralympics held in Seoul, ISMWSF decided to remove slalom from the Paralympic programme. The reason that I was given for this decision was that because slalom is not an Olympic discipline it also should no longer be a Paralympic discipline. Please, allow me to question this argument.

During this second decade the relationship with the other international federations intensified due to the development and establishment of the above-mentioned integrated classification systems, but also due to the formation of the IPC of which CP-ISRA was a founding member. Representatives from CP-ISRA played an active role at all levels when the IPC set up its structure and put together its aims and objectives.

In the early nineties CP-ISRA changed its logo: Instead of moving out of the world, CP-ISRA now moves into the world.

In 1983, CP-ISRA had 22 member nations. 10 years later, in 1993, we had more than 45. This year we have over 50.

Third Decade: 1998 and Onwards

At the beginning of the third decade it became obvious that CP-ISRA needed a new constitution. A draft of this new constitution was sent to our member nations early last year with the request to comment on it and to amend it where necessary. At the General Assembly held in Argentina last November the comments and amendments were discussed and, where necessary, the draft was changed with the majority of members present. The final constitution was then sent to the members. At the end of June of this year more than 60% of the national members and the individual and associate members responded positively to the request to give effect to the re-organisation of CP-ISRA. The new constitution became effective as of the 1st of July this year.

What is new or needs to be highlighted?

1. The name: Cerebral Palsy - International Sports & Recreation

Federation.

2. Purpose and scope: "The Federation is the ultimate international authority on sports matters for persons with cerebral palsy and related neurological conditions and shall not discriminate on the basis of political persuasion, religion, economics, race, sex or language. The goals and purpose of the Federation are to coordinate, promote and foster sports for persons with cerebral palsy and related neurological conditions, either directly or indirectly, through the authorities of each nation and international bodies or through any of the legally authorised channels ..." (Constitution, Article 2).

3. CP-ISRA retains the three forms of membership: national - individual – associate. As before, only the national members shall have the exclusive right to vote at the General Assembly and only the national members can appoint and elect members to the Federation.

4. The governing bodies of the Federation are: General Assembly - Executive Committee.

5. The elections and voting procedures have been changed. For example, the delegation of votes is no longer possible.

6. Major changes were made concerning the Executive Committee. Members were given specific functions. The Executive Committee consists of:

   - a President
   - a Vice-President for Regional Development and Communication
     - among countries represented by national members
   - a Vice-President for Marketing and Fund Raising
   - a Secretary General
   - a Treasurer

- a Sports Technical Officer
- an Athletes' Representative
- three members at large (Constitution, Article 10).

7. We now have an Election Committee which is nominated by the General Assembly.

8. We have dissolved the Recreation Advisory Group. Recreation became a part of the Sports Technical Committee, the former Sports Advisory Group.

According to the new constitution, the first election will take place in 2001. It will be proposed to the General Assembly held in Canada next month to have the elections in 2000. The Election Committee can be appointed during this next General Assembly. The new constitution is under Scottish law. We are in the process of formulating by-laws and will try to keep them as simple as possible. Our secretariat remains in the Netherlands. CP-ISRA will apply for charity status.

With this new constitution we are confident that we have fulfilled the demands and expectations of our members and we hope to be even more effective than we have been in the past.

In the near future CP-ISRA will focus on the following:

Firstly, we will try to encourage and help countries to build up sports programmes, and to increase the opportunity for our athletes - women and more severely disabled athletes included - to take part in events for athletes with cerebral palsy.

Secondly, we will endeavour to be pro-active in the development of integrated classification systems, for example the system for wheelchair athletes in track and field.

Thirdly, we will improve the present CP-ISRA classification system for different sports: cycling and soccer.

Fourthly, we will offer workshops and seminars in order to meet the educational demand.

Fifthly, we will endeavour to improve the relationships with the other international federations.

Sixthly, we will seek to be the right and strong advocate of the athletes we represent within the IPC.

Strategic initiatives of the IPC Sports Technical Department

Carol A. Mushett

Georgia State University, Atlanta, GA, USA

Since 1997, the IPC Sports Technical Department has been in a period of transition, challenges, and progress. Unforeseeable delays with the relocation of the Secretariat, restructuring of the Management Committee in 1997, ongoing clarification of the roles of the new officers, new professional staff, and accelerated growth of the Movement have, from time to time, caused disruption in service.

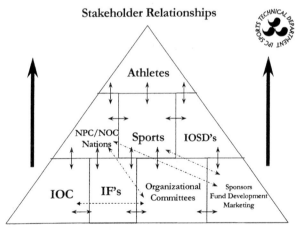

Diagram 1: Partnership and interconnectedness of the Paralympic Movement

However, these changes will provide the IPC with the organizational structure to better meet the challenges of the future. The new infrastructure will enable the IPC to provide the type and scope of services needed by member nations, athletes, IOSDs, and sports.

1998 was unprecedented in the level and diversity of sport activity. Beginning with the highly successful 1998 Nagano Winter Paralympic Games, athletes and nations were provided with more sports opportunities than ever before. By the end of the year, over 21 World Championship competitions had been held. These diverse competitions highlighted the partnership and interconnectedness of the Paralympic Movement (Diagram 1). World Championships have been organized by the IPC, the IOSD and Independent Sports.

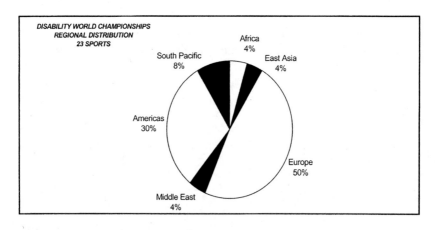

Africa	4%	1 Championship	Lawnbowls
East Asia	4%	1 Championship	Wheelchair Dance
Europe	50%	12 Championships	Archery, Athletics, Equestrian, Fencing, Goalball, Judo, Shooting, Table Tennis, Wheelchair Tennis, Volleyball, INAS Football, IBSA WC
Middle East	4%	1 Championship	Powerlifting
Americas	30%	7 Championships	Boccia, Cycling, INAS Basketball, Wheelchair Rugby, CP-ISRA Soccer, Sailing, IBSA Football
South Pacific	8%	2 Championships	Wheelchair Basketball, Swimming
	10%	TOTAL 24 Championships	

Diagram 2: Disability World Championships

The transition of leadership, and the rapid growth in sports have accentuated the need for systematic strategic planning in the Sports Technical Department. Strategic planning is an ongoing process which includes structured consultation and collaboration with all stakeholders. In order to meet the needs of the membership, present and future, sports must become more proactive and professional in providing services. Therefore, on June 5-6, 1998, the Sports Technical Department held a Strategic Planning Session of the Sports Council. This formal initiation of the process was facilitated by Dr. York Chow, IPC Vice-President for Policy, Planning and Development.

The outcomes of this meeting generated a Strategic Plan which was approved by the Sports Council in November, 1998. This plan will serve as a guide for the Sports Technical Department in this quadrennium and serve as a tool for ongoing self-evaluation. The Strategic Plan identified the following as critical factors for success:

- improvement in sport operations and development of sport infrastructures

- development of a diverse funding base to increase financial resources

- enhancement of marketing support

- recruitment of bids and organizing committees for championships

- improvement of internal and external communications

- coordination of championship program calendar between IPC Sports, IOSD and independent sports

- ensuring voting rights of the sports in the IPC General Assembly

- systematic evaluation of new sport/discipline applications for

Paralympic status within Paralympic Organizers' limitations on number of athletes and sports.

The Sports Council also identified a need for a concise mission statement to assist in prioritization of Sports Technical services. The mission statement is as follows:

> „ The IPC Sport Technical Department will promote elite competition and coordinate Paralympic Sport through an athlete centered, sport specific model which recognizes the diverse delivery systems serving athletes with disabilities and member nations. The focus of the Sport Technical Department includes:
>
> 1. fostering the growth of Paralympic Sport by increasing the number of athletes and nations while improving the caliber of athletic performance
>
> 2. enhancing the quality of Sport Technical operations and administration; and
>
> 3. ensuring diversity in Paralympic Sport. "

The process also required objective self-evaluation as to the strengths and weaknesses of the department which included the following:

Strenghts

- leadership - capable human resources
- sport technical knowledge
- commitment of sport leadership
- democratic process of decision making
- quality competitions
- diversity of sports
- athlete centered approach

- diversity in ideology.

Weaknesses

- limited depth of human resources and expertise
- limited economic/financial resources
- confusion in roles and responsibilities
- timeliness/inconsistency of responses in internal and external communications
- limited political influence (perceived)
- diversity in ideology - lack of consensus building
- lack of "cross-training" (knowledge of other Paralympic sports)
- deficiency in business management philosophy and strategies among the sport technical leadership.

The Sports Council expressed concern over the potential fractionalization of the Paralympic Movement, program stagnation, and the realization that accelerated growth has exceeded current resources.

Strategic goals were proposed in the following areas:

Human resources: to improve the quality and efficiency of our sport technical service to athletes, nations and games organizers by enhancing our human resource base

Financial resources: to increase financial resources for Paralympic sports and improve fiscal responsibility

Administration: to provide high quality, professional sport management and functional administrative support mechanisms in all sections of the IPC Sports Technical Department

Political area: to improve the level of influence of the sports within IPC through advocacy, education, and voting rights.

Short, medium and long-term strategic initiatives were developed to assist the Sports Department in achieving goals and realizing its mission. The Sports Council further emphasized its ongoing commitment to improved relationships and cooperation between the sports, IOSD's and regions. A copy of the Strategic Plan for the Sports Technical Department is available upon request from the IPC Headquarters.

Development and growth of Paralympic equestrian sport 1995 to 1999

Jonquil Solt

Loomington Spa, Warwickshire, United Kingdom; Chairperson,
IPC Equestrian Committee

Setting the Scene

How it started

Equestrian sport is fun. More and more people are realising this, and more and more National Paralympic Committees are linking in to the Equestrian Paralympic family.

IPC, the International Paralympic Committee, was formed in 1989. Two years later, in 1991, it set up the IPEC – the International Paralympic Equestrian Committee, among its first Sports Assembly Executive Committees. I joined the IPEC as its founder Vice Chairperson, and took over the chairmanship in 1995.

At that time there were sixteen nations widely practising the sport. Growth was slow and uncertain. Equestrian sport had the status of a Paralympic sport, but it was in danger of losing that status if it did not grow very quickly. We accepted the challenge this set us. Never in my wildest dreams did I think that by 1999 I would be in communication with over 40 nations. This rapid growth of interest did not happen of its own accord. My talk is about what we did, and what effect it has had.

About equestrian sport.

Let me start by saying that the growth could not have been achieved without the attractions that the sport offers:

- It is the only Paralympic Sport that involves two living beings, the rider and the horse.

- People can take part almost irrespective of their disability (at the last World Championships, 50% of the contestants were in the severely disabled category).

- Both men and women can take part on equal terms (70% of the contestants were women, 30% men).

- Athletes of all ages over 16 can compete (the youngest competitor at these Championships was 16, the oldest was 72).

- Working with a horse presents a mental as well as a physical challenge.

Striving towards the Paralympics offers a vision of what is possible and pride in the sport. Only dressage is so far recognised as a Paralympic sport. Other sports are also practised, particularly carriage driving. The first World Championship for drivers with disabilities was held at Wolfsburg in July 1998 jointly with the German National Four-in-Hand Championships. Gerhard Schröder wrote in the catalogue of the event that he welcomed it as making "an important contribution to the integration of disabled people". Over 5000 spectators came to see it.

Other equestrian disability sports include vaulting, endurance riding, and show jumping. The rest of my talk is however concerned with dressage.

About Dressage

There is a popular misconception that one rides a horse like a motorbike: You steer it by pulling on the reins, left or right; you kick the horse to step on the accelerator; and you pull back on the reins to put on the brakes. Nothing is further from the truth. In dressage, you use every part of your body to tell your horse what you want it to do: your legs, the position of your body, the movement of your seat, the position of your head and your hands, even what you think has an effect. The horse must respond instantly to what is asked of it, and the balance of the rider is crucial.

Many of you will be familiar with the Spanish Riding School in Vienna. It is the foremost exponent of dressage in the world. Few people reach that standard. At any level, however, horse and rider should achieve perfect understanding until the horse gives the impression that he does of his own accord what the rider requires of him. So this is the sport that we wanted to spread more widely.

What We Did

Our basic tools

To bring people into the Paralympic frame we needed a set of manuals as our basic tools. We already had a **Rule Book** that sets out what must be done, and how it should be done. We also produced a **Classification Manual**, and a range of **Dressage Tests**; more about both these later.

We then started a **publicity drive** for which we produced a brochure to tell interested people how the IPEC can help. We produced videos, circulated an IPEC newsletter, and set up a page on the internet. With the necessary material in place, we began to go out into the world, seeking out where dressage for people with disabilities was already being practised. We were sure that small groups or individuals were already riding dressage in many places all over the world, but our first challenge was to find them.

To establish contact we got in touch with a whole host of people and organisations: Equestrian Able Bodied Federations and Equestrian

Therapeutic Organisations; the National Disabled Associations, National Riding and Driving Organisations, and of course the National Paralympic Committees. We established links with individual riders and volunteers. Most of all, however, it was a matter of personal contacts through friends, new friends, and more friends!

Seminars and courses

As a result, we started to get invitations from all over the world to go and hold courses and seminars. My team and I offer our time and expertise for free but we ask that our fares and expenses are paid.

In response to these invitations, my colleagues and I have been to 25 countries 'spreading the gospel'. In and around Europe we have visited 17 countries, from Finland in the North to Israel in the South; and from Portugal in the West to Russia in the East. Further afield we made several visits each to Canada, to the USA, and to Australia. In the Far East we visited Hong Kong, Japan, Singapore, and Taiwan. In these visits we cover a wide field, but they include instruction for the specialists who are needed for the sport and whom we hope to accredit on behalf of the IPEC. To explain I must take you back and talk a little more about dressage.

Dressage: Classification, judging, and officials

Dressage tests are performed in an arena 20m x 40m. Dressage tests consist of a sequence of prescribed movements which the athlete must ask the horse to perform. Each test prescribes exactly where the horse has to go, and at what pace. You may ask it to go forward, sideways, back, or to halt; you may ask it to walk, trot, or to canter, and there are at least three different forms of each. The IPEC has written a wide range of dressage tests of varying difficulty. The most difficult have up to 26 prescribed movements.

Any impairment in the rider limits how he or she can control a horse.

So that athletes over a full spectrum of disablement can compete fairly, they are classified into four grades according to impairment. Riders compete only within the same grade. A set of graduated dressage tests has been written for each grade - the most demanding tests for the least disabled. It is important that the grading system is fair, so that widely differing disabilities are fairly matched and riders feel that they are competing on a level playing field. Where riders compete internationally, it is important that the grading system is competently and consistently applied across the world. We have adopted the **Functional Profile System for Grading** developed by top physiotherapist Dr. Christine Meaden. Accreditation as an IPEC classifier is open to medical doctors and to qualified physiotherapists.

Riders are classified into grades according to disability, but they are judged according to ability. One or more qualified judges mark each movement and the overall aspects of the test. Each judge has a sheet (a **Test Sheet**) which defines each movement of the test, and there is space to enter a mark for each. Judging dressage needs much practice and experience. Judging riders with disabilities is a little different from judging able-bodied riders. Inger Bryant and I lead conversion courses for officially listed national dressage judges of able-bodied riders. We will only accredit judges who demonstrate their competence to judge disabled equestrian athletes. As with classification, it is important that judging is fair, and consistent across the world.

Finally in our courses we provide advice to event organisers, to athletes' coaches, and to helpers in general. If the IPEC approves an event, a Technical Delegate is assigned to oversee it. We accredit people who can demonstrate the ability and the experience to do this.

What has been achieved?

I am now coming to the last part of my talk, where I shall list the main things that have come out of the work we have done over the last four years.

1. We have been successful in our drive to generate more international competitions. In the three years to 1996, there were altogether four such competitions world wide. In the three years 1997 to 99, there will have been twenty-six.

2. There are not only more competitions, but many more nations are taking part. At the 1994 World Championships, sixteen nations were represented. The same number appeared at the Atlanta Paralympic Games in 1996. At the next World Championship which has just been held in Denmark, twenty-eight nations have been represented.

3. I mentioned at the beginning that one very important effect of this growth concerns the status of equestrian sport as a Paralympic sport. In order to qualify, the International Paralympic Committee (that is our parent organisation) want to see a certain number of nations 'widely practising the sport'. Shortly after I took on the Chairmanship of the IPEC, the number required was raised from 16 to 18, and then to 24.

   To hold on to our Paralympic status we needed to have 24 nations 'widely practising the sport' by the year 2001. I did not really believe we had much chance to get there in the time, and I don't think anybody else believed it either. But one thing was certain: We would lose our Paralympic status if we didn't try. So there was no option but to go for growth, and so we just got on with it.

   We found large numbers of people all over the world who wanted to support us. We gave them all the support we could. And beyond all expectations we reached the magic number of twenty-four earlier this year, and have already exceeded it. We now have 27 nations 'widely practising the sport'. Altogether we are in contact with 41 nations in various stages of development.

4. The courses that we have run have enabled us to accredit classifiers,

judges, and technical delegates. As a result we now have an established network of over 120 such accredited people all over the world. It gives our sport a solid infrastructure, and competitors across the world can expect to be classified and judged to a common standard.

5. Now there are some benefits to which one can not put figures. As the number of international competitions has gone up over the last three years, the standard of competition from the established countries has gone up quite noticeably. In addition, the many countries taking part for the first time see what can be achieved and it raises their sights also. Some of the new countries are still at a very early stage of developing the sport and we all have to start somewhere - but standards are going up noticeably across the board.

It goes hand in hand with increased recognition and status. The recent World Championships were under the patronage of H.R.H. Princess Benedikte of Denmark. Different events elsewhere have been supported by other members of royalty, by Government Ministers, and by the wife of a President.

6. There is a huge range of equestrian organisations that are relevant to what we do in equestrian sport for the disabled. In Spain for example there are several local establishments helping riders with disabilities. Two Spanish riders competed at the last World Championship. As an example of a national organisation, the British Riding for the Disabled Association last year had 639 riders with disabilities competing to appear at their National Championships.

Along quite a different line, many of our riders have been through the therapeutic process and now want to compete. I am delighted that the DKThR – the German Therapeutic Riding Organisation – has offered to organise the World Championship for Disabled Riders with disabilities in 2006. At the other end of the spectrum, we are in positive talks with the International Equestrian Federation about some of their rules that are difficult to observe by riders with disabilities who want to compete with the able-bodied at near to Olympic level.

We have gone out of our way to establish links right across the board, and in some cases we have even been able to get local organisations to talk to each other! It has not always been easy, even within our own Paralympic organisation. We derive added support and strength from this network with organisations world-wide.

7. At the same time we don't lose sight of the real purpose of it all, the individual riders with disabilities wishing to compete and to realise their potential. The strengthened organisation, with the network that we have built up, has been able to open more and more doors, to more and more riders with disabilities, in more and more countries.

Conclusion

At the end of the day, that is what it is all about: To create opportunities for riders with disabilities to compete, and to compete better. I am going to let the riders themselves have the last word. We asked them for comments, and here is what they say:

> *"I have found myself and rebuilt my confidence."*

> *"Without equestrian sport I would have been in a wheelchair much earlier – it gives me a reason to live."*

> *"My horse and I are the only ones in the dressage arena – that's independence."*

> *"It is not until we dismount that people know we are disabled – that's very satisfying."*

"When I ride I am in charge of something, instead of someone being in charge of me."

"I can't do ballet on my feet, but I can do ballet with my horse."

"I can be an athlete on my horse."

One of them said simply:

"Joy!"

Finally, one of the letters I get from time to time said:

"Thank you for giving me the opportunity of a lifetime to represent my country."

It is not only the riders taking part in the sport, who are doing what they want to do. Everything I have described to you has been done as the result of voluntary effort. If it were not for the positive interest and the willing help of I don't know how many people around the world, it would not have happened. So I will confidently finish by repeating what I said at the start: **Equestrian sport is fun!**

FIG development strategy for Paralympic status for gymnastics

Marie Fisher

British Gymnastics, Newport, Shropshire, United Kingdom

British Gymnastics began its development initiative for gymnastics for people with a disability in 1984 with a change in its operating policy to a philosophy of providing integrated and inclusive activities for all at all levels. In the last fifteen years this aspect of the sport has come a long way. Today's gymnasts with disabilities have the opportunity to compete to a high standard in national competition and to trial for national squads in the disciplines of men's and women's artistic. Once in these squads the members train alongside their mainstream peers at the national training centre on several occasions throughout the year. This enables the squad to access the expertise and knowledge of the national coaching team and drive the quality of performance even higher.

The Organisational Structure of Gymnastics for Disabled People in the UK

In the UK there are two bodies which organise gymnastics for people with a disability, British Gymnastics and Special Olympics (Fig. 1). British Gymnastics is responsible for the regulation of gymnastics in the UK and is recognised by the international body for gymnastics, the Fédération Internationale de Gymnastique (FIG).

As the national governing body, British Gymnastics is a members organisation made up of approximately 900 clubs. Of these clubs 70 register as having disability sections or as clubs specifically catering for disabled performers. From these clubs we have identified around 1000 people with disabilities participating in gymnastics.

Gymnastics currently has six disciplines within it – men's artistic, women's artistic, sports acrobatics, rhythmic gymnastics, general gymnastics and sports aerobics. Gymnastics for people with a disability forms an integral part of all of these disciplines in British Gymnastics.

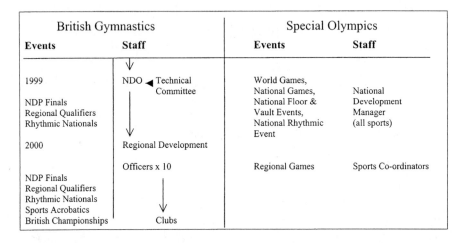

British Gymnastics		Special Olympics	
Events	**Staff**	**Events**	**Staff**
	↓		
1999	NDO ◄ Technical	World Games,	
	Committee	National Games,	National
NDP Finals		National Floor &	Development
Regional Qualifiers		Vault Events,	Manager
Rhythmic Nationals	↓	National Rhythmic	(all sports)
		Event	
2000	Regional Development		
	Officers x 10	Regional Games	Sports Co-ordinators
NDP Finals			
Regional Qualifiers			
Rhythmic Nationals	↓		
Sports Acrobatics			
British Championships	Clubs		

Key:

NDO - National Development Officer
NDP - National Development Plan

Fig 1: Organisation of gymnastics for people with a disability in the UK

The National Development Strategy

British Gymnastics is committed to providing quality gymnastic activity from foundation through to excellence for all its members. Since the appointment of the General Gymnastics National Coach in 1985 people with a disability have been a major target group for development. In 1998 this commitment was reconfirmed with the appointment of a National Development Officer responsible just for the development of gymnastics for people with a disability.

Competitions

The sport has progressed dramatically since 1985 with the development of a National Championship event in 1990 which has continued to grow in numbers and in standards of skills performed. In the beginning the majority of competitors in the event had an intellectual disability, they already had competed in the Special Olympics events and saw British Gymnastics events as another opportunity for competition. Nine years later and we are seeing a wider variety of disabilities entering the event, which means that from next year the gymnasts will be classified under International Disability Sports Organisations guidelines in order to maintain fair competition. As the interest for this event has grown (last year it had over 250 competitors), the need to develop the competition framework has become more apparent. To this end 1999 sees the first changes taking place.

New competition structure

National Development Plan Events take the form of regional qualification events for individuals, the winners will then form a regional team who will compete in the National Finals. The teams will be composed of a maximum of five people – the top three all around plus two specialists who compete on one piece of apparatus only (the specialists must be taken from gymnasts who are not able through their disability to compete on all apparatus). There will be three levels of competition across four age groups. The philosophy behind this is to provide a team in which all disability groups are represented.

These events will comprise set exercises on all apparatus plus a conditioning set. The set routines will be made up of skills that are essential to the development of gymnastics and will be graded.

The British Championships take on a new format mirroring the competition structure of mainstream gymnastics in the UK. The event is open entry with voluntary routines on all apparatus for men and women. This event will be introduced into the programme in 2000. This event will be the first event using the full new adapted code of points. This is a significant development in disability gymnastics in the UK.

Judging of routines in all events follows the adapted code based around the FIG code of points for each discipline. British Gymnastics hopes these will be adopted internationally as development of international competition becomes standardised. The voluntary codes have been adapted by a panel of people who specialise in judging men's, women's and rhythmic competition. The skills are graded from A to D (A = easiest, D = hardest); there is also a system for awarding bonus for combination of skills. This code follows the same format as the FIG code but the degree of difficulty of skills has been scaled down, for example a B in the FIG code becomes a C in the adapted code. At this stage the adaptations account mainly for gymnasts with learning disability, as they are Britain's main group of competitors, however, for other disability groups adaptations may only need to be slight, or the full FIG code may be used.

Rhythmic Gymnastics was launched competitively in 1998 where it attracted 35 people with varying degrees of disability. Currently the competition follows set routines, with the Special Olympic routines being used. These will be changing in 2000 as with Special Olympics.

In July this year British Gymnastics will launch a new programme for Sports Acrobatics. This is an adaptation of the mainstream scheme, which allows integration into mainstream events at all levels. Alongside this we have developed an entirely new programme which can also be integrated for wheelchair users. The scheme was well received at a preview event (a mainstream Sports Acrobatics Championships) and competition organisers are keen to integrate events from the start with competition beginning in 2000.

This programme has the potential to work to international competition in a very short time period and British Gymnastics feel that the scheme could be launched on a world level if FIG approval is gained and resources are available.

Technical Aspects of the Programme

1998 saw the selections for the first disability National Squad take place for women's and men's artistic gymnasts. In the 2nd year of operation the squad is made up of 7 senior and 7 junior men and 10 senior and 10 junior women. The squad members have a variety of disabilities. The men's and women's squads will come together 3 times each year to train at Lilleshall National Sports Centre. They will share the training venue with the mainstream National Squads, and have access to the support services in place for these squads. In addition to this the performance directors for the mainstream squads will run coach training sessions with the disability squad coaches thus improving the standard of coaching of the squads.

To date no international events have taken place, but British Gymnastics are looking for other teams to compete in invitational events in the next twelve months. The first planned event is scheduled for April/May 2000 with the Czech Republic.

Paralympic Development

In November 1998 John Atkinson, Executive Director of British Gymnastics, presented the case for development of gymnastics towards Paralympic status to the Executive Committee of the FIG. The FIG acknowledged gymnastics for people with a disability as a part of the gymnastics family, and appointed Great Britain through British Gymnastics as the lead nation for development to Paralympics. This acknowledgement was the first rung on the ladder towards the final goal of Paralympic status, and we feel that it is a significant step as unlike many sports already established within the Paralympic framework, gymnastics has the full support of its international governing body from the very start.

Since November 1998 British Gymnastics has begun the development by establishing a working party made up of key individuals from UK sport some of whom hold international posts and are IPC representatives. The working party's role is to identify the route and requirements for international development. They will act as advisors on key issues both nationally and internationally and identify forums through which to promote gymnastics as a future Paralympic sport. The working party has identified the need to consult internationally and identify interested nations who already have competitive programmes in order to adapt the FIG rules and regulations and agree formats for International competition.

In order to identify suitable members for this group the FIG working group and British Gymnastics are currently conducting an audit of gymnastics activity for people with a disability world-wide. The first route for this audit was through the INAS–FID General Assembly where an FIG representative spoke with 33 of the member nations to identify the levels of activity for people with intellectual disability. 23 of these nations had programmes in either artistic or rhythmic gymnastics taking place.

People with intellectual disability were identified as the first target group, as in the UK they form the largest participation group. In addition, there is also a strong Special Olympics gymnastics programme in the UK. Special Olympics also provides the only route at present for international participation. Within the Special Olympics programme in the UK there are regional and national games held each year. The programme alternates between artistic and rhythmic disciplines.

Every four years there are National Games for all sports and gymnastics has a large programme at this event. The event is at three levels for all apparatus and two lower levels for a floor and vault event for those who are not capable of working all apparatus. The rules for these games follow the Special Olympics International Rule Book.

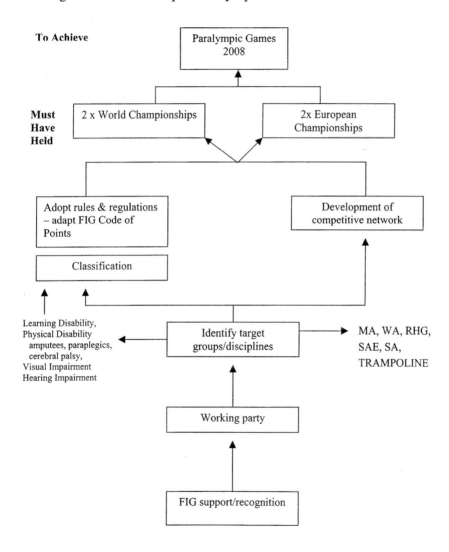

Fig. 2: Schematic of direction for development

The next part of the audit will take place at the Special Olympics World Games where the British Gymnastics/FIG representative will assess the level of activity and establish a world listing. A questionnaire will also be sent to other disability federations world-wide.

Conclusions

The schematic shows that the working party's main tasks will be to identify target disability groups and disciplines with which to take forward in the first phase of Paralympic development. It should be noted that the long term intention is to include all disciplines and all disability groups into the programme, but that initially the most widely practised discipline and the largest disability group should be targeted first. The progression of the other groups will be determined by their levels of development internationally. By following this pattern it should be possible to introduce one discipline at a time.

Once the working party has identified its lead group and discipline it will identify key people to adapt the FIG code of points to suit that group and to then adopt the FIG rules and regulations. The group will also have to adopt and develop, where necessary, the appropriate classification procedures for international competition. British Gymnastics are already establishing an adapted code as detailed earlier and this will probably provide a start point for establishing a code recognised by FIG.

As British Gymnastics have already established that other nations have competitors with a disability in gymnastics, the potential for the introduction of an international events programme within the next year is very real. By doing this it will allow the adopted rules and regulations to be tested. Throughout the development of the international framework British Gymnastics and the working party will be responsible for advising and reporting back to FIG via John Atkinson.

In order for European and World Championships to be included on the FIG calendar these events need to be identified at least four years in advance. British Gymnastics have outlined a projected time frame for inclusion within the Paralympic framework. In order to meet the criteria the working party need to have identified dates for the above events in the near future.

As displayed in British Gymnastics' national programme, the initial stages of the required changes to rules and regulations and codes of points are already being undertaken. The adaptation of the British Championships in the national event calendar mirrors the mainstream programmes. The voluntary competition is also the format used by FIG in international events. British Gymnastics hopes that in leading the way many of the changes made for national competition can be adopted internationally. This would save a great deal of time in the development process.

As new nations become involved and look to formalise their development structure for gymnastics for people with a disability British Gymnastics will look to use their development plan as a model for other countries. British Gymnastics have had several requests for this already.

The coordination of elite sport for athletes with disabilities in Australia

Jenni Banks

Australian Institute of Sport, Canberra, Australia

Background

The Atlanta Paralympic Games were a watershed for Australia. After finishing seventh on the medal tally in Barcelona and medalling in three of twelve sports competed, Australia finished second on the medal tally in Atlanta and medalled in ten of the thirteen sports competed. How was this possible? The structure of the Australian sports system and, in particular, its increasing provision for elite athletes with disabilities has been a major contributor for this elevation in the Australian Paralympic Team's performance.

The purpose of this presentation is to consider the structure of the Australian sports system with regard to elite athletes with disabilities. In particular, the paper will focus on the Australian Paralympic Committee's (APC's) Paralympic Preparation Program (PPP).

The Australian Sports System

The four major sources of support for elite Australian athletes with disabilities in the Australian sports system are: the Australian Paralympic Committee and the Paralympic Preparation Program; the Australian and State Institutes and Academies of Sport; the National Sporting Organisations; and the National Sporting Organisations for the Disabled. [1]

---

[1] In addition to athletes' personal support networks including family, partners, personal coaches, and individual sponsors.

Australian Paralympic Committee / Paralympic Preparation Program

The Australian Paralympic Committee is responsible for the selection, preparation, and assembly of Australian teams for Paralympic Games, IPC World Championships and other international multi-disability events. The Paralympic Preparation Program (PPP) was developed and implemented by the APC to provide athletes with the support and guidance required to perform at an optimal level. In addition to its own service provision, the PPP also has links with the institutes and academies of sport, national sporting organisations, and national sporting organisations for the disabled. As mentioned previously, the focus of this presentation will be on the development and features of the PPP.

Australian and State Institutes and Academies of Sport

In addition to the support provided by the PPP, the Australian and State Institutes and Academies of Sport provide scholarships for athletes with disabilities – including financial assistance (living, training and competition costs), sports science and medicine support, vocational guidance, and in some cases coaching support. The level of assistance tends to vary depending on performance level of athlete and also the institute or academy. Some institutes have separate "Athletes with Disabilities Programs" and provide support and services on this basis while others integrate athletes with disabilities into the appropriate able-bodied program (i.e. the program for their sport). There are advantages and disadvantages for each system. These will be discussed.

National Sporting Organisations (NSO)

Different NSO also provide varying levels of support/service for elite athletes with disabilities. This includes the organisation of national and Australian-based international competitions, the integration of athletes with disabilities in able-bodied events (camps, clinics, competitions), involvement in the APC Sport Advisory Committees, and exposure through NSO publications and posters. To date, Athletics Australia, Australian Swimming, Basketball Australia, and Tennis Australia have been the major contributors in this regard. More recently other NSO including Archery Australia, Cycling Australia, Soccer Australia, Table Tennis Australia have become more involved with athletes with disabilities. The Australian Yachting Federation has recently become the first NSO to incorporate a Paralympic Preparation Program within their organisation.

National Sporting Organisations for the Disabled (NSOD)

Seven NSOD - representing amputee and les autres, blind and visually impaired, cerebral palsy, intellectually disabled, and wheelchair athletes, and equestrian and winter sport - are currently full members of the Australian Paralympic Committee. The seven NSOD provide varying levels of support for elite athletes with disabilities.

The Paralympic Preparation Program (PPP)

The beginning

The September 1993 announcement of Sydney as the host city for the 2000 Olympic and Paralympic Games resulted in unprecedented financial support for Australian Paralympic sport. Keen to ensure successful Australian team performances in the 2000 Games, the Australian Government, via the Australian Sports Commission, poured an extra $135 million per year into sport. Paralympic sport received a small slice of this - $1.14 million for the period October 1994 to August 1996 (the 1996 Atlanta Paralympic Games). Whilst a small proportion of the overall allocation for elite sport, this represented a significant increase on funds previously received and allowed the Australian Paralympic Federation (as the APC was then named) to establish the Paralympic Preparation Program and employ a full-time staff member to develop and implement the Program.

PPP structure - pre-Atlanta

In the initial two years of the PPP's existence funding focussed on three major areas: coaching, training camps, and competition (domestic and international). In January 1995, National (Head) Coaches for each sport were appointed for fifteen sports, with assistant coaches and sport-specific support staff appointed at later dates, as necessary. Simultaneously, two PPP Squads - an Atlanta Squad and a Development Squad - were selected across fifteen sports and appropriate PPP for each sport were developed by the coaching staff, with assistance from the APF Director of Sport as required. Monitoring programs were implemented in each sport to chart athlete progress and the PPP Squads were reviewed quarterly leading up to the final team selection in April 1996. Advisory Committees for each sport were also developed to provide guidance in the development of the sport and on sport-specific and disability-specific issues. In January 1996, National Coaches and PPP Squads for the two demonstration sports of rugby and yachting were added to the PPP with a nominal amount of funding allocated to each due to their demonstration status.

Atlanta

As a result of the PPP and the contributions of the sports institutes, NSO, and NSOD, the the Australian team's preparation for the 1996 Atlanta Paralympic Games was without question the best ever of any Australian Paralympic team. Not surprisingly, the Australian Paralympic team achieved its best ever results at the 1996 Atlanta Paralympic Games. The 1996 Australian Paralympic team

- passed Australia's total medal tally from Barcelona on day five of the ten day Atlanta Games program,

- won the highest number of medals ever won by an Australian Paralympic Team - 106 medals (42 gold, 37 silver, and 27 bronze),

- won medals in ten of the thirteen sports competed (after medalling in only three of the twelve sports competed in Barcelona),

- led the medal tally until the second last day of the competition when we were overtaken by the host nation, the USA (a team almost twice Australia's size); and, significantly,

- a staggering 107 of 162 (66%) Australian team members medalled and/or performed personal bests in the Paralympic competition. This percentage was even higher in the sports of athletics (83% - 35 of 42 athletes), cycling (86% - 12 of the 14 riders), and swimming (100% - 30 of the 30 swimmers).

Important features of the PPP

The factors contributing to the success of the 1996 Australian Paralympic team included the development and implementation of the PPP - including the early appointment of National Coaches and the implementation of the PPP for each sport; the sport-specific nature of the team preparation and selection; the strict selection process; and the talents and commitment of the coaches, support staff and athletes selected. An increasing number of athletes understood the commitment required to be successful at international level and were prepared to make that commitment and adopt a professional approach to their training and competition.

The adoption of a sport-specific rather than disability-specific approach meant that the sport-specific needs of athletes were more closely met, while still taking into consideration any disability-specific requirements. The previous focus on disability-specific requirements often failed to meet the sport-specific needs of the athletes, particularly in the case of smaller sports, and limited their development. The focus of the PPP on sport and not disability resulted in a higher level of preparation and professionalism.

The support and cooperation of the APF member organisations, national sporting organisations, and the Australian Institute of Sport and state institutes and academies of sport was also critical, as was the dedication and commitment of the APF President and Board and the APF Office staff.

Post Atlanta review and re-structure

Following the Games a comprehensive review of the PPP was undertaken – with a survey of all stakeholders – and a number of areas for further consideration and refinement were identified. These included changes to APC staffing and management and to the sport PPP.

In terms of APC staffing there was a clear need to increase the number of professional staff responsible for the coordination, delivery, and review of the PPP, to establish a formal APC Sports Commission, and to review all APC sport advisory committees, coaching and support staff.

In terms of the sport PPP, it was clear that improvements could be made in all sports, with some requiring greater assistance than others due to their earlier stage of development. Areas identified for further consideration/refinement across the sports included:

- increasing our talent pool through **talent identification** (if we were to increase our talent pool, however, it was important to ensure that relevant support structures were in place to cope with increased athlete numbers),

- **more individualised preparation programs,**

- **increased domestic and international competition**, including a strengthening of Australasian ties, where appropriate,

- a greater emphasis on **coach development and coach support** with exposure to top international coaches and programs where required, and greater financial support for successful programs in Australia,

- ensure that all squad members have access to **top quality personal coaches**,

- **increased athlete support** - as the level of professionalism in disabled sport increases across the sports more and more athletes will have to train full-time in order to be successful at Paralympic level. Adequate mechanisms of support must be in place to allow this (Paralympic Employment Program - PEP),

- **increased liaison and co-operative working relationships with the institutes and academies of sport** regarding the provision of vocational, sports science and medicine support, and the identification and conduct of appropriate applied research projects and dissemination of findings

- **increased guidance to and monitoring of the less developed and newer sports**, including the sports in which we did not compete in Atlanta,

- **more flexible funds focus** – coaching, training camps, competition and other (e.g. equipment; individual needs).

Revised PPP structure and staffing

As a result of the review a number of changes were made to the PPP. In addition to the refinements mentioned above, the structure of the PPP – including the allocation of funds and selection of squad members – was revised so that PPP sport squads were selected and funded on a performance basis. Further details are available in the APC's "Paralympic Preparation Program 1997 – 2000. Background and Principles" document.

How's it going?

Results in 1998 and 1999 IPC World Championships suggest that, in general, refinements made to the PPP since Atlanta have been successful in enhancing performance in most, but not all, sports. Throughout 1998 and 1999, following each sport's World Championships / Paralympic Games, all sports are again being reviewed in preparation for the final lead-in to the Sydney 2000 Paralympic Games (summer sports) and the 2000 World Disabled Alpine Skiing Championships (winter sport).

Summary

In recent years, Paralympic sport performance has risen to a new level in Australia. The reason for this elevation has been the structure of the Australian sports system and, in particular, its increasing provision for elite athletes with disabilities. The four major sources of support for elite Australian athletes with disabilities are: the Australian Paralympic Committee and the Paralympic Preparation Program; the Australian and State Institutes and Academies of Sport; the National Sporting Organisations; and the National Sporting Organisations for the Disabled.

Importantly, whilst the level of performance of Australian athletes with disabilities has increased significantly in recent years as a result of the support provided through the Australian sports system, the support structure for athletes with disabilities can still be improved considerably and performances improved further as a result.

Creative movement patterns of persons with a disability in freeball

Birol Cotuk, Yasar Tatar, Bilsen Sirmen, Selda Uzun

School of Physical Education and Sport, Marmara University, Istanbul, Turkey

Introduction

Sport is accepted as a genuine part of the rehabilitation and recreation programs for persons with a disability. In most cases the affected persons share this insight, but nevertheless integration into a sports activity may not be achieved. One major reason for this discrepancy is the difficulty and complexity of movement tasks in sports. Therefore adequate sensomotor learning needs much time and effort. This is especially true for the handicapped novice, who is hindered both by his disability and his unfamiliarity with sports. To overcome these obstacles, movement patterns which motivate disabled persons and which they enjoy, are of particular interest (STROHKENDL 1989).

In this context ball games are of great importance. The ball has always been an object of fun in all cultures of the world. There is no historical epoch or place that has not created its own ball game (MENDNER 1956). This status of the ball is also reflected in the great efforts to adapt ball games for persons with a disability. These efforts resulted in adaptations of established ball games (basketball, volleyball etc.) for athletes with a disability or in designing novel ball games for special disability groups, e.g. goal ball for the blind. To our opinion this development has two shortcomings:

1. Segregation of athletes with different disabilities and exclusion of the family and friends from common sports activities (TATAR 1998). This point is of particular significance for children with a

disability (COTUK 1999).

2. Adaptation to regular techniques and movement patterns of established ball games present fixed models of movement patterns and thereby pose restrictions to body use. This is both true for able-bodied and disabled athletes. But for persons with a disability the engagement in sports is crucially depending on the preserved potential of creative body use, concisely called 'creative compensation' by Innenmoser (1999).

We followed this line of thought and propose that 'disability-independent' and 'creative' ball games be developed. So we adapted Freeball, a novel ball game, for persons with a disability.

Methods

Freeball is not only a new ball game, but also a fundamental concept in its own right and a challenge to all other ball games. Freeball was developed at the University of Marmara by Cotuk (1997). Freeball employs the "archaic" notion of using the whole body in a ball game without any restrictions. This is in striking contrast to historical and modern ball games. All these ball games tend to restrict body use, either by rules or norms of techniques and tactics. A high degree of specialized body movement is selected. Volleyball is a good example, allowing for only four basic techniques: spike, under-hand, over-arm passing, and block. The same is true for historical ball games as illustrated by the famous "hip ball" game of the Maya. If the ball game possesses ritual character, not only body restriction but also the right technique is highly formalized. The Japanese priests did not only kick the ball up only by foot, but did this also in a "kind manner". Remarkably, there has been no ball game played in the history of man without body restriction (COTUK 1998).

Freeball

- The aim of the player is to have a ball cross over a net.

- ***Every body part can be used for a shot.***
- Only catching and carrying of the ball is not allowed.
- One ground contact of the ball is allowed but not obligatory (except at service).
- Freeball is played either as single or double competition.
- In the single competition the player has to return the ball with a single shot.
- As for singles in the double competition only one player of the team is allowed to return the ball.
- Field measures are 24 m – 8,5 m for single competition and 24 m – 9 m for double competition.
- The height of the net is 119 cm, ball circumference is 63 – 64 cm and ball weight is 300 - 320 gr.
- The service must be carried out with the ball below shoulder level.
- At service the ball must touch the opponents service zone.
- Width of the service zone (SZ) is 6,5 m (Figure 1).

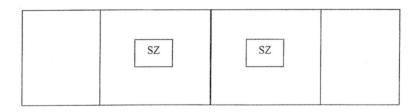

Fig. 1: Playing field for Freeball

- Each player uses 5 services in succession; the differences of scores are counted as points. At the score 4-1 the player may use an additional service if he/she wishes to do so. Possible scores and points are:

5-0 = 5 points   4-1 = 3 points   3-2 = 1 point
4-2 = 2 points   5-1 = 4 points.

Each set is completed at 11 points.

This way of scoring ensures variability of set length; a weak opponent is defeated in a very short time but not an opponent of equal ability.

The liberation of body use is unique to Freeball. This inevitably leads to an unlimited variety of shot techniques (!?) and forms of body movement. In this context 'technique' implies not a formalized scheme, but rather an individual movement pattern at the shot. The list of different movement and shot patterns has reached the impressive number of up to 50 (!) (KARAGÖZOGLU 1998). Almost every player creates his own 'technique(s)' and 'style' (the whole of his repertoire) in Freeball, but - and this is the crucial point - only to the extent he can liberate himself from acquired movement restrictions. Illustrative examples are the two players, who created C-shot and Z-spike.

The C-shot (Figure 2) is a fundamentally new movement form not found in other ball games. In agreement with this, a player who is not familiar with other ball games has created it. The C-shot is used primarily for aggressive attacking, but also variations of C-shot as spin and loop are used in the defense and for tactical reasons. The C-shot is an excellent example for the fact that new, creative and also highly adaptive movement patterns can emerge when prior learning does not restrict the body.

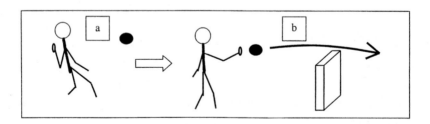

Fig. 2: C-shot. In a C-shot, the player pushes the ball on a straight-forward trajectory at the height of the net. By elevation of the arm the hand is held at shoulder level (a). The player hits the ball with the palm of his hand accompanied by an extension of the elbow (b). The abbreviation 'C' denotes the name (Cengiz) of the player.

The opposite case, namely that prior experience and learning structures new movement patterns, is best illustrated by the Z-spike (Figure 3). The Z-spike is a unique adaptation of volleyball spiking to Freeball. High-level volleyball players cannot "forget" their learned technique. By lowering the trunk they adapt their technique to the lower height of the net in Freeball. So they may play the entire game on their knees.

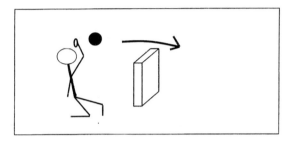

Fig. 3: Z-spike. The player is on his knee and performs a spike. The 'Z' denotes a folkloric dance in Turkey (Zeybek) where the dancer rhythmically falls on his knees.

Freeball for the Paralympics (Freeball-P)

The adaptation of Freeball to disability sport is easy and allows for diverse modifications. The following points need special emphasis:

- Freeball-P unites athletes with all types of disability. Segregation of different groups of disabled athletes is avoided. The blind, the deaf, the mentally retarded, the arm injured and the wheelchair athlete can join in one team.

- The person with a disability, his family and his non-disabled friends can play Freeball together. Therefore Freeball is best suited for integrative sport of persons with a disability (TATAR et al. 1998).

- For children with a disability it may serve as an important medium for integration in the world of sports, since no special talent or strength is required (COTUK 1999).

- Freeball-P is even more "free" than Freeball.

The Rules of Freeball-P

- In Freeball-P the aim of the player is to have a ball cross over the net.
- *Every body part can be used for a shot.*
- Only catching and carrying of the ball is not allowed. If the players are beginners or children, even this rule may be temporarily abolished.
- One ground contact of the ball is allowed but not necessary. More than one ground contact should not be allowed even for beginners or children.
- Only one ball contact is allowed for each team. But as this needs skilled and experienced players, this rule may be alleviated to allow for two ball contacts for each team. As rallies with passing in one team disturb the fluidity of the game, more ball contacts are not suited for Freeball.
- Allowed ball contacts of the players and ground contact of the ball may follow each other in all possible successions.
- There is no service zone. The service can be returned volley before the ball touches the ground.
- The wheelchair may be used for a shot, but not sticks or crutches for reasons of safety.
- The number of players in Freeball-P varies according to their skill level. The number of players of opponent teams have to be equal; thus a match of 3 to 4 or 4-6 etc is possible, if both teams' total "classification scores (CS)" are comparable (TATAR 1999) or both teams make a convenient agreement. This rule implies: anything goes as long it goes.
- Field measures may vary, but one half of the field (one team's area) should be rectangular. A usual volleyball field is appropriate in most circumstances.

- The height of the net is 119 cm, ball circumference is 63 – 64 cm and ball weight is 300-320 gr. For beginners and children a usual volleyball may be used.
- For the sake of safety there is a "safety zone" (SZ) for wheelchair players 60 cm aside from the net. Wheelchair players are not allowed to enter this zone (Figure 4).
- Scoring is the same as in regular Freeball.

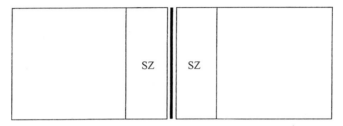

Fig. 4: Playing field for Freeball-P

Results

Players with a disability developed the following "techniques":

Service variations

A great variability of techniques is observed for service. We divided them into two main categories: individual and cooperative services.

Individual services

"Roller-Service" - This technique resembles the spike service of volleyball. The player throws the ball up and to his front while he lets his wheelchair roll to the ball.

"Lying Service" - The player lies on the ground and hits the ball with arm, hand, fist and foot (even overhead kicks) in numerous variations.

"Over-Chair-Service" - Wheelchair players use different hand or fist shots aside their chair. But for reasons of balance they prefer to turn their back to the field and loop the ball over their head.

Cooperative services

If a player has difficulties to serve he may cooperate with his team colleagues. He may use hand or foot, lie down, sit or stand upright.

Field techniques

For all wheelchair techniques the player needs a keen sense for the motion of the wheelchair. The main problem for the player is to be "in the right time at the right place". Especially smooth rolling to the place of anticipated ball contact enables the player to concentrate on the shot. If the player isn't able to time wheelchair motion and ball route, the ball will jump over him or he will swing his arm only through the air. The "jump-over" and "air-swing" situations are the result of coordination difficulties, which are typical for beginners. In the jump-over situation, talented players may turn their chair back and return by backhand shots. Wheelchair players use all possible shot techniques with arm, hand or feet; for example, the C-shot, spike, loop or half volley. The half volley of Freeball resembles that of tennis: the player swings his arm and hits the ball with his palm or fist while he is rolling his chair to the ball. A very strange maneuver with the upper arm is the "wing shot", mainly used as a sudden defense for unexpected balls. Both able-bodied players and athletes with a disability use this technique. The dorsum of the upper arm is used like a wing, as there is no time to stretch out the arm. The "rocket shot" is an acrobatic technique, which has been created by a wheelchair player who is able to push himself up with one leg but has difficulties in playing upright. Therefore he plays with a wheelchair, but "jumps to the ball like a rocket" and does not fear falling. Wheelchair players very often use different "underhand defense" techniques for balls touching down in front of them. They then simply bend forward and lift the ball up.

Players with a lower limb disability, who are experienced in wheelchair basketball, prefer to free themselves from the chair in Freeball. This is especially true for athletes with poliomyelitis who are able to use their weak leg for support, as well as for athletes with total amputation of the leg: without using a prosthesis they enjoy jumping on one leg. If a player is able to keep his balance upright, he may kick the ball with his healthy leg although he may fall. Moreover, he may develop this simultaneous kicking and falling into a new technique: the kick-fall technique.

Interestingly, players with lower extremity disabilities who are able to play upright, use head tossing very often. This can be attributed to their balance difficulties, which they compensate with arm movements. Therefore it is advantageous to have the arms free at the shot moment, when dynamic balance is at risk.

Conclusion

As a ball game Freeball is unique, because it gives the player the chance to create his own technique, the C-shot being the best illustration. There is no wrong technique! The player has to cope with the redundancy of each game situation in his own way. Despite his disability the player improvises, tries and experiments with various ideas. Athletes with a disability may use Freeball as an experiment to find out their own horizon of body movement, and even more important, to enlarge their body freedom. In succeeding, positive emotions will ensue. Freeball is not learning how to play a ball game but to find out or create one's own ball play.

Freeball also provides other advantages:

- Players with any kind of disability can participate in the game facilitating communication between groups. This is important for events with mixed participants, for example summer camps.

- Integration of the family and friends in the game is easy.

- Recruitment of children with a disability to sports will be facilitated.

It is for all of the above reasons that we propose to admit Freeball to the family of Paralympic sports in the future. For competitive purposes we have developed a specific classification scheme (Annex 1).

References

COTUK, B., KARAGÖZOGLU, C., KAPTAN, A., KEPOGLU, A.: Freeball: A novel ball game. II International Sports Congress, Istanbul 1997

COTUK, B., YORUC, M.: The historical process of body restriction in ball games. International Sports Congress, Ankara 1998

COTUK, B., TATAR, Y., CEKİN, M., UZUN, S.: Freeball in the recreation of the disabled child. Annual Congress of the European Society for Social Pediatrics, Istanbul 1999

INNENMOSER, J.: Results of motor behavior oriented research projects in track and field and swimming - adequate answers for some of the problems of classification? International Conference VISTA 99, Cologne (printed in these Proceedings)

KARAGÖZOGLU, C., COTUK, B., CİLOGLU, F., YORUC, M.: Unlimited and creative motion in freeball. Scientific Conference of the National Sports Academy, Sofia 1998

MENDNER, S.: Das Ballspiel im Leben der Völker. Münster 1956

STROHKENDL, H.: Rollstuhlsport für Anfänger. Lübeck 1989

TATAR, Y., COTUK, B., KARAGÖZOGLU, C., RAMAZANOGLU, N.: Freeball: A chance for communication. International Sports Congress, Sofia 1998

Annex: Classification Scheme of Disabilities for Freeball

Scope

Freeball, a novel ball game with total body involvement, is rapidly evolving to a fascinating competition sport. For its adaptation to athletes with disabilities we developed an appropriate classification scheme. We tried to integrate medical and functional aspects. Static and dynamic balance, speed, muscle force and shot accuracy are assessed on a scale accounting for all forms of disabilities.

Classification Scheme for Freeball

Muscle Force

Scale for assessment of muscle force:

0: total absence of voluntary contraction
1: absent; contraction not able to produce movement
2: weak; full range of movement if gravitation doesn't act
3: medium; full range of motion and contraction against gravity
4: good; full range of motion and light resistance against gravity
5: normal; full range of motion and full resistance against gravity.

The first and second degrees are considered non-functional and are not included in the classification.

Lower extremity

Hip	left	right
Flexion	5	5
Adduction	5	5
Abduction	5	5
Extension	5	5

Knee	left	right
Extension	5	5
Flexion	5	5

Ankle	left	right
Plantar flexion	5	5
Dorsal flexion	5	5

Upper extremity

Shoulder	left	right
Flexion	5	5
Adduction	5	5
Abduction	5	5
Extension	5	5

Elbow	left	right
Extension	5	5
Flexion	5	5

Wrist	left	right
Volar flexion	5	5
Dorsal flexion	5	5

Fingers	left	right
Extension	5	5
Flexion	5	5

The total lower extremity score is 40 + 40 = 80 points
The total upper extremity score is 50 + 50 = 100 points
The total extremity score is 80 + 100 = 180 points.

Speed

The speed of the players is assessed in an 18 m run at the lines of the field.

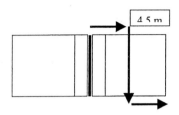

All players are tested in the way they prefer to participate in the game. This means they use wheelchairs, sticks, crutches, they run or crabble or jump at one leg.

Time	points
Below 6 seconds	10
6-9 seconds	8
9-14 seconds	6
14-18 seconds	4
Over 18 seconds	2

Balance

Dynamic and static balance are assessed. Static balance is assessed by the duration the player will be able to stand upright without and with aid.

Static balance	points
Over 60 seconds without aid	5
30-60 seconds without aid	4
Below 30 seconds without aid	3
Stands with one arm supported	2
Stands with both arms supported	1

Dynamic balance is assessed evaluating trunk lifting after the player has bent forward.

Dynamic balance	points
Full	5
With effort	3
Absent	0

Players who use a wheelchair or prefer to sit are evaluted in this position.

Dynamic balance	points
Easy and full lifting of the trunk	10
Lifting of the trunk with effort but without support	5
Lifting of the trunk with support	0

Shot accuracy is evaluated by 10 successive services. The field points are the following ones:

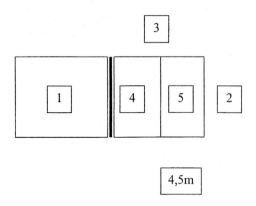

The points are given according to total shot scores.

Total scores	points
Over 45	10
40-45	8
35-40	6
30-35	4
Below 30	2

The total score in points is = Total Extremity P + Speed P + Total Balance P + Shot Accuracy P.

Maximal total points = 180 + 10 + 10 + 10 = 210 P.

For the following special conditions a defined percentage is substracted from the total score to yield the relevant "play score":

Special condition	percentage
Wheel-chair	30
Crutch	30
Stick	20
Orthesis / prothesis	10
Visual impairment	20
Blind	50
Hearing impairment	5
Deaf	10
Mental retardation (moderate)	30
Mental retardation (severe)	40
Female	10
Elderly (over 60 years old)	10
Young (below 18 years)	10
Sitting	40

Spasticity, athetosis and ataxia is assessed by medical classification in three classes:

Degree of condition	%
Weak	2
Moderate	5
Severe	10

The final score is obtained by adding all scores for each extremity.

Conclusion

Total and partial scores are good predictors for the players' game power. We compared various team combinations of athletes with different disabilities. We observed good correlations of classification scores with game power of team variations.

Improving the health and fitness of students and residents with complex learning disabilities

Bob Price

The Linkage Community Trust, Spillsby, Lincolnshire,
United Kingdom

Introduction

The invitation to participate in this second Vista conference was most welcome; all the more so because, whereas my contribution to Vista One in Canada derived from my leisure-time involvement with the Paralympic Movement, the request to do so this time focused on my 'real job' as Chief Executive of the Linkage Community Trust. Indeed, in many respects it could not have arrived at a better time. I joined Linkage three years ago – immediately after the Atlanta Paralympics – and I have now been there long enough to know what I want to happen ... even if not yet long enough for me to be able to report definitively on what has happened.

I will say more about Linkage later on in this presentation. For now, suffice it to say that we provide further education, residential care, and employment opportunities for people with complex learning disabilities. If this definition seems imprecise, that is probably a good thing because it covers many different conditions. For example, our current student and resident population includes moderate and severe intellectual deficits, visual and hearing impairments, locomotor and other physical disabilities and a broad range of emotional and behavioural disorders. The dominant feature, however, and the common denominator across all of our students and residents is what in America is called 'mental retardation' and what in England used to be known as 'mental handicap' but is nowadays more commonly described as 'learning disability'.

It is within this context, therefore, that my presentation today seeks to achieve four things: 1. to skim across the surface of what academics would call a literature review; 2. to provide some background to Linkage itself (what it is, what it does and what it hopes to do in the future); 3. to focus more specifically on Linkage's intended introduction of a new Health and Fitness curriculum; and 4. at least to touch on some of the possibilities for the future.

Literature Review

Messant et al. (1998) cannot have been the first to observe that it is now well accepted that physical activity is inversely and causally associated with the incidence of coronary artery disease. Indeed, back in 1992 the Allied Dunbar National Fitness Survey in Great Britain found that 70-80 percent of the adult population of England was at risk of coronary artery disease because of physical inactivity. According to this survey, the most common barriers to adult participation in regular physical activity in the general population were not access or facility related, but motivational, emotional, and temporal.

Although numerous studies have been conducted to demonstrate the long-term benefits of physical activity among people without a disability (POWELL et al. 1987; RUTHERFORD 1990; BOUCHARD et al. 1993), I am not aware of any comparable studies having been undertaken for people with disabilities. Nonetheless, as the Health Education Authority in England suggests in support of its Active for Life campaign, it is reasonable to expect similar health gains [from regular physical activity] for people with disabilities as for the general population.

With or without such research, there are at least three things of which we can be reasonably certain: 1. people with disabilities represent a significant proportion of the population at large; 2. physical inactivity is a major contributing factor in the deteriorating physical health of people with disabilities; and 3. people with learning disabilities represent a significant proportion of the disabled population.

There is anecdotal evidence aplenty to support the view that a large proportion of the learning disabled population exhibit physical and behavioural characteristics suggestive of a sedentary and unhealthy lifestyle. However, there is still a paucity of reliable research data to support this view and little 'hard' evidence of any causal relationship between such characteristics and either lifestyle or activity profiles. That research evidence which is available – in the English language – derives (not surprisingly) mostly from the USA and Great Britain.

A review of American literature points to the following conclusions:

- Persons with a learning disability have a higher mortality rate than the general population - 1.7 times as great (almost double) for individuals with mild to moderate learning disabilities (EYMAN et al. 1987).

- Young adults with learning disabilities who live in community settings demonstrate cardio-vascular fitness levels indicative of a sedentary lifestyle (PITETTI & TAN 1990).

- An inferior cardio-vascular fitness level is one of the main contributing factors for a shorter life span and higher mortality rates among those with a learning disability (PITETTI & CAMPBELL 1991).

- A disproportionate number of adults with a learning disability have been classified as obese (BURKHART et al. 1985; KELLY et al. 1996; RIMMER et al. 1993; SIMILA & NISKANEN 1991).

Studies in the UK have also highlighted the large proportion of people with learning disabilities who have relatively sedentary lifestyles:

- In a sample of young people with learning disabilities aged 14 to

22, the proportion taking part in sports was considerably lower than in a matched sample of young people in the general population - with much of their time spent in passive activities (FLYNN & HIRST 1992).

-   The 1995 Welsh Health Survey reported that, in a random sample of 4000 adults with learning disabilities, 65.4 percent engaged in no moderate or vigorous activity in any seven-day period (WELSH OFFICE 1995).

-   Among 2000 people with learning disabilities living in the community, 90 percent were inactive (TURNER 1997)

-   Adults with mild and moderate learning disabilities have disproportionately low levels of cardio-respiratory fitness compared with the general population - with 93 percent significantly below the recognised daily minimum levels of physical activity (MESSANT 1997).

The Department of Health (a government ministry with responsibility for England and Wales) recommends that thirty minutes of moderate intensity activity on most days of the week will bring significant health benefits. However, as Messant et al. (1998) were forced to conclude:

"Some people with learning disabilities have no alternative to a sedentary lifestyle and the health risks associated with physical inactivity, as there may not be enough moderate or vigorous physical exercise choices available in day and residential care settings to empower them to meet the minimum recommendations of the Department of Health."

Why it should be that so many people with learning disabilities compare so unfavourably with non-disabled people is uncertain. However, again according to Messant et al. (still in press), the barriers or obstacles which prevent such people from accessing meaningful physical activity seem to fall into two groups:

-   a set of primary barriers that prevent them from having a choice to adopt the Department of Health's recommendations for physical activity [including] unclear policy guidelines in residential and day service provision, together with resourcing, transport, and staffing constraints; participant income and expenditure; and limited options for physically active community leisure,

-   a number of secondary barriers that need to be addressed [including] how choice and rights are given; age appropriateness; and segregated versus integrated physical activity that may limit choice and opportunities for participation.

It is against this somewhat sorry background that Linkage is seeking to address the health and fitness needs of its students and residents. Our aims are 1. to raise their awareness and experience of health and fitness issues; 2. to enable them to make more informed choices about what they do (and do not do); 3. to provide a range of experiences aimed at increasing their levels of physical activity; and 4. through the above, to encourage them to adopt more healthy lifestyles. But what is Linkage?

Linkage Community Trust

Linkage is a company limited by guarantee and a registered charity situated in Lincolnshire, a rural county in the East Midlands of England. It was established in 1976 to address the education and care needs of young people with complex learning difficulties and currently administers a three-campus residential college serving approximately 200 students and two long-stay residential care facilities which provide permanent homes for some 80 adults. At the present time, it has a staff in the region of 280 people operating out of 30 properties, ranging from a network of eight-bed residential care homes to multi-acre college campuses and day care centres. The Linkage College aims to create a stimulating and challenging educational environment for young adults with complex learning difficulties, aged between 16 and 25 years. Courses are residential and based on a curriculum that provides a framework for academic, vocational, social, and personal development. Individual programmes are planned at a level and pace to match the varying abilities and disabilities of each student. An indication of the breadth of the current curriculum is given in Table 1.

Numeracy & literacy	Clerical & retail
Social skills	Horticulture
Communication skills/speech therapy/makaton	Grounds-care
Personal care & hygiene	Maintenance & building
Relationship skills	Painting & decorating
Sex education	Woodwork
Leisure, health & fitness	Sewing
Independent living skills (domestic skills)	Hotel & catering
Road safety & travel skills (mobility)	Fast food (café)
Leavers' programme	IT/Computer training

Tab. 1: Linkage College curriculum

The first of its residential care facilities was developed in close liaison with the local Health Authority back in 1986 and seeks to provide life-long care and support for 12 adults with severe learning difficulties who were previously patients in long-stay 'sub-normality' hospitals. At this centre, our aim is to provide community-based care within a stimulating and challenging environment for the lifetime of a group of increasingly elderly and infirm residents.

The second, more recent residential care development owes its origins to recognition of the fact that, for many young people with learning disabilities, there is a marked shortage, and in some cases a total absence, of suitable supported or sheltered living arrangements, either in the vicinity of their parental home or elsewhere. To address this need, Linkage was encouraged to develop a number of residential care homes specifically for graduates of its College, offering long-term security for those former students who have yet to attain the skills necessary to live independently and who, for a variety of reasons, have no other suitable 'home base' to which to return.

Students' and residents' lives are enriched as fully as possible by individually tailored programmes of occupational, recreational, and educational pursuits. Community-based resources are used, as well as Linkage's own comprehensive college and day-care provision, and there is a continuing focus on helping residents to acquire the independent living, social and vocational skills which will best equip them for as independent a life within the community as their disabilities will permit.

Since its first humble beginnings back in 1976, when a few founding members of the Trust agreed to provide further education in an ordinary house in Skegness for a similarly small number of young people with learning disabilities, Linkage's growth rate has been remarkable - from 5 students and 13 staff in 1979 to 216 students, 87 residents, and 280 staff in 1999 (see Tab. 2).

1976	Linkage established as a company limited by guarantee and registered charity
1979	First college campus opened in Toynton All Saints, near Spilsby (5 students and 13 staff; now 96 students and 89 staff)
1982	Second college campus opened in Weelsby Hall, Grimsby (36 students and 17 staff; now 106 students and 86 staff)
1986	First residential care project opened on Weelsby estate, Grimsby (6 residents and 6 staff; now 11 residents and 18 staff)
1992	Second residential care project opened at Scremby Grange, near Spilsby (7 residents and 5 staff; now 76 residents and 79 staff)
1999	Third college 'final stage' campus opened in Lincoln (14 students and 8 staff)

Tab. 2: Linkage milestones

Of particular significance this last year has been a decision to add to our existing education and care services a third 'core' service: the provision of a broad range of employment opportunities. This is an extremely exciting development – wholly consistent with the British government's latest attempts to move all unemployed people (disabled and non-disabled alike) off state benefit and into work – about which I would love to say more, but our main concern today is health and fitness not employment - although in many respects the one is a necessary prerequisite for the other.

Health and Fitness

At present, although it would be wrong to suggest that Linkage provides no activity programmes for its students and residents (see Tab. 3), it does not yet have a coherent and co-ordinated Health and Fitness curriculum. Advice on health and fitness is often haphazard and reactive and opportunities for physical activity (even though wide-ranging) are usually provided on a 'first come, first served' basis.

Football	Art & craft
Athletics	Tai chi
Karate	Aerobics/Step classes
Swimming	Table tennis
Gymnastics	Pool
Canoeing	Ten-pin bowling
Visits to cinema, concerts, theatre, etc	Horse-riding
Archery	Tennis
Duke of Edinburgh	Board games
Walking	Shopping

Tab. 3: Leisure activities offered to students and residents

Elements of the students' educational courses and of the residents' day-care provision **may** lead to opportunities for physical activity of the sort just described and, indeed, many of their day-to-day activities (gardening, painting, decorating) also contain an element of physical exercise. In addition, whenever possible, students and residents are encouraged to walk to college, to their work experience placements and to the local shops. Nonetheless, historically physical exercise **per se** has not been a day-time activity at Linkage being left instead to so-called 'leisure-time' during evenings and at weekends. Even when day-time activities **are** arranged - and they are generally very successful and well attended - they almost never reach the majority of students or residents.

A New Curriculum

Given the above, Linkage's ambition of introducing a coherent and co-ordinated 'health and fitness' programme probably needs little or no further justification. To achieve this end, all staff with interest or experience in these areas were invited to contribute and 22 members of staff offered their help. It is largely due to their efforts that a new Health and Fitness curriculum is now taking shape.

Over the past few months, a structure has evolved which provides for the instruction and practical involvement of students and residents in three broad areas: 1. healthy lifestyle; 2. fitness; and 3. nutrition. Each of these will be delivered – according to each student's and resident's abilities – through four levels of complexity. In very broad terms, the sorts of issues which will be treated through this new curriculum are as set out below.

Healthy Lifestyle – By increasing awareness of health issues and enabling our students and residents to take as much control as possible of the choices they make, we can do much to inform them of the potential consequences of those choices. We can also provide opportunities for them to work - with support - in group sessions where they can discuss issues of common interest, such as smoking, alcohol, and drug abuse, contraception, personal hygiene and how, when, and where to seek help or advice.

Fitness - It is intended to introduce a wide range of fitness activities into the curriculum – to reflect the inevitably wide range of personal interests - including walking, swimming, cycling, keep-fit, tai chi, and disco-dancing. We are also keen to develop life-style fitness opportunities such as walking to the shops, reducing dependence on our mini buses, active 'time-outs', gardening, etc., all of which are long-term, sustainable, and beneficial to health. To the extent possible, we would also want our students and residents to understand why fitness is important and to appreciate that different activities require different levels and types of fitness.

Nutrition - We are aware of large amounts of mis-information circulating not only amongst our students and residents but also within the staff. In settings like ours, food education needs to be simple, multi-sensory, and reliably reinforced. In the past, we have taken part in numerous 'Healthy Heart' projects, but a major re-assessment of food practice still needs to be made. A Health Education Authority model, known as 'The Plate', provides a simple and easily followed method of helping people to adopt healthy eating practices and will probably lend itself well to our circumstances. Given that most research suggests it is almost impossible to change people's eating habits successfully in the long term unless this is done before puberty, 'the Plate' encourages a gradual adaptation of the quantities of different foods eaten, adjusting the volume rather than the nature of the meal, to provide a healthy and nutritionally balanced diet which is suitable for almost everyone.

Of course, identifying the substance of a new curriculum is only part of the solution to our problem. It should be relatively straightforward to introduce the Healthy Lifestyle and Nutrition parts of the curriculum, but the introduction of Fitness programmes will be more difficult. At present, we have inadequate facilities (fitness halls, changing rooms, etc), little or no specialist equipment to support these activities and no specially trained staff through which to deliver them. What we do have in respect of all three areas – and this is invaluable - is an immense fund of goodwill on the part of Trustees and staff alike. I have no doubt whatsoever, therefore, that in the very near future these ambitions will be realised.

Future Possibilities

In due course, our Health and Fitness curriculum will be in place and our energies will be re-focused on evaluating and, where necessary, modifying both its content and delivery. Links will be established with local sports clubs (many already exist) and serious consideration will be given to the possible replication at Linkage of a scheme developed in Manchester by the Mancunian Community Health Trust. This provides advice and support for any individuals with a learning disability who have even a cursory interest in sport, enabling them to team up with a 'partner' who will 'show them the ropes', take them 'under their wing,' and introduce them to new activities and other like-minded participants.

There is also 'in the pipeline' an opportunity for Linkage to seek recognition by our national Health Education Authority as a regional Healthy Living Centre, but that is a subject for another day. For today, let me simply conclude with thanks for your interest and attention and with a request: If any of you has already embarked on the path which Linkage is now taking and has advice or information which you would be willing to share, please get in touch. The health deficits we are seeking to address cannot be exaggerated and it behoves us all to play whatever part we can in finding better ways to bring health and fitness to an extremely vulnerable client group.

References

BOUCHARD, C., DEPRES, J.P. & TREMBLEY, A.: Exercise and obesity. In: Obesity Research 1 (1993), p. 133-147

BURKHARD J.E., FOX, R.A. & ROTATORI, A.F.: Obesity of mentally retarded individuals: Characteristics and intervention. In: American Journal of Mental Deficiency 90 (1985), p. 303-312

EYMAN R., GROSSMAN, H., TARJAN, G. & MILLER, C.: Life expectancy and mental retardation: A longitudinal study in a state residential facility. In: American Association on Mental Retardation 7 (1987), p. 1-73

FLYNN, M. & HIRST, M.: This year, next year, sometime ...? Learning disability in adulthood. London 1992

HEALTH EDUCATION AUTHORITY: Allied Dunbar National Fitness Survey. A report on activity patterns and fitness levels. London 1992

KELLY, L.E., RIMMER, J.H. & NESS, R.A.: Obesity levels in institutionalised mentally retarded adults. In: Adapted Physical Activity Quarterly 3 (1986), p. 167-176

MESSANT, P.R.: The contribution of physical activity and exercise to quality of life of adults with learning disabilities. PhD thesis. Leeds Metropolitan University 1997

MESSANT, P.R., COOKE, C.B. & LONG, J.: Daily physical activity in adults with mild and moderate learning disabilities: is there enough? In: Disability and Rehabilitation 20 (1998), 11, p. 424-427

MESSANT, P.R., COOKE, C.B. & LONG, J.: Primary and secondary barriers to physically active healthy lifestyles for adults with learning disabilities. In: Disability and Rehabilitation (in press)

PITETTI, K.H. & CAMPBELL, K.D.: Mentally retarded individuals: a population at risk? In: Medicine and Science in Sports and Exercise 23 (1991), p. 586-593

PITETTI, K.H. & TAN, D.M.: Cardiorespiratory responses of mentally retarded adults to air-brake ergonometry and treadmill exercise. In: Archives of Physical Medicine and Rehabilitation 71 (1990), p. 318-321

POWELL, K.E., THOMPSON, P.D., CASPERSEN, C.J. & KENDRICK, J.S.:

Physical activity and the incidence of coronary heart disease. In: Annual Revue of Public Health 8 (1987), p. 253-287

RIMMER, J.H., BRADDOCK, D. & FUJIURA, G.: Prevelence of obesity in adults with mental retardation: Implications for health promotion and disease prevention. In: Mental Retardation 31 (1993), p. 105-110

RUTHERFORD, O.M.: The role of exercise in the prevention of osteoporosis. In: Physiotherapy 76 (1990), 9

SIMILA, S. & NISKANEN, P.: Underweight and overweight cases among the mentally retarded. In: Journal of Mental Deficiency Research 35 (1991), p. 160-164

TURNER S.: The health of people using learning disability services in Tameside and Glossop. Manchester 1997

WELSH OFFICE: Welsh Health Survey. Cardiff 1995

The use of community-based rehabilitation (CBR) as a model for integrated sports activities

Majed Abdul-Fattah

Palestinian Sports Federation for the Disabled, Ramallah, Palestine

The provision of services for Palestinians living in the Palestinian territories is still considered underdeveloped. The long history of occupation is generally considered the main reason for this bleak picture, especially in the last 32 years during which the country was ruled by Israeli military occupation. The military administration at that time made few improvements itself, but also tried to prevent any meaningful development undertaken by national non-governmental organizations. Especially at the level of health and rehabilitation services there being few adequately functioning hospitals and rehabilitation centers. This underdevelopment of the services sector, together with other socio-economic factors, impacted negatively on disadvantaged groups, especially persons with a disability.

Historically, as is the case elsewhere, people with an impairment – especially a mental impairment – were viewed as worthless and were left to fend for themselves on the streets. Only the "lucky" ones were sent to what was generally referred to as the "crazy hospital." This practice showed the lack of a policy of equality which in turn affected how the public viewed persons with a disability. As a result, these persons were prevented both from receiving adequate services and from being included in daily life activities.

Children with a disability were excluded from mainstream schools and child and youth clubs, both on the mistaken grounds that they could not cope with the other children, or that similar opportunities including the practice of sports, were inaccessible to them. The extension of health services, as well as social services, formed the basis of the development of the rehabilitation system, as the main route to meeting the needs of persons with a disability on a "cure" basis. By the end of the 1980s this led to the approach of building new well-organized rehabilitation centers to meet the new demands, especially urgent as a result of the Palestinian intifada-related injuries. Most of the staff working with persons with a disability at the time had some medical background.

Although this new care system was built almost solely on medical and care needs, it represented a milestone in recognition of the needs of people with a disability and led to an improvement in policies which affected them.

In the early 1990ies health care providers and the general public began to recognize the importance of integration of the disabled into mainstream life. The establishment of a community-based rehabilitation program, or CBR, was the first step towards social integration of persons with a disability. At the same time, sports for such persons were introduced as a means of improving the quality of life and of furthering integration.

The CBR model depends on principles such as making use of local resources, for example, schools, youth clubs and local clinics. Later this approach was adopted by the Palestinian Sports Federation, and led to the development of local sports clubs for persons with a disability. The introduction of sports for these persons was viewed by the disabled themselves and by organizations that work with them, as a major step toward what came to be called comprehensive rehabilitation.

Development of the Movement of Sports for the Disabled

Following the movement towards comprehensive rehabilitation and better living standards for the disabled, some people with a disability began, together with professionals, working in the field of rehabilitation and to develop structures for organized sports. In 1993 a sports camp for the disabled was held, out of which the idea of forming a body to plan and sponsor sports was developed.

Due to limited resources, a lack of national policy, the small number of sports clubs, and inaccessibility of community centers and public places, the movement began by a top-bottom approach. Professionals together with the disabled formed a national body for sports called the Palestinian Sports Federation of the Disabled (PSFD). To begin with the PSFD depended on external donations and worked directly with the disabled who used the rehabilitation services, and tried to form national teams. At the very beginning those living in rural areas were excluded. With the experience gained from the CBR, by 1995 the movement reached a wider range of communities and disabled people. The introduction to the community of sports for persons with a disability proved popular and the capacity of the limited members volunteering to develop the idea was quickly exceeded.

As a result of the limitations of existing sports clubs and their lack of accessibility to persons with a disability, the PSFD decided to encourage the idea of sports among those centers working mainly in rehabilitation in the various Palestinian districts. Such centers are usually easily accessible and have staff with considerable experience in dealing with disability-related issues. The approach of introducing sports and lobbying at the same time for the rights of the disabled created community focal points that recently developed into local clubs. There are now 12 clubs which specialize in sports for persons with a disability of which two are integrated with mainstream clubs. Another 8 sports sections are practicing sports at rehabilitation centers.

Management Structure and Integration

With the introduction of the CBR as a concept of comprehensive rehabilitation, the PSFD planned its strategy upon this concept. Meetings and promotion methods to create clubs concentrated on adopting the same strategy of integration.

Beginning with the structure of the clubs, the approach was to include sport activities in mainstream clubs. By this approach disabled people were integrated into the management committees of two mainstream clubs, while others became members of the general assembly. Special committees for supervising the technical side of sports for persons with a disability were created in order to include the non-disabled side. Players with a disability have now begun to use the same facilities and equipment that other non-disabled players use. Due to accessibility barriers at other clubs this model was only successful at the two clubs already mentioned.

In order to secure integration in management and administrative structures at other specialized clubs for persons with a disability, the general assembly as well as the management committees decided to also include non-disabled members. These were drawn from various backgrounds such as professionals in the field of rehabilitation, sports and youth sectors, as well as local business people. To ensure the integration structure in sections practising sports at rehabilitation centers, special management committees were created to include disabled and non-disabled persons both from the rehabilitation centers and from the outside community.

The principles of integration are also used in planning activities; sports-related activities for persons with a disability, for example, are planned to take place simultaneously with other social and sports activities. Activities are situated at mainstream clubs or mainstream centers. Most of the activities are planned, managed and supervised by special event committees. These committees include club members as well as all other related institutions in the community, such as youth clubs, rehabilitation institutions and local schools.

Local businesses provide the funding for these activities. Some of the local business people are members of the clubs' management committees and others fund activities on a charitable basis; the majority make contributions as a business promotion. Budgets of the last year for both the PSFD and the clubs show that 65% of the donations came from the local community, thus financing 85% of the cost of activities.

The successful experience of the Palestinian Sports Federation for the Disabled in fund-raising has been pioneer work compared to that of similar institutions working in the field of rehabilitation or sports. They, like most sectors working in the interim period following military occupation, have depended on governmental or external funding.

Although local youth and sport clubs have put up some barriers in their management structure that prevent the integration of sports for persons with a disability - usually because of a lack of financial resources or inaccessibility factors - the clubs have always been ready to integrate by other means, mainly by human resources. Trainers, classifiers and referees of the mainstream clubs have shared the same mission with the disability clubs over the last three years: 60 trainers of various sports for persons with a disability have attended training courses to upgrade their skills; 30 others were trained as classifiers; at least 50 as referees, and all are working on a voluntary basis.

Results

Palestinians working with persons with a disability and people with a disability themselves believe that the current period is crucial to the formation of future society. This belief is reflected in the way that services for persons with a disability are structured, in order to promote the empowerment of these persons and strengthen their movement.

The structure of the PSFD and its clubs which include disabled and non-disabled members is significant to the launching of the movement for persons with a disability. Clubs at community level are viewed not only as centers for sports for the disabled, but rather as community centers using sports as a means for integration and empowerment.

People with various disabilities and from all age groups visit the clubs on a regular basis to practice sports, not only for the purpose of developing their sporting abilities, but also to encourage their hopes as other non-disabled people do. Activities are not limited to sports or the sport-related aspects, but also include activities which tackle other aspects of the life of a person with a disability.

Club members work in local communities as animators rather than sport teachers. They plan club activities including sports and other social activities in order to address issues which concern the whole community. Some examples are social activities including sports for the Day of the Disabled, Environment Day, and school openings and graduations. Other activities are used to celebrate national days such as Independence Day. These activities make the clubs move from the strategy of integration to the strategy of inclusion. This strategy of inclusion has made sports for persons with a disability part of the activities planned by other institutions, e.g. for youth or for social activities. The athletes and club members are always welcome to be part of these activities. This practice of inclusion has moved the issue farther forward. At the time being, clubs are represented on an equal basis within local cooperative structures serving different social issues. This inclusion of clubs in mainstream structures allows to increase the level of community participation and community financial con-tribution.

Conclusion

Palestinian development in general is at a transitional stage where the building of infrastructure is being constrained. Services such as leisure centers for the public (including disadvantaged groups, such as people with a disability) can accommodate the new inclusion approach. This approach was developed as a result of the fast movement of services for persons with a disability as well as the fast growth of the disability movement, which is struggling for its own autonomy. The provision of such services is viewed as progress towards the achievement of more rights for people with a disability in the coming Palestinian self-rule.

In relation to policy concerns, sport is an important factor in social status, and is paid considerable attention to. But there are many problems. Overall, the long period of occupation has caused a deterioration of infrastructure, low sport standards, inaccessible sport buildings, the absence of people specialized in sports for the disabled, as well as a low priority given to sports for people with a disability both inside and outside the mainstream Palestinian sports structure.

Although people at policy level have limited initiatives to promote sport for persons with a disability, as well as other rights, the long struggle that the disability groups (like PSFD and its local clubs) have gone through over the years for the recognition of their civil rights, has influenced the views of policy makers. This change has encouraged the understanding and acceptance of a social model of a disability rather than the medical model that viewed the people with a disability as defective.

In recent years this has led to the realization in many countries around the world that inclusion of people with a disability at all levels of daily life is a society need.

The strategy involves all community levels within the structure of the clubs and its activities. The use of clubs as community centers using sport for the development and empowerment of the lives of persons with a disability has directly affected Palestinian policy makers. All newly-built sport centers set up by the Palestinian Authorities serve the strategy of inclusion. Such centers are built to be accessible and having some if not all necessary sports equipment for persons with a disability.

Making a difference: Using sport and recreation in the Guyana project for people with disabilities

Colin Higgs

School of Physical Education, Recreation and Athletics, Memorial University of Newfoundland, St. John's, Newfoundland, Canada

Sport for persons with a disability can be either a goal in itself, or a means of creating societal change; through wider social acceptance of athletes with disabilities within society in general, and through providing persons with disabilities opportunities for greater visibility within their communities. It is this latter use which has, for the past several years, been the focus of the Canadian Paraplegic Association's international development activities. Since 1995, the CPA had delivered international development programs in Trinidad and Tobago, Cuba, Costa Rica, the Dominican Republic, and Guyana. It is the work in Guyana that is the focus of this presentation, and to understand that work it is necessary to understand both the nature of international aid projects (known as official development assistance or ODA) and that terrible, wonderful, country Guyana, formally British Guyana.

Guyana

Nestled on the Northeast shoulder of the continent, Guyana is the only English speaking country in South America. Bordered by Venezuela to the north, Brazil to the west and Surinam to the south, Guyana has a population of less than one million people with a diverse ethnic composition, and crippling economic problems.

Guyana is the second poorest country in the Western Hemisphere, and while accurate figures are difficult to obtain, the per capita income is approximately one third of that of the small island developing states of the Caribbean, at about \$600 per year. This is about 1/50th the per capita income of North America and Europe, and places Guyana in the same category as Haiti. However, it is its ethnic make-up that is perhaps its greatest challenge.

There are six well-defined ethnic groups in Guyana, and each has its own attitudes and beliefs about both the reasons for disability and the way that persons with disabilities should be treated. These groups are the Amerindians (native indigenous people); the Afro-Guyanese (descendants of slaves brought to the country before emancipation); the Indo-Guyanese (descendants of indentured labourers brought to the country to work the plantations after the abolition of slavery); the Chinese (who arrived in Guyana during the late 1800's): the Portuguese (who were the early European settlers); and the Europeans (which generally means those of British descent). It is the explosive mixture of poverty and ethnic differences that make the country both fascinating and difficult to work in.

Official Development Assistance

Governments in developed countries expend approximately $40 billion annually on Official Development Assistance (ODA), and while each individual country has its own ODA agenda, the global goals of ODA are remarkably similar. In general, the purpose of ODA is to assist countries and people who are most in need, with assistance provided for the basic necessities of life: sustainable food sources, shelter, employment and human rights.

The Canadian International Development Agency (CIDA) has goals that are consistent with those of other government aid programs. Those goals are:

- provision of basic human needs (approximately 25% of Canadian Official Development Assistance)
- advancement of women in development
- infrastructure services

- human rights, democracy and good governance
- private sector development
- protection of the environment.

Persons with Disabilities in Developing Countries

Within developing countries there are massive needs that cannot all be met by government, and in this environment the needs and aspirations of persons with disabilities (PWD) have low priority. Unemployment among PWD is almost universal, and in many countries to be disabled means to be a beggar. This situation is created and reinforced by the exclusion of persons with disabilities from even the most basic opportunities, with many PWD being denied access to basic education, housing, and other social services.

In the absence of government assistance, non-government organizations (NGO) in developing countries have become important change agents. Canada has recognized this and, through the Partnership Branch of the Canadian International Development Agency, funds initiatives brought to it jointly by Canadian and developing country NGO. The present project is a partnership between the Canadian Paraplegic Association (CPA), and the Guyana Mini-Olympic and Projects Committee.

The Guyana Project for People with Disabilities

The Guyana project for people with disabilities has followed a model used by the CPA in several other countries, including Trinidad and Tobago, Cuba, Costa Rica and the Dominican Republic. In each case, a project proposal has been developed jointly by the CPA and the in-country NGO, and, once funding has been secured, a needs assessment undertaken. The purpose of the needs assessment was to 1. identify the topics to be covered by the proposed workshops, 2. identify the in-country groups and individuals with whom we would work, and 3. to identify the roles and responsibilities of the Canadian and in-country organizers. In the model used, a reiterative process fine-tunes the delivery, with the lessons learned in one phase of the project determining the offerings in the next.

In Guyana, five phases were funded by CIDA. They were the needs assessment, three delivery phases of approximately one-week duration each, and an independent external evaluation. During the needs assessment, the joint Canadian-Guyanese assessment team identified a number of areas in which work was needed. They were, 1. the need to establish a facility for the repair and maintenance of wheelchairs, and possibly for the construction of wheelchairs from locally available materials, 2. peer counselling, 3. advocacy, 4. employment readiness, 5. barrier-free design, and 6. sport for persons with disabilities. In addition, the project donated 20 modern wheelchairs for distribution in the country so as to provide immediate high visibility for the project.

Negotiating Workshop Content

For each workshop delivered, the workshop content needed to be negotiated. This was due to a simple, but profound problem that had been identified during previous projects. The problem stems from the different perspectives taken by the Canadian workshop leaders and the in-country community leaders. By virtue of their extensive knowledge and experience in developed and developing countries, the Canadian workshop leaders knew the possibilities for improvement in the lives of persons with disabilities, but were unaware of the specific local economic, political and social barriers facing the in-country workshop participants. The local leaders, on the other hand, were very much aware of the problems and difficulties faced by the local participants, but were unaware of the range of possibilities for the solution of those problems. Under these conditions the Canadians frequently over-estimated the range and speed of possible change in Guyana, while the local participants frequently under-estimated the possibilities for change.

Since leading workshops in which the leaders and the participants have such different expectations of change was fraught with danger, there was a need to spend considerable time negotiating common goals. Although this was time-consuming, there is no doubt that these negotiations were one of the major reasons for the success of the project.

Workshop Delivery

Each of the three delivery phases of the project consisted of a team of Canadian volunteers visiting Guyana to deliver week-long workshops. Generally the Canadian team consisted of 5-6 people, all but one of whom were responsible (alone or in partnership) for leading a workshop. During the first delivery phase, workshops were delivered in the areas of wheelchair repair and maintenance, grant writing, peer counseling, and sport for persons with disabilities. In addition, an assessment was undertaken of the possibility of establishing a wheelchair construction facility in the country. The selection of the topics throughout the project was based on the needs assessment previously undertaken, predicated on a model in which the advancement of the position of PWD in society was seen as dependent on 1. being mobile – thus the need for mobility aids such as wheelchairs, 2. being able to move around the community – thus the need for information on barrier-free design, and 3. confidence to go out in public – helped by workshops in peer counseling, advocacy, dealing with the media, and wheelchair sports. Only when the more pressing issues of mobility, access, and confidence are addressed, can sport participation be a realistic expectation. In order to assist in sustainability, a workshop was also held on grant writing.

It was the responsibility of the Canadians to organize and deliver the workshops in partnership with key local leaders, and it was the responsibility of the local organizers to arrange for 1. the event venues, 2. the selection and transportation of participants, and 3. the provision of lunches during the workshops. This joint responsibility moves such projects out of the realm of charity, into the realm of partnerships, and appears to be a key factor in developing a commitment to continue the work after the Canadian funding was exhausted.

In a typical one-week workshop the Canadian team having convened in Toronto on a Friday evening would arrive in Guyana on a Saturday after long and frequently difficult flights from various cities across Canada. Sunday would be an orientation day for the Canadians, with an opportunity to visit the site of the workshops, and to become familiar with the conditions under which they would be working.

The workshops would be held from 9:00 am to 4:00 pm from Monday to Thursday, with Friday reserved for one-on-one meetings with participants who required more in-depth consultations. The team would usually take Saturday as a day to play "tourist", and would fly home on Sunday. All the workshop leaders were volunteers, and most were able to take a week off work with the blessing of their employers, frequently without having to use vacation time. Although longer workshops might have been more valuable to the Guyanese, longer stays would have necessitated prolonged absences from work, and probably would have meant that the project would have had to pay the workshop leaders.

A full description of the topics covered by the workshops in all of the phases can be found in Table 1.

Following the three delivery phases an independent, external evaluation of the project was undertaken by Dr. Mary Blueschadt of the University of Regina, Canada. In the evaluation, Dr. Blueschardt determined that the project had been successful, and that this was due in large measure to the way in which the project had listened and responded to the needs of the Guyanese. Another, perhaps the, major reason for success was the use of Canadian workshop leaders who were themselves persons with disabilities.

Use of Persons with Disabilities as Workshop Leaders

To understand the profound impact of using workshop leaders who were persons with disabilities, it is necessary to consider in some detail the lives of persons with disabilities in Guyana.

Phase	Workshops
Needs assessment	Meet with key local stakeholders and plan workshop offerings
Phase 1 workshops	Construction and maintenance of wheelchairs Peer counseling Grant writing Introduction to wheelchair sport
Phase 2 workshops	Employment readiness Peer counseling Advocacy Dealing with the media Creating a vision and strategic plan for the future of persons with disabilities in Guyana
Phase 3 workshops	Maintenance and set-up of wheelchairs Barrier-free design and effective home design for persons with disabilities Training participants to be workshop leaders Wheelchair basketball
Evaluation	Independent external evaluation of the project

Tab. 1: Guyana Project for People with Disabilities

Persons with disabilities in Guyana are almost invisible. Shut away at birth, hidden from the outside world, ignored by the educational system, unrecognized by the government and social agencies, it is almost as though they do not exist. In the Afro-Guyanese community, the visitation of a child with a disability on a family is frequently seen as retribution for earlier evil acts by one or both of the parents. In the

Indo-Guyanese community it is simply Karma – to be accepted. In both societies, which together make up about 95% of the total population, there is a fatalistic view that the disabled child is somehow "God's Will" and, for many individuals, there is a belief that to improve the lot of the disabled child is in some way "working against God".

Once the child has reached school age, another barrier appears – the School Principal (or Headmaster). With almost dictatorial power over what goes on in his or her school the Principal merely has to decline to take the child into the school to prevent that child from ever receiving an education! Social services and support are lacking, and legal challenges to the system unheard of. By age five, the child, denied an education, is already destined for a life of dependency on the government, or on charity.

If the uneducated child with a disability reaches adulthood, they are frequently denied access to government housing and will receive a government "disability pension" of $700 Guyanese per month – approximately $5.00 US. Under these conditions it is not surprising that most live with reluctant relatives, to whom they may become part servant, part slave. Physical and sexual abuse is commonplace, and, for those with physical disabilities, the home in which they live may well become a prison.

Most Guyanese live either along the coast, or on the banks of the country's massive rivers – after all the translation of Guyana is "Land of Many Waters". The coastal strip is reclaimed from the ocean, and in many places is 6-8 feet below sea level. The rivers are prone to massive flooding during the rainy season, and for both these reasons the typical house, and all of the "official" government and municipal buildings are built on stilts, with the primary living and working areas on the second floor. Elevators are virtually unknown (electric power is unreliable), and ramps are almost non-existent. Physical barriers to movement are horrendous! There is NO accessible transportation!

For all of these reasons, local persons with disabilities have NEVER SEEN a successful person with a disability – unless that person by luck of birth comes from a wealthy family and has traveled abroad. What they have never seen is a person with a disability who, through the own efforts, has become successful. Knowing this, our project specifically recruited successful, predominantly female, workshop leaders. Women who had careers, and families, who were eloquent spokespersons, and who were not afraid to be seen in public in their wheelchairs! In the evaluation of the project this use of leaders with disabilities as role models, showing what could be done, was cited by every participant as one of the major accomplishments.

Using leaders in wheelchairs was not without difficulties. In a country that made even simple logistical operations like getting leaders to the workshop site difficult, the effort of supporting wheelchair-using leaders was very high. During one phase, the Canadian team was made up of three wheelchair users, one walking workshop leader, and a logistical coordinator: this proved to be exhausting – for everyone.

Lessons Learned

Many lessons were learned during this project. We learned the critical importance of selecting the right workshop leaders and participants, and what to look for in a venue. We also learned how best to adapt materials to the needs of local participants. And perhaps most of all we learned the need to be very clear in identifying the reasons that participants were present in the workshops, since that was a critical determinant of the role that they might play following the completion of the project. It became clear to us that some of the participants were there primarily for their own education, while others were there as future in-country workshop leaders. Knowing who was who at the start would have greatly simplified the logistics of workshop delivery and would have had an impact on the teaching methods used. Table 2 shows the critical considerations that need to be taken into account by teams engaged in delivery of international development workshops.

For the sake of completeness, notes have been added to indicate the additional considerations that would need to be taken into account if the workshop delivery is not in the language of the workshop instructors.

Why Use Sport?

In a paper delivered in a conference predominantly concerned with sport, there has, up until now, been little discussion about sport itself. That is both a decision, and the inevitable consequence of working in a developing country. Sport simply cannot occur until more basic needs have been met. Without mobility aids such as wheelchairs, without access to building and transportation, and without a social acceptance (or at least tolerance) of their participation, the person with a disability cannot become an athlete with a disability. Thus sport became the end-point of the program – not the starting point.

As the last component of our workshops in Guyana we offered a workshop on wheelchair basketball. Everyone turned out for it, including people in wheelchairs who could not push themselves from one end of the court to the other, but who wanted to be there to watch their colleagues. We drew a crowd of on-lookers, and the players were watched; not with sympathy, but with admiration. The new converts to the game have since formed their own wheelchair basketball team, have sought and received permission to train at the national gymnasium, and are planning to enter a team in regional games for persons with disabilities. They are, for the first time in their lives, VISIBLE in their community.

Area of Concern	Consideration	Key Points
Participants	Selection process	Who will select? What criteria used? Have people been included/excluded for political reasons? When will they be selected?

	Nature and extent of disability	Will special needs have to be met? What support will be required? Single disability groups v multi-disability group?
	Availability	Will desired participants be available? Will they lose wages because of participation? Will they be able to afford transportation?
	Learning styles	What is their preferred learning style? Will a range of preferred learning styles be present?
	Role they will play	What role will the participant play? Are they present to meet their own needs, or as future workshop leaders?
Instructors	Selection process	How will instructors be selected? For their skills and knowledge or for their affiliations?
	Expert knowledge	Do they have a broad knowledge base applicable to the developing country? Can they apply their knowledge to new and novel situations? Greater expert knowledge is usually required towards the end of a project.
	Teaching effectiveness	This is particularly important at the start of a project when participants will frequently feel threatened by working with outside "experts"
	Use of a variety of teaching techniques	Can teaching techniques be matched to the learning styles of the learners? Will there be enough variety to keep participants' interest?
	Adjustment of language level	Can the expert/teacher adapt their presentation to accommodate the language level of participants who may have a low level of education?
	Adjustment of materials to the level of the participants	Can teachers/experts adjust their materials to best meet the needs of the participants? Can they "read" their audience's response to materials and adjust the material accordingly?
	Flexibility	Since conditions are rarely what are anticipated, can the experts/teachers adjust to uncertainty and to constantly changing conditions?
Workshop venue	Accessibility	Is the venue accessible to persons with different types of disability?
	Transportation routes	Is the venue on accessible transport routes? Can people arrive independently or will transportation need to be arranged?
	Environment	Does the power work? Is the lighting adequate. Is there good ventilation? What is the sound level from outside noises? How good are the acoustics?

	Rest rooms	Are they accessible? Are they clean? Are there enough?
	Audio-visual aids	Are they available? Are they compatible in terms of video format (PAL, NTSC), voltage (120, 240 volts) and frequency (50 Hz or 60Hz)? Can the environment be changed to permit the use of audio-visual aids? Can you close the blinds for darkness without cutting off all ventilation?
	Rooms	Are there both main presentation rooms and smaller break-out rooms or areas for small group work? Is there room for private meetings when personal details need to be discussed?
Materials	Content	Is it appropriate? Is it culturally sensitive? Is it economically sensitive – inexpensive solutions?
	Readability	Is the language and type size appropriate? Is it suitably illustrated?
	Availability	When will it be available? Will there be a chance to pre-read the materials before the workshop starts? How many copies will there be? Will everyone have one? If not, how will the decision be made about who should have copies?
	Where will it be held	Where will reference materials be held? Who will have access? Will having the materials give a person or group power over others – since knowledge is power?
Objectives	Participant roles	Are the participants present to learn for themselves, their organizations or to be future workshop leaders?
	Clarity	Are the objectives of the workshop clear? Do the participants and the leaders have the same objectives? Do the participants support the objectives?
Translators	Selection	Who will select translators? Who will certify their competence?
	Pre-workshop glossary	Since many words used to describe conditions and equipment for persons with disabilities are not in general use, translators need to know the correct words to use, and the meaning of technical terms.
	Pre-read materials	Translators need access to workshop materials so that they can pre-translate difficult or technical passages.

	Number	Translation is a difficult and tiring process. An adequate number of translators need to be available to provide adequate rest periods, bathroom and meal breaks.
	Continuity	Because of the technical language used in workshops it is better to use the same translators during a series of workshops. Translators also get used to the style and pace of particular teachers, and establishing a longer term relationship helps both.
	Acoustics	The quality of room acoustics needs to be much higher when translators are used. They must be able to hear the instructor and be heard by the participants over the voice of the instructor. Outside noise makes this almost impossible.
	Linguistic competence	Translators must be very good to convey the subtle meaning of workshop interaction. Non-professional translators should be used with caution.

Tab. 2: Considerations in workshop delivery

There are, however, some lessons for sport that should be taken from this work.

Sport, the IPC and Developing Countries

When such as in Cologne, we have international conferences on disability sport, it is important to remember that the majority of participants, and almost ALL of the new presenters come from the developed world. We talk technology, innovation, new sports and new techniques. We consider the nuances of classification and the ethics of our modes of action – and we see all of these issues from a privileged, eurocentric point of view. We make our decisions, and we implement change – and frequently forget the life realities of athletes in developing countries.

We need to remember that a technology that frees and empowers its owner and user may make a prisoner of the sport opponent from a developing country who has no access. Wheelchair racing is now out of the reach of many – probably most – athletes in developing countries, and the high technology artificial limbs used by affluent runners and jumpers are beyond the dreams of people who must work, live and compete with hand carved wooden limbs. At this conference (Vista '99) we saw demonstrated an innovative and technically exciting guidance system for visually impaired runners that would alleviate the need for guides and/or lane callers. A wonderful idea. Or is it? Let us consider who might benefit from the introduction of this technology.

Clearly the beneficiaries will be the athletes who live and train in facilities that incorporate this (or other similar) systems. They will be familiar with the system, will be able to use it to train independently, and as a result will likely improve their sport performance. For the athlete in a developing country the situation is vastly different. The system simply will not be available in-country. That means that EITHER the system will not be used at major international games, or, if it is, the athlete from the developing county will be at a major disadvantage only having the opportunity to learn the system in the few days before the Paralympics. The freeing technology that helps the athlete from the developed nation keeps the athlete from the developing country imprisoned as a second class citizen, with a reduced chance of achieving success.

We must also be conscious of, and sensitive to, the cultural differences between athletes from different countries. For example, will Western standards for doping control be seen as so invasive of personal privacy by individuals (particularly women) from developing countries that they feel compelled to withdraw rather than submit to such scrutiny?

We also need to get classification expertise into the developing countries. Local, available, experts capable of accurately classifying local athletes are needed so that there are no surprises when they finally make it to major international games. Local coaches with knowledge of disability sport are also needed, but what is needed most for the advancement of sport in developing countries is the removal of the systemic barriers to participation. This means the provision of mobility and other aids for persons with disabilities, to enable them to move independently in their communities. It also means making advances in barrier-free design of both community transportation and sporting venues. Also required are changes in societal attitudes that permit - and even encourage - participation by persons with disabilities in recreation and sport. Lastly, it also requires knowledge of, and expertise in, sport for persons with a disability. Taking this holistic approach is probably the only way to move forward, and was the plan that provided the foundation for the Guyana Project for People with Disabilities.

Postscript

Every year the developed nations of the world invest approximately 40 billion dollars in official development aid. By using sport as a tool for advancing the position of people with disabilities in developing countries, organizations involved in disability sport can seek ODA funds, and can advance both persons with disabilities and sport. If we want the Paralympics to truly take in the whole world, this is the route we have to take.

Sporting with visual impairments.
An initiative to develop sports activities for persons with visual impairments in Uganda

Nina Kahrs[1], Nayinda Sentumbwe [2]

[1]Norwegian University of Sport and Physical Education, Oslo, Norway;
[2]Tambartun Resource Centre for Visually Impaired, Trondheim, Norway
(in association with Brian Scoobie and Ilona Melonowa, International Blind Sport Association)

Introduction

The Uganda Mobility and Rehabilitation Programme

The Sporting with Visual Impairments project is an initiative of the Uganda Mobility and Rehabilitation Programme for Persons with Visual Impairments. Sport is one of the four main initiatives which the Mobility and Rehabilitation (MBR) Programme has started and focused on in an attempt to enhance the life quality of visually impaired Ugandans. The idea is to achieve this objective through enabling people with visual impairments (PWVI) to get involved and participate in social, cultural, economic and other activities at various levels of society. Therefore, the important approach has been competence provision and capacity building of relevant rehabilitation service bodies and networks related or linked to such bodies, and competence provision to the visually impaired individuals and their social networks within their home and community environments.

The MBR programme started as a result of Norwegian contacts with the Uganda National Association of the Blind (UNAB), the Uganda

Foundation for the Blind (UFB), The Ministry of Gender, Labour and
Social Development (GL&SD), The Ministry of Education and Sports -
Education Assessment Resource Services / Special Needs Education
(EARS/SNE), and the Uganda National Institute of Special Education
(UNISE). The Programme's direction and agenda were set during a
seminar held in Kampala in August 1995. In the course of the seminar,
Working and Steering Committees comprising representatives from the
five Ugandan programme partners were formed to take charge of
programme activities in the country.

The Programme is 80% and 20% funded by NORAD and the
Norwegian Association of the Blind and Partially Sighted (NABP),
respectively. Tambartun National Resource Centre for the Visually
Impaired is the implementing body, and Norwegian Peoples Aid
(NPA) is the administrative authority. The University of Oslo,
Department of Special Education, the Norwegian University of Sports
and Physical Education (NUSPE), and the International Blind Sport
Association (IBSA) are other associate European partners of the
programme. (ELMESKOG & TELLEVIK 1998).

The Sporting with Visual Impairments Initiative

"Sporting with Visual Impairments" is a sports and adapted physical
activity initiative. The main objective is to make sport and adapted
physical activity integral parts of all programmes that aim at improving
the life quality of visually impaired individuals in Uganda. With
respect to the MBR Program, sport was to be used to enhance the
orientation and mobility capacities and social profile of visually
impaired Ugandans. Implementation was to be through MBR Program
channels (existing structures and programmes of or for persons with
visual impairments) and those for sports at local and national levels
(KAHRS & SENTUMBWE 1997).

The role of sport in life quality enhancement became more obvious to
MBR Program partners when representatives of the Working and

Steering Committees participated in the 8th International Mobility Conference (IMC8) held in 1996 in Norway. During their stay in Norway, members of the Ugandan delegation visited NUSPE where they became aware of different aspect of "disability sports". As a result, sport for PWVI became perceived as an important activity which the MBR Programme should initiate and promote. This interest in sport is, for instance, reflected in one of the resolutions passed by the UNAB general assembly held in 1997 (UNAB GENERAL ASSEMBLY REPORT 1997). A project proposal and plan of action for implementation of the desired sports activities for PWVI were developed and presented to the MBR Programme by Kahrs and Sentumbwe in 1997 (KAHRS & SENTUMBWE 1997). The co-operation and participation of IBSA in the project was also sought and obtained by January 1998.

Objectives and goals

Sporting With Visual Impairments is to be perceived as a multi-purpose enterprise. Its principal objectives are to:

- introduce, develop and promote sports and physical activities so that participation or non-participation in them is by individual choice rather than lack of opportunity or availability in the country,

- involve and provide relevant competence in the field of "blind sports" and adapted physical activity to the MBR Programme partners and relevant sports bodies so that they become solid and valid structures for spreading and sustaining such activities,

- use different aspects of sports and physical activities to positively influence the stereotypical beliefs, conceptions and attitudes of visual impairment at individual and societal levels,

- provide a working model for the development and enhancement of "disability sports" in general through strengthening the sports and physical education curriculum for educational and training institutions in Uganda with respect to the special needs of people with disabilities.

In order to realise some of the objectives above, activities related to a range of significant short-term goals were to be carried out and achieved in a proposed pilot project.

The pre-project sports situation for PWVI

It is relevant that at this juncture one grasps the general situation of sporting opportunities people with disabilities experience, particularly prior to the Sporting with Visual Impairments Initiative. In their home environments, the exclusion or inclusion of persons with a disability in the games and sporting activities enjoyed by their peer groups is normally determined by a range of factors, in particular the type and degree of physical or sensory impairment. For those with greatly restricting disabilities, participation depends not only on their own resolution, but also on whether they have had any sporting experiences in the course of a schooling or rehabilitation career.

Generally, Ugandans with visual impairments experience little or no sporting opportunities compared with their compatriots with physical and other kinds of sensory disabilities. For instance, until the mid-80s football, wheelchair racing, table tennis, etc. were activities in which some sections of the physically disabled population could participate at recreational and competitive levels. Uganda was even able to send competitors to the Stoke Mandeville Games a number of times and was represented at the last Paralympics held in Atlanta. Uganda has also been represented for many years at the Special Olympics.

At schools and training centres for the blind, Ugandans with visual impairments used to participate in different physical activities. These normally included rope-pulling (tug-of-war), ball games, sack-racing, sprinting, etc. However, no effort has ever been made to involve visually impaired Ugandans in organised recreational or competitive sports activities.

Given the health, social, cultural, and economic merits of sports activities, it is imperative that PWVI as well as other categories of disabled persons in Uganda have the opportunity to participate in at least one sports activity. This, moreover, is in line with UNESCO's 1976 resolution which stipulates the relevance of physical exercise for all people.

The Pilot Project

Objectives and goals

The principal objective of the pilot project was to create the nucleus and model for the development and promotion of "blind sports" activities in Uganda. Therefore, the goals and tasks to be carried out during its implementation included:

- information dissemination to PWVI, other persons with disabilities, and non-disabled Ugandans about the sporting needs and athletic potential of visually impaired Ugandans,

- imparting basic technical knowledge and skills to, and ensuring the creation of, a core or pioneer group of "blind sports" personnel,

- the introduction, adaptation and promotion of a selected number of sports and physical activities,

- the organisation of exhibitions and regular sporting arrangements at local and national levels,

- the identification and establishment of bodies and networks to co-ordinate, promote and sustain the activities.

Implementation

Implementation of the project commenced in the third quarter of 1997, when a sub-committee was appointed and given the responsibility to register and identify suitable districts and institutions throughout the country that would participate in project activities. However, the bulk of activities started in 1998 and was outlined in a project action plan.

Target groups

According to a Pilot Project Action Plan and the main project proposal, institutions of learning were to be the primary target groups for project activities. Taking institutions of learning as the points of departure for the development and promotion of sports activities for PWVI in Uganda has several advantages:

-   PWVI and relevant personnel to be trained and to foster the activities are available and, therefore, readily accessible.

-   Educational and vocational establishments have as their clientele young aspiring people of all ages. Consequently, there is great opportunity for their athletic interest and talents to be discerned, aroused, and developed at an early age.

-   Resources and facilities at the institutions may be used. For example, the physical education prescribed by the national school curriculum can provide a springboard for the kind of recreational, and thereafter competitive, sporting activities envisaged by the project.

-   Institutions of learning also have the potential to provide an amicable sports environment, and an even greater potential for sustaining sports activities for PWVI.

The success experienced in the short period the project has been running vindicate the implementation approach with respect to the pioneer target group of "blind sports" in Uganda. The activities have not only been embraced with great enthusiasm by both PWVI and personnel at the participating institutions, but also by the mother ministry and its relevant sports bodies.

Public awareness/sensitisation initiatives

A two-day workshop was held at UNISE in April 1998. The primary objective was to raise public awareness and to sensitise participants about "disabled sports", particularly sporting activities for PWVI, in order to create an understanding and relevance of the enterprise. Participants included officials from the MBR Program partner ministries and organisations, officials from the Sports Department of the Ministry of Education, representatives of sports bodies and the mass media, and the pilot project institutions. The workshop was conducted by Nina Kahrs, Ilona Melonouva, and Nayinda Sentumbwe. It is possible to assume that the positive attitude the project has experienced at all levels since its conception is partly attributable to the understanding generated at the workshop.

Sport courses for pioneer personnel

Two two-week courses were conducted at UNISE 1998 and 1999 respectively. Each of the courses had a praxis component, and together they comprised the first ever "blind sport" course at the Mobility and Rehabilitation Section at UNISE. A total of sixteen teachers from the pilot project institutions plus UNAB participated in the course. The practice component of the course as running, throwing, long-jumping, goalball, and showdown, were to be implemented at the participants' respective institutions.

Sports competitions and arrangements

Already by October 1998, the first ever Primary School Sports

Championships for Children with Visual Impairments were being organised. This quick start to "competitive sport" was prompted by the fact that both the Ministry of Education and Sport and the Uganda National Council of Sport were planning to organise a primary schools competition for children with disabilities. After their experiences at the Public Awareness and Sensitisation Workshop, officials decided that the envisaged arrangement should be limited to participants in the pilot project. After the interest and success of the first arrangement, the competition is now officially entered on the regular school sports calendar with this year's activities scheduled to take place in October. Plans are also under way for an inaugural National Open Sports meet. About 100 visually impaired sportspersons are expected to take part in each of the arrangements. Besides, EARS/SNE now requires the regular physical education activities to be part of all schools and annexes of the blind. Another interesting aspect of the project is the training opportunity that UNAB's Kampala Sports Club for PWVI provides for blind sports enthusiasts who are outside the educational institutions.

Establishment of sports structures and networks

A number of sports formations, the objectives of which are to provide sporting opportunities and to promote sports activities for PWVI, are already in existence. The UNAB Kampala Sports club has already been mentioned. This has resulted in the Makerere students with visual impairments to exploit ways of forming their own club on campus. Besides, a national association for blind sport activities was formed at last year's primary school competitions of October. On top of this steps have been taken to found the Uganda Blind Sports Association (UBSA). Both IBSA and the MBR Programme have supported this move and the Uganda National Council of Sports has also given its support. An assembly at which UBSA is expected to be formed, is scheduled for mid-September. With a draft constitution already in place, it is expected that UBSA can participate in organising the previously mentioned sports activities scheduled for October.

It is also positive that IBSA has committed itself to supporting the process of establishing relevant structures for blind sport in Uganda, both at governmental and non-governmental levels. The role of UNAB through its sports should also be an important factor in this process.

Sustainability of activities

To ensure sustainability, IBSA has accepted to be a full partner in the MBR sport initiative. "UBSA" will be entitled to full membership of the National Council of Sports and, internationally, IBSA. It is also expected that UBSA will benefit from the fact that it will also be an associate member of UNAB. It is also to be noted that "blind sports" is to be a two-credit component of the two-year Mobility and Rehabilitation Diploma Course at UNISE. However, perhaps the greatest guarantee for sustainability is the enthusiasm and interest which surrounds the Sporting With Visual Impairments initiative.

Concluding remarks

For leisure or competition purposes, the Sporting with Visual Impairments activities carried out so far in Uganda indicate that PWVI desire to have the opportunity of making the choice of participation or abstention on their own. This is indicated by the fact that at the project institutions, the activities are very popular and the demand for them at the institutions where they still have to start is great. It is also worth noting that the Ugandan model of implementing blind sports is being adopted in Zimbabwe, and that other countries in the region expressed interest in it during the recently held Second Forum for Africa.

References

ELMERSKOG, TELLEVIK: Mobility and rehabilitation programme in Uganda. Tambartun 1998

KAHRS, N., SENTUMBWE, N.: Sporting with visual impairments, project description. Oslo 1997

KAHRS, N., SENTUMBWE, N.: Sporting with visual impairment, report. Tambartun 1998

KAHRS, N., SENTUMBWE, N.: Sporting with visual impairment, report. Tambartun 1999

Research generation and information dissemination

Walter R. Thompson

Center for Sports Medicine, Science and Technology, Georgia State
University, Atlanta, GA, USA

There is a need to bridge the ever-widening gap between science and practice. The failure of scientists has been that high quality relevant information is gathered, yet the people who need it the most have little or no access, or the information is not presented in a user-friendly format. One of the great challenges of scientists is to present this important information to those who need it - coaches, athletes, technical officers, team management and venue operations personnel. Besides, the proceedings of Congresses and summaries in lay publications are often inadequate and do not capture the essence of the research. A new and innovative approach to information distribution must be discussed, debated, and implemented. Strategies should be developed that address the important issues. These strategies should include the identification of research questions that include athletes, coaches, and other sport officials. Scientists should be identified that can carry out the research plan. Finally, the distribution of research findings in a format that is easily understood and usable is of great importance. Above all, if data are to be collected during competitions, the research plan must not interfere with the athlete's ability to compete at the highest levels.

There are a number of issues that need to be discussed, and then policies developed to ensure that the proper type of research is accomplished and that the results are widely distributed.

If data are to be collected during the Paralympic Games, a time schedule must be developed in the years leading to the Games. Because of funding issues, the process should start upon the completion of the previous Games (that is, four years prior to the start of the next Games). A standard application form should be developed for all research projects. The application should carry the seal of the International Paralympic Committee, not the local organizing committee. Approval for the research has to come from a number of places, which are to be placed in a hierarchical organizational chart. The originating institution must first approve the project, followed by a Scientific Inquiry Board, and finally by the governing body of the International Paralympic Committee (presumably the Sport Science Committee).

Finally, the local organizing committee, working with the Sport Science Committee, develops the logistics necessary for the conduct of the research project. A Human Subjects Protection Review Committee at the originating institution must have approved all research prior to submission. A budget should be developed by the International Paralympic Committee to help support the research efforts. Finally, guidelines must be developed to direct the research teams on how to submit final reports in a timely manner. The IPC Sport Science Committee should then address how this information will get to those who need it the most.

At the center of all research should be the athlete. It is the athlete who must assist the scientist with relevant research questions. Once a research question is identified, the series of steps necessary to collect data should be instituted. These research questions must be comprehensive and have some direction. Data must not be collected if they are not relevant and important to the athlete. In addition, the sports must be consulted to determine relevance to their sport and to gather their support.

In summary, research on and for athletes with a disability is crucial to success, not only of these athletes, but also of those who work with them. Success can be measured in many ways, and can also impact on those who may have a disability but do not wish to engage in sport. It is the responsibility of research scientists to make these data available. It is the responsibility of teachers and coaches to apply the results in an appropriate way. In summary there are seven points that need to be addressed when developing a comprehensive research program for Paralympic athletes:

- quadrennial time schedule preceding the Games
- funding (budget)
- standard application forms
- organizational approvals (including Human Subjects Review Committees)
- logistics for data collection
- final report submission to the IPC Sports Science Committee and
- wide distribution of results.

Information technology: A solution for effective administration of sport for athletes with a disability

David Grevemberg [1], Christian Lillieroos [2]

[1] Atlanta, GA, USA;
[2] IPC Director of Sport, IPC, Bonn, Germany

„If teamwork is the key to effective organizations, information is the key to effective teamwork" (Susan G. Cohen, Center for Effective Organizations, University of Southern California).

Sport Administration and Information Technology

As the international sports community continues to grow, effective, responsible, and equitable administration of the diverse systems that support, it is imperative. According to Berend Rubingh from the European Association for Sport Management, there are three categories of sports administrators: the federation administrator, the sport policy-maker, and the sport entrepreneur. Each of these categories has their own distinct framework, scope, and responsibility. The federation sport administrator is typically responsible for the management and maintenance of sport infrastructures, including organizational member-ships, competition management, financial management, and external relations. Sport policy-makers are responsible for creating fair and equitable sport infrastructures for management by federation administrators. These individuals, some elected to their positions, seek to establish policies and procedures that progress towards the accomplishment of the organization's mission and objectives. Lastly, the sport entrepreneur takes a creative, innovative, and sometimes interdisciplinary approach to the development and evaluation of the sport movement. This individual may play multiple roles, including fund-raising, working for private enterprises or creating independent initiatives. With sources of funding becoming evermore competitive to obtain, and increases in alternative forms of entertainment, sport administrators must collectively harness the qualities and skills of all categories in order to effectively promote and manage their sport.

According to Alain Loret (Center for Research of Sport Management and Innovation), the ultimate sport administrator is one that can balance their attributes to accomplish two primary obligations:

1. to produce knowledge and solutions appropriate to the distinct needs of the respective sports movement,

2. to train effective and efficient management personnel for future growth.

The ability of an international sport organization to harness these multiple approaches to sport administration is based on the following general business attributes:

- the ability to **identify** organizational leadership, based on cultural influence and area of functional expertise,

- the ability to **empathize** collectively with multicultural perspectives, customs and ideas, while **integrating** a company's performance objectives with cross-functional approaches to management and evaluation,

- the ability to **implement** education and informational programs which provide the basis for organizational management, and

- the ability to **utilize** information technology systems to increase productivity.

According to Tora Bikson, Susan Cohen, & Don Mankin, authors of „Teams & Technology: Fulfilling the Promise of the New

Organization", the final point in the above list is imperative to the overall effectiveness of the three other attributes. „Information technology (IT) refers to the information and communication technologies, systems, and tools used by individuals and teams in their work"; it is „the link that provides access to diverse sources for specialized information and enhances our ability to analyze, manage, and apply this information to our work."

Therefore, one can assume that the ability to harness diversity in an international sport organization is through the effective management of sport administrators combined with integrated IT systems. By integrating IT systems with sport administrative responsibilities, sport organizations can expect the following general benefits from these diverse relationships:

- attracting and attaining the best available human talent
- enhanced marketing efforts
- higher creativity and innovation
- better problem solving
- more organizational flexibility.

Very few international sport organizations have used IT as their means of creating global sustainability and development like the International Olympic Committee (IOC). The IOC example showcases the convergence of federation administration, sport policy-making, and entrepreneurism.

The Olympic IT Connection

> „*For a worldwide project as complex as the Olympic Games, it takes a global reach and local presence to make it happen*" (Toshihisa Shibata, IBM Japan General Manager, Nagano Olympic Games Project Office).

In 1960, the International Olympic Committee began its formal relationship with global technology giant, International Business Machines (IBM). In 1993, the IOC and IBM formed an unprecedented seven-year agreement as „Worldwide Partners." With the goal of establishing an IT foundation for future Olympic Games, the Atlanta Games marked the first Games where a single IT sponsor provided „end-to-end solutions" for all technology needs. IBM provided not only the technology, but also the human resources to implement their „business solutions." At the 1998 Nagano Olympic Games, a joint sponsorship effort was established with IBM, Seiko, NTT, Xerox, Kodak, Panasonic, and Samsung to deliver the management tools needed to coordinate and operate the Games. Additionally, Nagano marked the first Olympic Games where network computing through internet and intranet (on site at the Games) technology provided integrated tools that fans (at the Games and abroad), delegations (athletes, coaches, and administrators), organizers (staff and volunteers), the media (broadcasters and journalists), and the „Olympic Family" used synonymously. IBM agreed to continue its sponsorship through the 2000 Sydney Olympic Games (INTERNATIONAL BUSINESS MACHINES 1998).

On December 7, 1998, the IOC's Executive Board announced that the Olympic Movement's 2001 through 2008 IT partnership was awarded to the SEMA Group. The agreement marked the largest sports-related IT contract ever awarded. „The company will provide and operate a comprehensive, cost-efficient IT solution to support the preparation and staging of the Olympic Games, and will be the key participant in the new Olympic Information Technology Group (INTERNATIONAL OLYMPIC COMMITTEE 1998).

Additionally, the IOC has currently developed two Internet sites used for information distribution and accountability (the official sites of the International Olympic Committee and the Olympic Museum). The IOC site provides general information on the modern Olympic Games, the Olympic Charter, current and past press releases, financial reports, marketing reports, special initiatives (i.e. anti-doping), and global programs (i.e. Olympic Solidarity, United Nations efforts). The Olympic Museum's site is dedicated to the artistic, cultural and historic significance and impact of the Olympic Movement on our global society. The Museum site also maintains current links and information on all disciplines of Olympic research.

Both the IOC and Olympic Games Organizing Committees have lent IT resources in the past to assist with the organization of Paralympic Games. However, these systems are seldom evolutionary for future use by the International Paralympic Committee, Paralympic Sport Committees and Federations, and future Paralympic Organizing Committees.

IT: A Solution for Paralympic Sport Administrators

By nature, Paralympic Sport Administrators (PSA) take an interdisciplinary perspective to their jobs. PSA must incorporate social, environmental, and economic values of sport, culture and disability with that of organizational management. Additionally, PSA must combine functional areas of planning, organizing, directing and controlling together with those of their communication, decision-making, and motivational skills. The very integration of these internal and external factors places PSA in multiple roles as federation administrators, policy-makers, and entrepreneurs. Faced with moderate to null budgets, shortages of staff, volunteers, equipment, and adequate office supplies, the large majority of organizations for athletes with disabilities must be innovative, creative, persistent, and unconditionally committed to their constituents. This extraordinary combination of diverse considerations combined with high levels of demand by athletes, coaches, members and sponsors can sometimes lead many PSA into a „survival management" mode. In this mode, administration, policy-making, and entrepreneurism become reactive, as opposed to proactive, activities.

This reactivity can lead to mismanagement, lack of informational continuity, and loss of organizational credibility. The current and future solutions to these challenges may lie in the establishment of integrated functional IT systems. Within Paralympic sport, IT can be used to integrate the following functional areas:

- event management
- data processing
- information distribution
- general administration.

Once established, functional IT systems will provide all Paralympic stakeholders access to information critical to their respective needs. Examples of Paralympic stakeholders by category include:

Athletes
- Developmental (2nd Tier Elite)
- Elite

Coaches
- National Certified
- International Certified

Officials
- National Certified
- International Certified

Event Organizers
- National Championships
- Regional Championships
- World Championships
- Paralympic Championships

Federation Administrators
- International Organization Sport
- for the Disabled
- International Sport Federations
- International Paralympic Committee

Media Personnel
- Journalists
- Photographers
- Broadcasters

Technical Delegates
- Regional
- International

Sport Scientists & Researchers
- Sport Sociologists
- Sport Historians
- Sport Physiologists
- Sport Biomechanists
- Sport Psychologistss

Sports Doctors & Classifiers
- National Certified
- International Certified
- Doping Control

Sponsors & Suppliers for
- National Championships
- Regional Championships

Leadership
- IPC Executive Committee
- IPC Sport Council
- IPC Committees
- National Paralympic Committees
- Regional Committees

- World Championships
- Paralympic Championships
- Sanctioned Events

Fans
- Youth
- Adult

In a survey conducted by the International Paralympic Committee in 1996 on the status of IT in National Paralympic Committees, International Organizations of Sport for the Disabled, and Sport Chairpersons the following results were found from the respondents (96 respondents out of approximately 140 total):

NPC respondents   72% had a computer
                         38% had Internet access
                         46% had CD-ROM capability

IOSD respondents   100% had a computer
                         75% had Internet access
                         46% had CD-ROM capability

Sport chairperson respondents   100% had a computer
                         91% had Internet access
                         100% had CD-ROM capability.

Recognizing that statistics have changed since 1996, this data emphasizes that various levels of IT capability exist throughout the Paralympic Movement.

Integrated IT systems change traditional hierarchical organizational structures into „virtual structures." Virtual structures encourage both vertical and horizontal lines of communication, and prepare information based on their functional effectiveness and relativity to the organization's mission and objectives. Therefore, IT systems provide a high degree of global flexibility for the management, processing, distribution and administration of magnitudes of diverse sports data.

Event Management

The 1998 Nagano Winter Paralympic Games marked the pinnacle in Paralympic event management IT systems. The Nagano Paralympic Organizing Committee (NAPOC) used an integrated structure that divided the Games into three interdependent systems:

- operation and maintenance systems (internal NAPOC logistical coordination & management)
- results & information distribution systems
- support systems for competition related operations

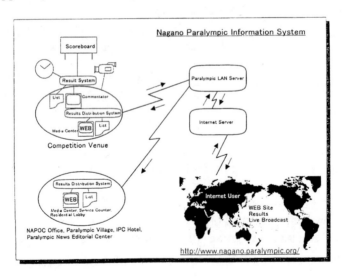

Diagram 1: NAPOC 1998

Operated by 26 students from Shinshu University with professional instruction and support by 36 personnel from IBM Japan, the system was fully integrated and fully accessible to all the Paralympic stakeholders mentioned above via the Internet (see diagram 1).

Realistically, the majority of disabled sport event organizers have limited capacities in resources or the need to devise such complex IT systems, as at the Paralympic Games. However, simple IT solutions still exist for the logistical coordination and management of all games operations for no matter what size event. The typical coordination and management areas of event management include:

- games staffing (volunteer scheduling)
- accreditation
- accommodations
- arrival & departure
- classification
- transportation scheduling
- medical services.

The majority of these tasks can be accomplished with basic office applications such as spreadsheets, word processors, and simple databases. Coordination of these services can be accomplished through e-mail communications. According to IBM, the single most important concern for event organizers of a global sports event is the dissemination of facts and information. During any event, information that is current and accurate is essential for effective athlete preparation, on-site promotions (commentary), and public relations. Such information includes:

- player profiles
- competition schedules
- start lists
- registration
- results
- rankings

- world records
- Paralympic records.

The IT solution for event information distribution is an integrated system that combines data from spreadsheets, databases and/or competition specific software packages with that of Intranet (internal networked information) and/or Internet (external World Wide Web publication) base applications. Both types can either be extremely cost-effective or expensive, depending on the complexity of the event and the need for „real-time" versus non-real time" IT solutions.

The last area of the event management IT support structure are systems for competition related operations. These systems gather the raw data from competition sites and filter them into final results „ready-made" for the above information distribution. Raw data includes information gathered from the following event evaluation areas:

- timing
- measuring
- scoring
- judging
- statistics.

The competition related operations systems are heavily dependent on both the hardware and software available to the event organizer. Most competitions use a combination of automation and handwritten procedures to collect and utilize competition data. Several popular non-disabled sports have developed competition management programs that interface with data collection equipment. However, many of these programs must be creatively adapted to interface with disability sport classification systems. In return, non-standardization systems have been developed that occasionally create confusion in the interpretation of results and performances. Unfortunately, the automated IT solution for competition related operations is subject to an organizer's access to personnel, equipment, and the facilities that support this technology.

A simple IT solution is to develop competition-related forms, which are hand-entered into results tables. The primary difficulty with this is the possible margin for error, depending on the amount of data processed and the training of personnel.

Sport administrators are responsible for interfacing with and/or organizing sport events for people with disabilities, and must analyze, plan, and implement management systems that incorporate IT as the solution for integrating and maximizing their organizational efforts. This proactive approach to event management provides valuable data for use by Paralympic stakeholders.

Data Processing

The importance of accurate, secure, and timely data for use by PSA is essential for the development of the Paralympic Movement. Whether administering a sport federation, working on sport policy/procedures, or developing new and innovative sport initiatives, it is essential for PSA to recognize the value of IT solutions that data processing offers in terms of assessing sport specific environmental, sociocultural, and economic impact. In marketing terms, this information is the core product of any sport organization. Information that may currently be useful to the IPC for example, include:

- sport participation rates by region and sport
- sport participation rates by National Paralympic Committees by region and sport
- sport participation rates by disability - regionally and world competitions
- male to female athletes participation rates and developments
- performance progressions by event, classification, and gender, and
- sport sponsorship information by level of competition and event location.

The term „data processing" was originally defined by a financial analyst as „the transformation of data into a form that is useful for a specific purpose." When organized, maintained and processed according to the needs and IT designs of a Paralympic organizations and events organizer, information databases can provide a wealth of collective knowledge for developing reports and statistics for any organization. Examples of the IPC divisions that may benefit from such information include:

- marketing
- finance
- legal
- public relations
- member services
- sport science and medicine
- sports technical
- development
- standing committees & volunteer leadership.

Beyond generating reports and statistics, data processing can also be used to track and maintain administrative records for archival purposes. Examples of data record types include:

- outstanding information tracking systems
- sanctioning and bid procedure tracking systems
  Paralympic
  world
  regional
  national
- event and meeting calendar information tracking systems
  Paralympic
  IOSD
  invitational
- assembly & meeting coordination & management tracking systems
- committee & member directory systems
- rules & regulations tracking systems

- event result filing systems
  Paralympic
  IOSD
  world
  regional
- world ranking tracking systems
- world record tracking systems.

The IT solution for data processing systems is again an integrated mix of spreadsheet, word-processing, and database management software. The important aspect for PSA to consider is the area of standardization. Depending on the confidentiality of the information or its intended use, customized database programs can provide an effective solution for highly standardized data processing. PSA must recognize areas that can be standardized, and thus tracked, to those that must be individually assessed. The words „diversity" and „global" are seldom synonymous with standardization. Standardized data from results, rules, criteria, and event statistics must be supported by accessible and equal information distribution systems that allow for discussion and feedback from Paralympic stakeholders.

Information Distribution

One of the most critical areas for success in any sport organization, and thus for its administrators, is the ability to effectively communicate information both internally and externally. IT provides many solutions for distributing facts, figures, and guidelines. Whether in the form of presentations, printed reports, e-mails, faxes, or via the Internet, IT is the essential component for these delivery systems.

The three most widely used IT systems for distributing data and general correspondences are the Internet, facsimile, and e-mail. These electronic solutions have various benefits and disadvantages, which PSA should be cognizant of when developing information dissemination plans and procedures. These include the following (see Table 1):

SOURCES	BENEFITS	DISADVANTAGES
INTERNET	• Global distribution • Multimedia capability • Centralized information source • Easily updated and modified • Cost-efficient • Centralized stakeholder feedback	• Not accessible to all • Time consuming at start-up phase
FAX	• High accessibility rate • Ability to copy original information • Immediate confirmation of information receipt	• Expensive • Time consuming • Must file information via paper system • Security (depending on environment)
E-MAIL	• Personalized • Ability to attach additional applications and documents • Ability to create mail groups for select mailings, segmentation, and information distribution • Ability to file information electronically • Ability to confirm receipt	• Not accessible to all • Security (dependent on user environment) • Reliability • Tangible copy of document

Tab. 1: Benefits and disadvantages of IT systems

Keeping the above in mind, PSA should develop policies that support these IT solutions emphasizing preferred lines of informational feedback and discussion. As noted earlier as a key component in event management, information distribution creates accountability through action-oriented leadership. By making critical information accessible to stakeholders, PSA help create knowledge and empowerment thus ultimately improving performance.

Information that is critical for the development and credibility of Paralympic sport and thus must be distributed accurately and timely, includes:

Decisions   systems that report minutes, timelines and decisions from organizational meetings

Directories   systems that organize, maintain and report contact information for organizational leadership and administration

Calendars   systems that report annual event information (dates, places, contacts, and additional information if appropriate and available).

The five R's:

Regulations   systems that report organizational governance structures, constitutions, legal control mechanisms, event selection criteria, and codes of eligibility, conduct and ethics

Rules   systems that report technical rules for the officiating and management of the respective sport's competitive events

Rankings   systems that report and place athlete/team performances based on results and competitive criteria into numerical order from first to last place.

Records   systems that report the best performances ever accomplished by athletes/teams within competitions, time periods, or overall

Results   systems that report the final standings and performance statistics from competitions.

The Internet provides the best possible IT solution for globally distributing such critical information.

Currently PSA use diverse IT resources to distribute information and manage general feedback. Unfortunately, many individuals and organizations have limited access to adequate IT resources and information can become irrelevant or outdated using standard mail systems. It is therefore essential in this time of technological growth, that PSA recognize and encourage that the various national and regional IT capacities of their constituents may differ. Accommodations on an individual basis may be necessary for information distribution systems to work.

General Administration

PSA may evaluate the effectiveness of their IT systems based on their cross-functionality with general administrative activities. Examples of general administrative PSA activities, include:

- budget preparation
- program planning, implementation and evaluation
- general accounting
- proposal writing
- committee management and organization.

The first four activities can be solved using typical office applications such as spreadsheets, presentation software, project planners/daily organizers, and word-processors. This fifth example, committee management and organization is integrated with the first four activities. establishment of a clear team mission and vision. The mission provides the foundation for a committee's development through its tasks in problem solving, program development, and service delivery. However, when a committee is of multinational base, organizations must be aware of the structural needs of the members. IT can provide flexible methods by which PSA can assist committees in collaboration,

---

Internet Committee Meeting
Protocol & Conduct

1. All Committee Members are to check in to the appropriate meeting location/ medium (i.e. Yahoo Pager, Microsoft Messenger) during the scheduled meeting time (preferably 5 minutes prior to the meeting's start time).

2. The Chairman will record the order by which Members sign on. The speaking order for the Meeting will be determined according to the order by which Members sign on.

3. The Chairman will start the meeting with a Roll Call and designate to each Member his or her respective number in the speaking order.

4. The Chairman will then motion to approve the adoption of the Meeting's Agenda. The motion is approved upon a second motion from one of the Members. (If appropriate, minutes from prior meetings will be approved).

5. The Chairman will then begin with the first item on the agenda.

6. The Chairman will discuss the item in full, and then put the item on the floor for discussion. Discussion will be conducted in-turn according to the pre-determined speaking order. Once the item has been discussed through the Committee's Roll, the Chairman will ask if there is any further discussion. Upon receipt of a yes or no the Chairman will conduct the following actions:

   If Yes: The item is placed on the floor for another turn through the Committee's Roll. Members having no further discussion will simply type the word PASS.

   If No: Depending on whether the item needs a course of action, the Chairman will either call a motion for a vote (which will be made in the appropriate speaking order), or a motion to close the item and move on.

7. The process is then repeated until all items are complete.

8. In the case of a secret ballot, votes will be e-mailed or faxed to the Chairman for tallying. Upon receipt of the ballots, the Chairman will determine the results and report the decision.

Tab. 2: Operational guidelines for IT correspondence

but initially operational guidelines for correspondence must be established (see Tab. 2).

By using IT solutions such as virtual committee meetings, automated chat services, monthly intranet committee reports, and the internet, committees are able to distribute workloads more effectively and thus take more proactive approaches to their responsibilities.

While creating global IT solutions on paper may be structurally impressive, the administration and management of these integrated systems is a constant balancing act. Monitoring the need for equal representation, recognition of individual perceptions, customs, and ideas combined with that of the sometimes diverse access to IT resources, PSA must consider technology not as a purpose, but as a tool.

The Reality

One example of a Paralympic sport using computer technology to maximize its information outflow and committee management and communication is IPC's International Table Tennis Committee. Since 1996, the Committee has increased its nations widely practicing table tennis by 45%, has increased the number of athletes by 75%, and has increased its number of competitions by 363%. Table tennis has used a two-tier strategy: 1. provide current/accurate information to its constituents, and 2. maintain effective global committee management.

Future Recommendations

Understanding that multiple perceptions and opinions toward the development of the Paralympic Movement exist, the following suggestions are merely considerations, based on the factual basis that IT plays an important role in the future of sport in general:

1. that IPC establish a formal relationship with the United Nations

Educational, Scientific and Cultural Organization (UNESCO) to develop a joint program that assists IPC Regions and NPCs with obtaining IT resources and training,

2. that IT be incorporated as an integral part of the operational functions of the IPC and its relationships with POCs and member constituency,

3. that IT become an integral part of the planning, operating, and evaluation processes of IPC Championship sport,

4. that training documents for Paralympic sport administrators be developed that encourage IT as a cost-effective and efficient solution to management, policy-making, and entrepreneurial activity.

References

BARNER, R.: The new millennium workplace: Seven changes that will challenge managers and workers. In: The Futurist (1996), p. 14-18

BARR, C.A., HUMS, M.A. & MASTERALEXIS, L.P.: Principles and practice of sport management. Gaithersburg, MD, USA 1998

BIKSON T. COHEN, S. & MANKIN, D.: Teams & technology. Boston, MA, USA 1996

BOVET, S.: Building an international team. In: Public Relations Journal (1995), p. 26-31

CASTON, A. & TAPSCOTT, D.: Paradigm shift: The new promise of information technology. New York, NY, USA 1993

CONVEY, S.: Performance measurement in cross-functional teams. In: CMA Magazine (1994), p. 13-15

COPELAND, L. & GRIGGS, L.: Going international: How to make fiends and deal effectively in the global marketplace. New York, NY, USA 1985

COX, T.: Cultural diversity in organizations: Theory, research & practice. San Francisco, CA, USA 1993

CRONIN, M. J.: The Internet as a competitive business resource. In: The Internet Strategy Handbook, Boston, MA, USA 1996

FAIRCLOTH, A.: Really important things you need to know. In: Fortune (1996), p. 36-37

GRIECO, P.: Team leaders. In: Executive Excellence (1997), p. 17-18

HATCH, E.: Cross cultural team building and training. In: Journal for Quality & Participation (1995), p. 44-49

KAPPOOR, J.R., HUGHES, R.J. & PRIDE, W.M.: Business. Boston, MA, USA 1991

KIEFFER, L.: Building a team. In: Nonprofit World (1997), p. 39-41

NAGANO PARALYMPIC ORGANIZING COMMITTEE: 1998 Winter Paralympic Games Nagano Official Report

SARROS, J., WOODMAN, D.: Leadership in Australian and organizational outcomes: Leadership and Organization. In: Development Journal (1993), p. 3-9

Media / Marketing / Sponsoring

Marketing sport for persons with a disability

Robert Wanzel, Hughues Gibeault, Angelo Tsarouhas

Optimé International, Ajax, Ontario, Canada

Introduction

The development of sport opportunities for persons with a disability has a remarkable history but it is really in the last ten years that dramatic growth has occurred in opportunities for aspiring Paralympians. The formation of the International Paralympic Committee (IPC) in 1989 has provided a central focus for the development of the Paralympic Movement's sports events worldwide and for its Paralympic Games.

The IPC decided that the time had come for the world business community to learn more about the sponsorship opportunities within the Paralympic Movement. This was a calculated decision by the IPC to move aggressively towards the corporate marketing budget as opposed to the traditional contributions or donations budget. An International Marketing Program was developed to provide stability, continuity and growth to the Paralympic Movement while showcasing the abilities and achievements of people with a disability. The ultimate objective is to use sport as a vehicle to expand opportunities for any person with a disability around the world. The International Marketing Program provides a powerful global business partnership opportunity for leading worldwide corporations.

Societal acceptance of people with a disability is building like a "wave" around the world. People with disabilities will be employed in greater numbers in the future; technological advances are eliminating barriers; education rates are increasing; media attention is much greater; the population base is aging and disability increases with age;

and an economic and social power group is forming. For example, in the USA, people with a disability have greater disposable income (approximately $200 billion USD) than the entire teen population. The Paralympic Movement provides a growth opportunity partnership for corporations as the "wave" builds momentum.

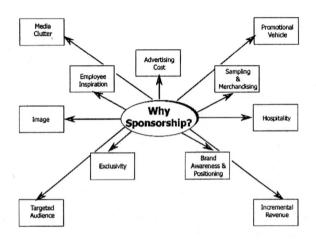

Fig. 1: Why sponsorship?

Figure 1 highlights the varied reasons why a corporation would consider sponsorship in general. Corporations consider the following elements when making a decision to use sponsorship as part of the marketing mix:

- Credibility
  - Consumers see corporate or brand identification in programming and media coverage. They view this as more credible than advertising, perhaps because there appears to be no selling message. In addition, 86% of consumers are more likely to buy a product that is associated with a cause or issue.

- Direct Customer Contact

- Events provide an opportunity for corporations to be face to face with consumers, corporate prospects and brokers. This is an unmatchable opportunity to build relationships, offer information and demonstrate product leadership.

- Continuity
  - Investment in an ongoing program provides continuous exposure.

- Leverage
  - Millions of athletes, officials, administrators, volunteers and corporations contribute time and energy to worldwide sponsorship initiatives. Sponsors benefit from this work, and over time these people become committed supporters and often spokespeople for the company at no cost.

- Strategic Flexibility
  - A sponsorship can support a corporation's changing sales and marketing priorities, including brand awareness building, customer business development, and loyalty programs.

- Exclusivity
  - Sponsors generally get category exclusivity. Unlike regular media, this is an environment where competitors cannot dilute your message. However, you must be prepared to address ambush marketing.

Figure 2 highlights varied reasons why a corporation would consider sport over other types of sponsorship.

Why Sponsor the Paralympic Movement?

There are very few truly global marketing opportunities in the marketplace today. Sponsorship of the Paralympic Movement provides a consistent global positioning, with relevant local activation. A partnership can support corporate activities in marketing and

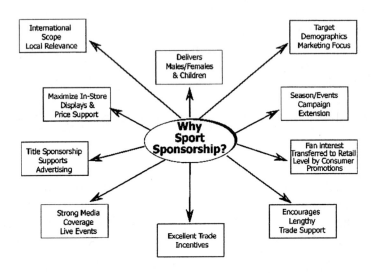

Fig. 2: Why sport sponsorship?

advertising, public relations, sales, employee recruitment, diversity and human resources. Consumers and a corporation's customers will fully understand why the company is partnering with the Paralympic Movement - it makes good business sense!

More than 3,500,000 people have attended Paralympic Games in the 1990s. This compares favorably to many other major sporting events in the United States and globally. For example:

- 2,780,000 fans attended the 1998 FIFA World Cup in France
- 2,950,000 fans attended New York Yankees home games during the 1998 season (World Series Championship season)
- Combined attendance at all American football Super Bowls equals 2,700,000 fans
- 650,000 attended the 1999 FIFA Women's World Cup in the United States.

The Sydney 2000 Summer Paralympic Games (4,000 athletes; 125 nations)
- were larger than the 1956 Melbourne Olympics
- had more nations competing than at the 1972 Munich Olympics
- were larger than the 1998 Kuala Lumpur Commonwealth Games
- were 10 times larger than the first Paralympic Games held in Rome, 1960.

The Nagano 1998 Winter Paralympic Games (1,200 athletes; 32 nations)
- were larger than the Sapporo 1972 Olympics
- were double the size of the first winter Paralympic Games held in Sweden, 1976.

The Paralympic property provides a company with a growth opportunity partnership. Examples of other properties that needed corporate support to grow are:
- the Olympics
- the National Football League, the National Basketball Association (USA)
- Senior and Ladies Professional Golf Tours
- women's sport activities
- the Opera, live theater, art galleries and museums.

Social change history reveals many examples of global enlightenment, understanding and acceptance of the 1 billion people with a disability (one-sixth of the world's population):
- A vault in Kansas City, USA, contains every Hallmark greeting card ever printed, neatly organized in chronological order, providing a history of social change. Only recently has the climate-controlled room held cards for people with disabilities. Increasingly, corporate America is looking to the market that Hallmark Cards discovered – as individuals, consumers and valued employees.

- In 1995, the National Organization on Disability learned that there was no planned depiction of President Franklin D. Roosevelt's

disability in the National Memorial that was under construction in
Washington, DC. N.O.D. Chairman Michael Deland requested that
FDR be shown in his wheelchair in the Memorial. He presented
N.O.D's position that by depicting FDR in a wheelchair, the world
would know that a person with a disability can become President of
the United States; and not showing his disability would perpetuate
antiquated stereotypes about limitations of people with disabilities.
Mr. Deland's request was subsequently approved.

The 1990 Americans with Disabilities Act led to increased media,
corporate and government attention on this issue in North America and
globally.

The world population base is aging and, since disability increases with
age, many more people will become disabled at some time in their
lives.

A global partnership with the Paralympic Movement makes good
business sense - plus a corporation can make a real difference in the
world.

According to the National Family Opinion Inc. 1994 survey:
- 77% of households with a disability and 71% of households without
  a disability would be likely to switch brands to support the
  Paralympics
- 61% of households with a disability and 56% of households without
  a disability would be somewhat to extremely likely to buy a
  product(s) of a company that sponsors the Paralympics
- Households with a disability and without a disability rated the
  importance of corporate involvement in addressing the following
  issues:
  - people with disabilities at 82% and 76% respectively, compared
    with
  - crime problems at 68% and 65% respectively
  - homelessness at 50% and 48% respectively.

Obstacles to Sponsorship of the IPC

- Diverse movement - various disability groups, NPC differences, event weaknesses
- Paralympic Games follow Olympic Games - lack of complete host broadcast production
- lack of awareness of the Movement - media, spectators, lack of national sponsors
- overcoming a corporation's trepidation about actually sponsoring disabled sport rather than just making a donation
- difficulty in making a sponsorship work globally in corporate strategic market areas
- convincing a corporation that event corporate hosting opportunities would be attractive to its customers, prospects and employees
- funding requirements to allow the whole Paralympic Movement to grow are expensive vis-à-vis the perceived IPC property worth
- huge number of sponsorship alternatives in both marketing and social responsibility areas
- world social change attitudes still not fully receptive to persons with a disability.

Overview of the Paralympic Movement

160 IPC Member Nations (e.g. Japan Paralympic Committee)	23 Sport Federations (e.g. International Wheelchair Basketball Federation)	5 International Organizations of Sport for the Disabled (e.g. Cerebral Palsy)

Selected Paralympic Games Legacies

- 1998 - A $288 million USD legacy fund for people with a disability was developed by the Japanese Government as a result of the increased awareness created by the Nagano Winter Paralympic Games.

- 1996 - 300,000 children participated in a Paralympic youth and education program that focused on people with a disability during the Atlanta Paralympiad.

- 1992 – The Barcelona Games resulted in an urban renewal program that included the building of 1,000 barrier-free apartments that incorporated numerous features for ease of use by people with disabilities.

IPC International Marketing Program

The vision:
- The inaugural IPC International Marketing Program has been developed to provide stability, continuity and growth to the Paralympic Movement while showcasing the abilities and achievements of people with a disability.
- The ultimate objective is to use sport as a vehicle to expand opportunities for any person with a disability around the world.

Guiding principles:
- new marketing and public relations initiatives to drive corporate business results
- long term, equity building opportunity
- a maximum of four (4) corporations will be involved worldwide "Less is More"
- creative and flexible program to be designed in partnership with a corporation
- fully integrated program encompassing all marketing properties of the Paralympic Movement to maximize corporate leveraging possibilities.

Corporate Partnership Concept

The idea:
- A corporation utilizes a global partnership with the Paralympic Movement as a catalyst to:

- build relevant brand awareness and exposure worldwide
- maximize return to work initiatives
- promote return to life opportunities
- support the corporation's international growth strategies – build business
- inspire and engage employees, customers, shareholders and the general public

Possible program components:
- IPC activities
- Corporate Brand Equity Program
- Paralympic Games
- IPC World/Continental Championships
- IPC Founding Patron Program
- IPC General Assemblies
- IPC non-sport activities

International Paralympic Committee:
- worldwide Sponsor status and significant recognition at IPC Headquarters
- broad-based recognition and exposure throughout all IPC media, public relations, communications and web site activities
- direct activation/link to the corporation's internet-based products, services and activities
- on-going access to IPC/Paralympic Movement research.

Paralympic Games (subject to IPC bylaws and pre-existing contractual agreements):
- VIP corporate hospitality packages
- identification and advertising in collateral material
- direct response activities
- identification on international television programming
- identification on athlete competition bibs at the Sydney 2000 Paralympic Games
- identification on athlete competition bibs and athlete, coach and

support staff uniforms at the Salt Lake City 2002 Paralympic Games
- identification on athlete competition bibs and athlete, coach and support staff uniforms at the Athens 2004 Paralympic Games.

IPC World & Continental Championships (subject to IPC bylaws and pre-existing contractual agreements):
- international sponsor status at select IPC World or Continental Championships
- corporate flexibility in choosing strategic markets for sponsorship
- identification on athlete competition bibs
- corporate strategic signage
- identification on collateral material
- activation opportunities for a corporation's local operations and product groups.

IPC General Assembly:
- involvement (case-by-case) at the IPC General Assemblies
- direct response initiatives.

National Paralympic Committees (NPCs):
- corporate identification on collateral material of participating National Paralympic Committees, subject to pre-existing contractual agreements.

IPC non-sport activities:
- cultural festivals, educational programs, congresses, government projects, etc.

The possible corporate contributions include:

- guaranteed base financial contribution

- brand equity program
  - a share of a corporation's commitment to a joint equity-program would be applied against the rights fee

Fig. 3: Possible corporate contributions (case-by-case flexibility)

- media initiatives
  - a share of corporate media activities which directly support the partnership would be applied against the rights fee

- value-in-kind (VIK)
  - budget-relieving corporate products and services, e.g. travel, cars, equipment

- performance-driven initiatives
  - opportunity to offset costs through a joint fund-raising campaign.

Summary of International Marketing Program Key Benefits

- Build global awareness, exposure, and business for (a) corporation(s)
- generate resources for the Movement's stability and growth
- increase opportunities for people with a disability who aspire to become athletes
- inspire and engage people globally about the Movement's potential

to make a difference.

Conclusion

The competition for corporate sponsorship funding is intense but the Paralympic Movement is an underdeveloped property with excellent potential. The IPC International Marketing Program provides the integrated marketing platform that corporations can benefit from while supporting the growth of the IPC member nations' activities.

Perspectives of marketing and sponsoring in disability sports - a different approach

Reinhild Moeller

Incline Village, NV, USA

Introduction

The recognition of disability sports has come a long way since the first steps of organized international competition. Despite a delayed start of our movement in comparison to the Olympic Movement we see an upward trend. Social acceptance has played a major role in the struggle for recognition and support for disability sports. Integration in terms of social awareness plays therefore a key role for further success of the Paralympic Movement.

I am proud to present a unique and successful educational program called "Behinderte helfen Nichtbehinderten" (people with a disability help able-bodied people). Over the years the disability community has put tremendous effort in seeking to fit into the mainstream of society. Most projects for integration are focussed on persons with a disability and, to enable them to be as normal as possible, to adjust them as much as possible to the mold that society has cast for them. According to Dr. York Chow (VISTA 1993), "it is important to realize that integration is for people with disabilities to join society at large and not to be isolated into their various disability groups. It will be much easier for people with handicaps to adjust their lives in the community if they model their social behavior on that of non-handicapped persons." But how about going the opposite direction and trying to change the social behavior of the able-bodied society towards the needs of the people with a disability? For example Tom Wittacker states in WE-Magazine, March/April 1999: "My analogy has always been that most medical rehabilitation programs are a steam catapult and society is a brick wall. No matter how much you tune up the catapult, you still don't achieve integration. You must make a bigger splat". Tom Wittacker believes that the solution lies in education. He states that education is about softening the wall and pulling it down. If we can (and our experiences have shown, WE CAN) impact the value system of children growing up today, we will create a more empathetic society where disabled people are seen as capable individuals.

Instead of referring to a brick wall, we describe the able-bodied person as the person with a disability, while meeting a disabled person. Most able-bodied people feel uncomfortable in personal relations towards a person with a disability. We are a group of German Paralympians who founded the educational program "Behinderte helfen Nichtbehinderten e.V.". The name of the program reflects the confidence and self-esteem of the disabled involved in this program and project.

After a brief history of how the program initially got started, I will talk about the aims and goals of the program, give an overlook of the structure, and present some of the activities as well as the most important accomplishments of the first four years of operation. My conclusion is, this is a worth while program to be started.

Behinderte Helfen Nichtbehinderten – a Different Approach

History

Some things might start with a big bang; but our program grew slowly in the beginning. And once it acquired definition it gained momentum. During my years as a Paralympic athlete beginning in 1980 I have been travelling and experiencing how the status of disability sports varies in different countries and I have seen the profound effect of people with disabilities in able-bodied people's minds. I also earned a degree in Sports Science and Adapted Physical Education at the University of Heidelberg in 1986, which gave me an inside view of the able-bodied and disability sport organizations and the interaction between sports, education and society.

After I had spent some time in the United States and had heard about some people with disabilities with remarkable accomplishments giving motivational speeches in different settings, but always on an individual basis, I thought these efforts could be more effective if the presentations were planned in a more structured way. Over the years many people, with disabilities, able-bodied, athletes, non-athletes, coaches and officials have helped to put this puzzle together; into what is now a very established program. The timelines of the development of this program are outlined below:

October 1994: After talking to several insiders and key persons in this field over a period of two years the Ministry of Culture and Sport of the State of Baden-Württemberg (MKS) asked me if I could present them with a proposal concerning my ideas. I had expressed my thoughts at one time when I was writing for the MKS in a brochure about disability sports.

December 1994: Events were moving rapidly. At a ski race camp in December 1994 a few German athletes with a disability sat together and discussed the possibilities and structure of the program. A so-called 'Project Design' was put on paper during the weeks to come.

January 1995: I was able to introduce the idea and a detailed project design to the Secretary of State and several other experts in the MKS. The response to this introduction was very positive and cooperation and support of the MKS was promised after the meeting.

February 1995: A program is only as good as the people who run it. Just two weeks after the presentation at the Ministry I met Wahl at the German Alpine Ski Championships in Berchtesgaden observing the competition as an independent reporter. I introduced him to the BhN-Program and told him about the need for good executive management.

Shortly afterwards Mr. Wahl became the executive manager of BhN.

May 1995: Meanwhile the BhN program had been formed into a structured movement and all involved were very motivated and wanted to get this program going. It was important to select and find the right businesses as sponsors. Although beggars can't be choosers, we decided to only approach companies, which would not have any negative influence on the education of the youth, for example alcohol or tobacco. It was also important that the company would be present throughout the entire Federal Republic of Germany in order to provide an easy start for the program in other parts of the country.

Alexander Spitz, former World Champion in disability ski racing, contacted his former sponsor 'DIE SPARKASSEN' which is a nation-wide financial group. This first contact led to a lasting relationship. The idea and the proposal which we presented to the sponsor was so convincing that it took very little time for him to commit himself to this different approach to merging the able-bodied and disability worlds.

October 1995: The international trade show for adaptive equipment 'REHA' in Duesseldorf was the hosting location for an informal meeting of people with an interest in and an ambition for the program. In this meeting, we made plans for the official start of the non-profit organization 'Behinderte helfen Nichtbehinderten e.V.' and prepared a work schedule for those who wanted to be involved in the program. Further plans were made for developing positions in the proposed organization.

January 1996: A press conference in Stuttgart was held to introduce the original project (BhN), which is supervised by the Ministry.

May 1996: The foundation of the non-profit organization 'Behinderte helfen Nichtbehinderten e.V.' (BhN) became a reality at the sponsor's headquarters in the 'Haus der Suedwest LB'.

Aims and goals

The program's main goal is to enable society to reach new levels of understanding and competence towards people with disabilities. It is not about the basic recognition and acceptance, a state wherein people with disabilities are tolerated without the awareness of what it really means to be different. Able-bodied people need to learn about adaptations, increase their sensitivity for diversity and become experts in the daily integration process. This means that the program's effort is aimed towards the able-bodied society.

In order to reach these new horizons in the effort of integration, the members of the program BhN have started to turn things upside down. First it was necessary to do a brainstorming, or should I say: a brainwashing to erase the existing concept of the terms integration and inclusion. The first task was to motivate self-confident people with a disability who also have potential as a role model to join this program as advocates for their less assertive peers. These advocates may be athletes with a disability, artists or other persons with a disability who have other outstanding skills or accomplishments.

The program provides the opportunity for able-bodied children, teenagers and adults to meet these advocates, to ask them about their disability, to learn about their lives and to experience an uninhibited interaction. This is done mainly through school visits but also through other events like in a day camp or at a school district event.

After qualifying for this educational program and before making presentations, the advocates get training and coaching in how to prepare and give presentations and how to speak in front of a school class or a large number of people. In order to be able to put a qualified curriculum together and earn more experience in this subject, advocates are supposed to prepare a written report after each school visit. They are asked to consider the different age groups, or grades they are visiting and the intention of their presentation. The program is also designed to support athletes with a disability in other important ways. Every advocate receives a fee for each written report of a school visit. And it is recommended that the advocates try to have the local news paper reporting about his or her involvement in the program and personal accomplishments in sports. This public coverage will give athletes with a disability more publicity, which might reach potential sponsors, and the advocate will make fans in the school as well as promoting athletes with a disability.

The main goals of the program are:

- to reduce insecurity in able-bodied people when meeting persons with a disability

- to accomplish a positive change in social awareness towards a diversity of people

- to develop higher levels of understanding and increase competent behavior towards people with disabilities

- to help to obtain knowledge about adaptations and diversity

- to create experts for the daily process of integration

- to prepare a qualified curriculum as a guideline for the advocates and educational material for the students.

This poem from the 'Behinderten Sport Nordrhein Westfalen' (BSNW) is an excellent tool to approach the tasks listed above:

NORMAL

Lisa is too tall.
Anna is too short.
Daniel is too heavy.

Emil is too thin.
Fritz is too quiet.
Flora is too frank.
Cornelia is too pretty.
Erwin is too ugly.
Hans is too stupid.
Sabine is too clever.
Traudel is too old.
Theo is to young.

Everybody is somehow too much.
Everybody is somehow too less.
Everybody is somehow not normal.

Is someone here,
Who is totally normal?
No, here isn't anyone,
who is totally normal.

That is normal.

Structure

The organizational framework of the program is the non-profit organization 'Behinderte helfen Nichtbehinderten e.V.' (BhN). This organization oversees all tasks of the program in the State of Baden-Württemberg and intends to initiate the extension of the program into other States of Germany. The Ministry is the governing body in terms of educational and school-related affairs of the program only in the State of Baden-Württemberg. The BhN is a democratically founded organization with its own statutes and rules. It is a non-profit organization with the right to accept charitable donations. The executive committee consists of the first and second chairperson, a treasurer, two auditors and a secretary. One representative of the

Ministry and one representative of the SPARKASSE are members of the BhN. There is a general assembly once a year and every other year executive committee elections are held. Those advocates who are receiving a fee for their school visits can not be members of the non-profit organization.

Activities

The advocates are very independent in their plans and choices of how to design their school visits. The possibilities can be put into a structure as follow:

The settings: "Where or what population?"

- visit a school class
- visit a whole school
- visit a school project
- visit an event of a school district
- visit a teacher's training session
- visit a parent's meeting

The contents: "How?"

- theoretical presentations and lectures
- practical presentations like sports lessons and demonstrations with a subsequent discussion

The time: "How long?"

- one-hour to two-hour school lessons
- one-day events
- multiple-day camps.

In the first year of operation we still only had a small number of qualified advocates who were able to start with some school visits.

Although the official start of the program was not until May of 1996, the year was concluded with a total of 13 presentations.

There were a total of 19 activities in 1997. The program began to get more and more popular during these first 18 months. The public response and interest in the program is reflected in the rising numbers of activities (49) and the number of over 20 advocates in the third year of operation:

1996: 13 activities

1997: 19 activities

1998: 49 activities.

Members of the BhN present the program at other events to promote the idea and motivate other groups to join us. By now there is a two-day seminar every year for all advocates. The seminar gives everybody the chance to exchange their experiences, ask questions and give input in the scientific research and development of a curriculum especially designed for the BhN program. Members and advocates of the BhN present the program at other events such as the international trade show of adaptive equipment REHA-Duesseldorf, the Paralympic Revival, the conference 'Kooperation Schule und Verein '98' which took place at the 'Institut für Sport und Sportwissenschaft' in Freiburg and at regional meetings of the youth program 'Jugend trainiert für Olympia'.

Accomplishments

With the generous support of the sponsor 'DIE SPARKASSEN' the BhN was able to start the program in a very effective way. It was possible to pay professionals to create our logo, a brochure and two separate posters and T-shirts were made with the BhN logo and the name 'Behinderte helfen Nichtbehinderten'. The BhN is financing a scientific study, which is the first and most important step towards the development of a curriculum and educational material.

The BhN program now has its own website: www.BhN-online.de. School teachers and principals, students' parents and the media have shown high interest and have given much positive response which also resulted in an increasing demand for school visits for the next year.

Conclusion

Over the years sport has been promoted as an ideal medium for integration. Sport was one way to try and adapt to the able-bodied society and to be as conforming as the (dis)ability would allow it to be. But full integration has not yet been accomplished. The reason might be the lack of knowledge of the so-called able-bodied society. Equality can hardly be reached without educating society. The so-called able-bodied are to be taught in consciousness, integrity and congruency by the seemingly disabled.

In order to fulfill this task a group of Paralympians founded the program 'Behinderte helfen Nichtbehinderten' (BhN). The founders were athletes with a disability who had gained self-esteem and confidence through their athletic or other accomplishments in life.

This program is innovative and unusual in that it goes in opposite direction in the effort of integration. The overwhelming response towards the activities of the program validates our initial assumption. The progress of integration will be propelled and broadened by this educational program from the grassroots up, which is trying to change the way of how society is looking at disability. We plan that the popularity of the disabled sports movement will grow by the number of students we talk to. The recruitment of children with disabilities into sports will also grow in the same portion.

The program 'Behinderte helfen Nichtbehinderten' is a worthwhile program to be started wherever there are a few self-confident people with disabilities willing to start this program. This is a program to be created and run by people with abilities for people with a disability.

Synopses

VISTA '99 – a synopsis

IPC Sport Science Committee

Introduction

The second International VISTA Conference on Sport for Athletes with a Disability was held in Cologne, Germany, on August 28 – September 1, 1999. VISTA '99 was hosted by the German Sport University, Cologne, and held under the patronage of the International Paralympic Committee (IPC) and the International Council of Sport Science and Physical Education (ICSSPE). Six years after the first VISTA Conference held in Canada, 170 athletes, coaches, administrators, and sport scientists from 38 countries and all the continents of the world gathered to explore and discuss new horizons for disability sport.

In co-operation with the hosts, the Sport Science Committee of the International Paralympic Committee (IPCSSC) under the leadership of Dr. Gudrun Doll-Tepper prepared a balanced and high-quality scientific program. Consistent with VISTA '93, the Conference was organized around a number of major themes including: sport performance, classification, integration/development/recruitment, ethics, organization/administration, and media/marketing/sponsoring. Sport performance was subdivided into 4 areas: exercise physiology, advances in training techniques, technical developments/equipment, and sport medicine. Time was allotted at the end of each oral presentation for questions and discussion. In addition, participants were able to view a sport demonstration of wheelchair rugby, new technological developments of sport equipment, and new technology for visually impaired athletes. Poster and film presentations provided opportunities to delegates for in-depth discussions and interactions. The round-table discussion of representatives from the International Organizations of Sport for the Disabled (IOSD) and the IPC provided a unique opportunity for participants to learn of the challenges facing disability sport around the world.

At the final session, each moderator was asked to provide a summary of each of the 16 sessions including: major issues raised by the presenters, challenges for the future and recommendations to the International Paralympic Committee. Below is a summary of the major issues arising out of the Conference.

Themes emerging from the Conference

An overriding theme: The athlete's voice in an athlete-centered organization

Perhaps the most prevalent and overriding theme arising out of the Conference was that of the need for an athlete-centered approach to disability sports in all aspects and the maintenance of a strong relationship between athletes and administration. This was highlighted by Dr. Robert Steadward, President of the International Paralympic Committee, who in his opening address reminded the audience that Vista '93 had called for the development of a sports environment that was: ethical, consultative, equitable, communicative, and analytical. At the center of each of these themes is the athlete as an active participant, not only in competition, but in the development of the institution of disability sport itself. As Dr. Steadward noted: The athlete cannot exist without the institution, nor can the institution exist without the athlete. The role of the athlete in co-operating and assisting in technical development; the athlete developing as autonomous individual in his/her sport and assisting in the design of training programs; the responsibility for athletes in acting in an ethical manner and the impact on the image of the Paralympics; the role of the athlete as an ambassador for disability sports in marketing efforts – all were points raised regarding the athlete-centered model in sports.

Key Conference themes

In addition, a number of key themes emerged from the Conference including gender equity, ethical issues (including doping and boosting), objectivity in classification, optimization of sports performance, progress in integration and inclusion, challenges for developing countries, and marketing and funding realities.

Gender equity

Issues of gender equity and participation continue to be raised and were addressed throughout the Conference and, for the first time, specifically in an oral presentation session. Presenters noted that although participation by women is high in some sports – e.g. equestrian, and that participation by women has increased during the last 25 years, there continues to be far lower participation rate among women than men in the Paralympics. It was noted that although participation will increase in Sydney, female participants will still be outnumbered approximately 1.7:1 by men. A number of issues including role expectations, socialization experiences, perception of women inside and outside of disability sports, under-representation at the decision-making level, financial and logistical concerns, and culture were raised as reasons for the disparity. Issues surrounding participation in sports and administration still need to be addressed. An emphasis was also placed on men and women working together in order to solve this issue.

Objectivity in classification

The medical-disability specific versus the functional-integrated classification system continues to spark vigorous discussion. It was generally agreed that classification should be a fair and objective system that places athletes on an equal playing field, but at the same time maximizes the opportunities of persons with a disability for participation. Concerns raised by the speakers and the audience were often aimed at the apparent disparity between these two objectives in that as the numbers of classes fall, so do opportunities for athletes. Also, the degree of subjectivity in functional classification continues to raise concerns. One of the most powerful presentations was by an athlete who discussed the psychological impact of late cancellation of events.

Ethical issues

A number of key issues were discussed which are most appropriately grouped under the general heading of ethics.

A code of ethics

Dr. York Chow presented a draft of a code of ethics for the International Paralympic Committee. This was consistent with the recognition of the relativistic ethical environment which pervades the business and entertainment model of sports in general and which has led to so many ethical problems for athletes and administrators alike. There was a general agreement that the code of ethics of the IPC must be firmly grounded in sound ethical theory; that it must be tested regularly; that it must be associated with a sound ethical decision-making process; and that it should apply to administrators, volunteers, officials, coaches and athletes alike.

Performance enhancement – legitimacy in performance optimization

Performance enhancement continues to be an issue in discussions of disability sport. While clear rules exist regarding performance enhancing substances such as androgenic anabolic steroids, there continues to be a vigorous debate over the practice of boosting. Considerable discussion was heard regarding the safety, legitimacy, and ethics of this practice. Some argued for the facts: that boosting simply returns to the high spinal cord injured that which was lost through injury; that boosting has not been associated with deleterious health effects in athletes; that it is a naturally occurring event; and that it simply cannot be controlled. Some also argued that other practices in sports are equally potentially harmful. However, others argued strongly from an ethical view point, that it is morally wrong to engage in potentially self-injurious behavior and that it is a potentially serious health issue. It is clear that the IPC must establish a consistent policy with regard to the practice of boosting for moral, ethical and legal reasons.

The second concept of technical boosting was a novel and tantalizing concept that emerged during discussions on performance enhancement. New technologies might be perceived as giving athletes an unfair advantage over each other particularly when resources are not equally distributed among athletes and among developing nations.

Progress in integration and inclusion

The move to inclusion at many levels in sport and culture continues to be a major source of vigorous debate. A variety of new initiatives were presented during the Conference as examples of progress in integration and inclusion. However, the most important point arising regarding integration and inclusion was that it cannot be achieved without considering all of the parties and factors involved: All levels of organizations, administration, the mandates of organizations, social attitudes in organizations and at large, were given as examples.

Challenges facing the developing countries

It became clear that in a variety of areas such as training opportunities, access to technology, funding of athletes and organizations, scientific research and medical support, participation of women, developing nations continue to be disadvantaged and that the International Paralympic Committee should strive to support efforts to assist the development of disability sport and disability sport organizations around the world.

Realities of funding the elite sport model

It was evident form a number of presentations that certain realities face the International Paralympic Committee in terms of establishing a firm funding base. It was stressed that in the absence of major sponsorship, the International Paralympic Committee faces enormous challenges in achieving its true potential as a world class sport organization serving athletes with a disability. The presentations on the future marketing strategies of the International Paralympic Committee clearly had an impact on the audience and necessitated an accommodation of the ideology and philosophy of disability sport with the hard reality of the need to raise the profile of the IPC and national sports organizations through sponsorship programs. The need for sponsorship at an international level was described as a crossroads and the analogy of a wave about to break on a shore was also used. At the same time the realities of an elite sports model versus an all inclusive participatory model will clearly continue to raise questions.

Conclusions

There is little doubt that Vista '99 was an enormous success. Continuing the tradition of Vista '93, a number of key recommendations emerged, perhaps the most important of which was that a mechanism be established for an ongoing discussion of issues between VISTAS and the operationalization of recommendations arising out of the VISTA Conferences. The recommendation was that VISTA be held every four years and also that an ethics in disability sport conference, symposium or seminar be convened in the year 2000 in association with the development and publication of the International Paralympic Committee code of ethics.

Sport Performance – Exercise Physiology

Session A1

Presenters: Yagesh Bhambhani
                    Andreas Schmid et al.
                    Georgia Frey
                    Marco Bernardi et al.

Moderator: Donald Royer

On a general note, the four speakers presented excellent and very stimulating papers but very diverse in nature. Therefore it is not easy to tie these four papers together and to draw conclusions and to offer recommendations for the future.

The paper presented by Dr. Bhambhani pointed at the urgent need to bridge the gap between research and practice in Paralympic sport. The paper offers a list of recommendations (10) to achieve this goal. If high quality important data are to be gathered on athletes with a disability, then we must make sure that this information is channeled to the people who need it the most – athletes and coaches. This is an issue a future VISTA Conference should address.

The other three papers, as mentioned before, dealt with different aspects of exercise physiology but prompted very interesting discussions:

1. The paper presented by Dr. Schmid investigated glucose, insulin, cortisol and catecholamines in trained and untrained spinal cord injured persons at rest and during exercise. He stressed the fact that despite the reduced functional mass and the interruption of sympathetic pathways, physical activity resulted in positive hormonal adaptations of spinal cord injured.

2. Dr. Frey talked on the subject of physical activity and people with disabilities. She addressed the issues surrounding physical fitness assessment, physical activity assessment, and physical activity programming for people with mental retardation. Her opening remarks pointed at the fact that people with disabilities may have a higher risk for developing chronic diseases associated with physical inactivity compared to people without disabilities.

3. The paper given by Dr. Bernardi presented results on the cardiac and energetic cost of wheelchair basketball and offered some practical considerations, therefore 'bridging the gap'. One consideration emphasized the fact that the results can be of critical importance in recruiting athletes and designing their training schedule.

Over the years, sport physiologists have played a major role in enhancing testing and training techniques for athletes competing in national and international sporting events for able-bodied individuals. However, according to Dr. Bhambhani, the contribution of this field in Paralympic sport is minimal and even though the level of performance has steadily improved over the years much could be gained with proper coaching that is based on sound physiological principles.

Everyone will agree that exercise physiology must be an integral part of conferences dealing with the performance of disabled athletes. However we must make sure that the information dissemination is done in a way that is easily accessible and understandable for our athletes and coaches. Hence it is necessary that qualified sport physiologists work with Paralympic sport organizations in order to bridge the gap between research and practice.

Sport Performance – Advances in Training Techniques

Session A 2

Presenters: Karl Quade
                Chris Nunn
                Daniel Daly et al.
                Simone Zimmermann, Jürgen Innenmoser
                Trish Bradbury

Moderator: Yves Vanlandewijck

This first session on 'Sport Performance - Advances in Training Techniques' was characterized by a variety of contributions:

Karl Quade (Federal Institute of Sport Science, Cologne, Germany) stressed the need for a science-based supporting system for elite athletes with a disability.

Chris Nunn (Head coach, Australian Institute of Sports, Canberra) introduced 'water based training' as an excellent and safe alternative for the development of athletes at all levels, classes and sports.

Based on video-analyses of the swimming events at the Atlanta Paralympic Games, Dan Daly (Catholic University of Leuven, Belgium) provided novel scientific information, documenting the manner in which Paralympic swimmers achieve swimming speed. Also the monitoring function of this approach towards the functional classification of athletes was stressed.

Simone Zimmermann (University of Leipzig, Germany) presented preliminary results of a complex motion diagnostic system, in order to reveal the causality between various racing propulsion parameters.

Trish Bradbury (Massey University, New Zealand) provided a set of research based strategies and steps which are considered to be successful in 'self-coaching'.

It is surprising that only few conference contributions were made addressing new training and coaching strategies, both from a trainer/coach perspective, demonstrating new field evaluation and intervention techniques, and from a scientific perspective, evaluating the reliability and validity of the assessments, and looking for explanations for the effectiveness of the interventions.

This session addressed the cornerstones of the optimization process of elite sport performance: assessment, training, and coaching. As sport for people with a disability has reached the level of elite sports, the IPC is challenged to set up a framework for a science-based supporting system for the elite athlete, to be implemented in each country. It is clear that such a support system should be multidisciplinary and athlete-centered, optimizing the interaction between the scientist, trainer/coach, and athlete.

Sport Performance – Technical Developments/Equipment

Sessions A 3 and A 7

Presenters: Brendan Burkett
                         Ewald Forner
                         Christiane Bohn et al.
                         Robert Tinker
                         Luc van der Woude, A.J. Dallmeijer
                         Yves Vanlandewijck
                         Rory Cooper et al.
                         Kees van Breukelen

Moderator: Yeshayahu Hutzler

Equipment development, disability and sports

Equipment development is a specificity of the human being. It is typically developed in order to overcome human disadvantages such as lack of force, speed, endurance, range of motion, and to conserve energy. Thus, equipment has traditionally been a source for improving man's motor function, his well being, and socialization potential. Individuals use equipment in sports to push against their own limitations (which could be classified as disabilities compared to other species). In "disability sport" proper equipment is often critical for accomplishments, perceptions of mastery and participation. Improper use or misuse of equipment often causes immediate dropout from activity, and/or may increase risk of acute and long-term injury. Therefore the task of equipment development is to enhance performance and reduce risk. Adapting equipment (as well as the environment, rules and instruction strategies) is a major task of Adapted Physical Activity, thus providing an avenue to inclusion and participation of more individuals in a healthy lifestyle (SHERRILL 1995).

Presentations

Eight presentations were included in the two "Equipment" sessions. They covered the following topics:

- 4 papers concerned technical developments affecting the wheelchair user athlete. They comprised a complete session.
- 2 papers concerned methods for improving the running ability of athletes with AK amputations.
- 1 paper concerned a method for improving running ability of athletes who are blind, and
- 1 paper concerned rule and equipment modification for increasing participation in bowls.

Wheelchair development

Luc van der Woude et al. presented alternative modes for manual wheelchair propulsion, including discussions on the hub-crank, lever, and arm-cycle solutions. The physiological advantages of these modes of propulsion were described in much detail, permitting significant increase of power output, oxygen uptake, and mechanical efficiency. Yves van Landewijck reviewed methods for optimizing wheelchair arm propulsion, and finally proposed a simulation model based on forward dynamics. Starting from muscle activations, this model will calculate muscle forces through which segmental motion could be deduced. Rory A. Cooper et al. have proposed a range of sophisticated technical solutions, including the SMART^{wheel}, SMART^{hub}, SMART^{caster}, for collecting forces, moments, accelerations, velocities, displacements and cardio-respiratory parameters in real life situations of wheelchair use. Goals are to improve sport performance, reduce fatigue in daily and prolonged sport activity, design training programs, and reduce injury risk. Kees van Breukelen went through 8 different categories of wheelchairs and 4 categories of hand-cycles, ranging from standard via hybrid to high performance wheelchairs. His presentation clearly describes the practitioners' tendency to use stiffer wheelchairs in order to minimize losses of energy.

Non-wheelchair technical developments

Brandan Burkett as well as Christiane Bohn et al., concentrated on improving running efficiency and performance in persons with AK amputations. The typical problems facing both the experienced and the beginner athlete are increased loads on the remaining leg, causing asymmetry and compensation. One solution proposed in Burkett's study was to modify the vertical position of the knee axis, leading to significantly faster velocity and exacerbated asymmetry.

Forner & Primsch dealt with the problem of dependence on personnel (guides or callers) for athletes with total loss of vision being able to run. The proposed solution: A track guide consisting of 1. copper wires bounding the track; 2. a power control unit; 3. the sensor system integrated into a belt; and 4. headphones.

Equipment and environment adaptation as a means of increasing accessibility and participation were the main concerns of Bob Tinker's presentation. After being excluded from Paralympic games, bowls and court for playing lawn bowls were adapted in order to permit a more accessible environment. By means of increasing weight and friction to the bowls, the game could be practiced on any hard court facility rather than on a special carpet.

Conclusions

- Present research and development of equipment in disability sport are strongly related to wheelchair propulsion.
- Performance enhancement seems to be the major issue attracting researchers' interests.
- It is suggested that in future development and adaptation of equipment, studies should also concentrate on increased participation and reduced injury risk.

Sport Performance – Sports Medicine

Session A 4

Presenters: Michael Ferrara
                   Hartmut Stinus
                   Michael Riding (2 presentations)

Moderator: Markus Zimmer

To prevent trauma and overuse syndromes it is necessary to know the mechanisms of their genesis. The injury risk in sports for persons with a disability was therefore the first main topic of the session.

M. Ferrara gave an excellent overview of the state of the art of injuries in athletes with disabilities. His detailed literature review showed that there are limited data reported in different structures and mostly not comparable. As a member of the IPC Sport Science Committee, Ferrara made clear what information about sports injuries is necessary and which data have to be collected by whom in which form in order to allow relevant conclusions.

The following evaluation of Alpine skiing injuries in disabled competition skiers by H. Stinus, the team physician of the German Alpine skiing team, reviewed the time from 1994 to 1999. Although there were four major injuries at the Paralympics in Nagano, the overall injury rate – calculated over the whole period of the review – was comparable to data of able-bodied skiing and other data shown also by Ferrara. The injuries were sport-specific and not disability-dependent.

The two presentations triggered an intensive discussion. The following results can be presented:

1. According to the available data, sports for persons with a disability

involves no higher risk of injury than sports for able-bodied athletes.

1. Because of small samples, there are no valid data about the correlation between the injury rate and the kind of sport or the type of disability.

2. Investigations about sports-related injuries are important to inform the athlete about his/her risk of injury and possibilities of prevention, to provide best health and medical care, to improve the sport environment, for example rules and venues, and to educate and support coaches and administrators.

3. We need a standardization of the collected data, bigger samples and more data.

The second part of the session, concerning the limits of performance enhancement, was based on two presentations of the IPC Medical Officer M. Riding.

His ethical considerations concerning boosting showed that medical knowledge is fundamental, but that it is not the only criterium to decide about how to deal with this practice. Psychological, athlete-centered and practical arguments were at the center of this progressive presentation. Boosting is the unphysiological provocation of autonomic dysreflexia which may improve performance, but which can also cause an uncontrolled rise of blood pressure with danger for health or even for life.

In the discussion of Dr. Riding's presentation, there was no clear opinion as to whether boosting should be banned or not. The majority of the audience was in favor of a greater flexibility of the IPC rules. The following arguments were brought forward against banning boosting:

Boosting is giving back to the athletes what they have lost. Autonomic dysreflexia is a normal finding in high spinal cord lesions. Risks in sport cannot generally be avoided. Boosting in training and during competition is hard to control.

The arguments for banning boosting were the well-known clinical data, the unphysiological and unpredictable and therefore dangerous reaction, the possible reflux in the urinary system and the dangerous different types of stimuli to provoke dysreflexia.

In his second presentation M. Riding reported about the development in the doping control procedures of the IPC. Except for one positive testing result in Barcelona, the Paralympic Games were doping-free until today. Despite financial problems, the doping control program is performed flexibly and effectively.

Beside the dangers caused by the drugs, the ethical responsibility towards the athletes is one of the major reasons to continue the fight against doping.

Ethics

Session A 5

Presenters: York Chow
                    Garry Wheeler (2 presentations)
                    Jill Le Clair

Moderator: Gudrun Doll-Tepper

The session might best be summarized as having raised and addressed a number of key questions pertinent to the area of ethics.

What are ethics?

Often the word "ethics" is used without a real understanding of what is meant by the term. Jill Le Clair referred to the Oxford Dictionary. She defined the term ethics as: relating to morals, treating of moral questions, morally correct, honourable. Dr. Chow defined the concept of a code of ethics as a set of rules and principles that govern conduct and behaviour and are based on a set of moral standards regarding what is considered right and wrong.

Codes of ethics are based on ethical theories.

Dr. Wheeler pointed out that codes of ethics are ultimately based on ethical theories (e.g. utilitarianism). From ethical theories principles are derived for directing human conduct. Principles are utilized to establish sets of guidelines specific to certain situations or professions, e.g. doctors, psychologists, coaches, and athletes. Out of this, constitutive, regulative and auxiliary rules develop which govern the way in which games are played and how athletes perform, the consequences of breaking the rules, and other unwritten conventions in sports.

Four classic ethical theories were of relevance to the discussions. These were:

- **Kantian theory** – considers that every person is important and that persons are ends in themselves and not just means to an end. Out of this theory arises the principle of universalizability which basically states that one should act consistently in all situations of a similar nature and accord equal respect to all.

- **Utilitarian theory** – is based on the consequences of actions and stating that a moral act is one which results in the most good for the most people and the least harm to the most people.

- **Cultural relativism** – is a process of moral decision-making based on the particular beliefs of a specific society or culture, i.e. ethics and morals are relative to cultural beliefs and therefore based on facts of law for example.

- **Personal relativism** – is a stance in which it is believed that even culture cannot determine how one should act. Personal relativism is based solely on how an individual feels about a certain act or behaviour in determining whether the act is moral or immoral or unethical.

Why is a code of ethics required in disability sports?

Dr. Chow noted that the need for a code of ethics in disability sports arises out of the rapid progress and establishment of the IPC and the experiences of those involved. However, both Dr. Chow and Dr. Wheeler noted that increased commercialism in all areas of sports have led to increased temptation at the level of administrators, coaches and athletes to engage in unethical behavior. These pressures threaten fair play and integrity upon which true sports are based. Dr. Wheeler noted that such problems have „intruded" into the realm of disability sports and necessitate the development of an ethical code.

Citing a classic paper by Thomas and Ermler (1988), Dr. Wheeler noted that able-bodied sports have become increasingly utilitarian in nature and based on a business and entertainment model in which the athlete is a commodity used by the system. The athlete is often embedded in a power dependency relationship with coaches and the institution.

The intrusion of business and entertainment ethics into able-bodied sports has resulted in a form of ethical relativism in which decisions are made based on situations, the needs of individuals and organizations in relation to results and profit, and independent of a higher set of moral standards and decision-making processes. He went on to describe a number of forms of ethical relativism in able-bodied sport including sport sub-culture, personal, national/cultural, and institutional relativism. Examples were given to illustrate each of these such as: differential rules regarding fighting in sports, the choice of athletes to take performance-enhancing drugs, and the recent IOC scandal. Jill Le Clair also highlighted such issues, as e.g. the Ben Johnson affair in her presentation.

The impact of this state of ethical relativism was assessed in both able-bodied and disability sport. Therefore a clear code of ethical guidelines for administrators, coaches, officials and athletes is required. In addition, it is clear that the ethical code must balance the needs of the individual (athlete, coach, official, volunteer) with the needs of the organization, i.e. encompassing the essential aspects of Kantian and Utilitarian theory.

What should the code of ethics comprise?

Dr. Chow presented a draft of the IPC code of ethics to the audience. This code is preliminary in nature and is based on fundamental principles including: fairness (fair play), honesty, integrity, human rights, and justice, comprises a set of general principles and specific ethical guidelines for the conduct of athletes, coaches, team officials, classifiers, sports officials, and sports leaders and administrators.

What ethical challenges are facing disability sport today?

The challenges can be viewed in relation to the transitional process model of disability sports as suggested by Wheeler et al. (1996, 1999) which has been referred to on a number of occasions during the week. This model describes sports as a process of initiation, development, composition, retirement.

Examples of issues and challenges arising from the discussion are as follows. This is not a comprehensive list but illustrates the diversity of ethical challenges facing the IPC and its Ethics Committee.

Initiation and development

Issues include the development of:

- an early and reliable classification system that is fair and equitable
- safe training programs for young athletes with a disability
- coaching programs
- criteria for the successful integration and/or inclusion of athletes with a disability in able-bodied sports organizations.

Competition

Classification: Fairness and efficiency of the process; recognizing the psychological impact on the athlete.

Performance enhancement: Here the ongoing issue of "boosting" was addressed, and Dr. Wheeler pointed out that we must not simply look at "facts" when determining the desirability of this practice but that we should appeal to ethical theory and principles in the decision-making process.

Retirement

Counselling programs: The development of comprehensive counselling programs to assist athletes in making a transition from sports to the non-sport world was discussed.

Integration in swimming as an ethical issue

Jill Le Clair highlighted the important issues surrounding the concept of inclusion. Swimming Canada addressed the ethical issue of inclusion by passing a Memorandum of Understanding in 1993. The purpose was to integrate able-bodied athletes and athletes with a disability within one organization. The aim was to have greater equity for all athletes. However, to have full inclusion it is necessary to include all aspects of a sport organization including: mission and goals, media and information distribution, governance, funding and grants, education, events and programs, awards and recognition (WOLFF, 1999). Words are not enough, it is the programs and organization that are key. From interviews with coaches, administrators and athletes it is clear that Swimming Canada is actively implementing its new approach.

How are codes of ethics implemented?

A final question dealt with the operationalization of a code of ethics. Dr. Wheeler suggested a two-phase ethical decision-making process based on four fundamental theoretical constructs including: phase 1: questions based on autonomy, universalizability (consistency), consequences, and intentions. In phase 2, a jurisprudential and ethical decision-making process is used. Boosting was used as an example.

Conclusions and recommendations

1. The session made it clear that a code of ethics is of crucial importance to the IPC.

2. This code of ethics should be continually developed and refined in the future and be treated as a working document.

3. The code must be continually tested for adequacy and efficacy as situations arise.

4. Finally, although there have been many hundreds of ethics conferences world-wide in 1999, it is recommended that an ethics symposium be convened in the area of disability sport early in the next millennium.

Classification

Sessions A 6 and B 1

Presenters: Horst Strohkendl
Christian Brunner et al.
Jürgen Innenmoser
Norma Lorincz
Aart Kruimer
Ronald Davis
Lutz Worms

Moderator: Rebeccah Bornemann

The two sessions on classification certainly presented a diversity of views on the topic. Generally there was consensus that classification systems exist to create a level playing field for athletes with a disability, and allow them to compete at the highest level possible. Classification should be fair, equitable, accurate and credible; it should also allow for the development of both athletes and sports.

There is, however, a fundamental difference between classification for athletes with physical disability/visual impairment and intellectual disability. As Dr. Worms pointed out in his presentation, eligibility is the single most important factor in the classification of athletes with intellectual disability. While all Paralympic sports have minimum disability requirements, the INAS-FID system has one open classification for all those athletes eligible for competition. The major challenge is that it is difficult to measure intellectual disability precisely, and standards vary worldwide.

The degree of precision needed for an effective classification system was debated generally. Some, such as Dr. Strohkendl, suggested that classification is given too much importance, and thus should be simplified. In contrast, Dr. Brunner presented a study demonstrating the need for more in-depth physiological analysis in certain circumstances, and an expansion of classification practices to include an evaluation of the activation of the sympathetic nervous system in individuals with incomplete quadriplegia. This factor appears to have a significant impact on the performance potential of these athletes.

Further discussion arose concerning the organization of classification systems. Classification could be based on sport (e.g. fencing or swimming functional classification systems) or on disability (e.g. intellectual disability or visual impairment). And while there was a prevalent view that classification should be constant from grass-roots development to elite competition, and that classification should be based on disability and not on performance, others suggested that it could be organized around skill or athlete development level.

Expanding upon the theme of rationales for classification, Dr. Kruimer suggested that all classification for athletes with a disability should be based on force magnitude impairment and force control impairment. Such distinctions could allow for different types of disability and lead to greater equity in classification.

A common theme that developed was that classification should not penalize athletes for training or innovative techniques. Dr. Innenmoser introduced the idea of "creative compensation" – defined as a specific motor adaptation that could not be found through normal (or traditional) means. He further suggested that traditional rules from mainstream sport could be changed to allow for greater flexibility in innovation, such as allowing the use of the dolphin kick in the breaststroke.

In the second session, Ms. Lorincz and Dr. Davis talked about the process and impact of classification, from an athlete and organizational perspective, respectively. The common themes that emerged were striking. Clear communication, respect for athletes and their preparation, education of everyone involved, and the need to do as much classification as possible prior to and away from major games (particularly Paralympics) were stressed. Concern was also raised about the "numbers game" of events running (or not), cancellations, and personal and system impact – both internationally and nationally – of classification changes just prior to competition.

From these two sessions, a number of recommendations or ideas for the future of classification emerged. These include:

- better communication

  - between sports and disability groups to find solutions for classification challenges and to refine classification systems;
  - to educate all participants, including the training of classifiers, and awareness raising for all athletes, coaches and administrators;
  - between IPC and local organizing committees, and for the distribution of classification results in a calm, orderly and sensitive manner.

- commitment

  - by the entire Paralympic community to basic principles of fair, equitable, accurate, and credible classification;
  - by the IPC, sports, the IOSDs and countries together to adapt classification practices and consequences to help ensure that the system does not continue to marginalize female athletes and those in lower classes;
  - by the IPC, sports, the IOSDs and countries together to develop classifiers and provide competitions and classification opportunities so that athletes can get permanent classifications before World Championships and (in particular) Paralympic Games;
  - by the IPC to provide standard information about classification to local organizing committees via handbook;

- by local organizing committees to plan well and to ensure that proper spaces and personnel are available so that classification can proceed in a dignified and respectful manner;
- by sport scientists and classifiers to look into other factors which could have an impact on performance so as to improve classification systems (such as the sympathetic nervous system);
- to clarity and consistency: "We cannot ask athletes to try something out at a competition", nor should classes be split up or combined because of confusion.

- cooperation

  - between classifiers and current and retired athletes to get feedback on classification systems, and to recruit their expertise;
  - by the use of information technology to streamline and enhance the process;
  - between countries and INAS-FID to standardize evaluation and eligibility for athletes with intellectual disability.

Important and constructive discussions about classification have occurred during the conference. The presenters and the audience are to be commended for their contribution to our understanding of this area, and it is our hope that the Paralympic community will continue to work together to better improve classification systems and processes.

Integration / Development / Recruitment

Session B 2

Presenters: David McCrae
                Colin Rains
                Ted Fay
                Ray Allard / Rebeccah Bornemann

Moderator: Maura Strange

The presentations made during this first session focussed in the main on integration or inclusion and a range of experiences in this area.

David McCrae provided the conference with an example/model as currently practised in the UK at World Class level, which indicated partnership and finance (particularly parity in access to funding) as key factors. He identified these factors as leading to quality and credibility for athletes with a disability within the UK. Access to the very best input from service areas (coaches, sports scientists, technicians, medical staff, core management and administrators) is required if athletes are to have the "edge" to win. Social inclusion is now very high on the agenda of many senior nations in the Paralympic Movement in the governance of their countries as well as sport.

Colin Rains, as an exception to the theme of inclusion in this first session, pursued the expansion of provision of opportunity at all levels as a crucial and fundamental requirement. He promulgated the theme of the negative impact on recruitment, motivation and participation by the reduction of events programmed at Paralympic level for the more severely disabled athletes. During the subsequent discussion, it was suggested that national grass roots programmes should be broader based to stimulate and maintain opportunity levels, particularly for females and the more severely disabled. Cultural conditions were also considered a limiting factor in this area. A call was made for the IOSDs to investigate this further through their membership organisations. It was felt also that the IPC, perhaps through the Sports Science Committee, could give further consideration to the situation facing females and the more severely disabled relative to strategies or incentives that could be employed to maintain events on the Paralympic programme.

Ted Fay introduced the conference to the relevance of critical factors identified as fundamental to change, which could be considered universal to a range of minority groups. His study explored the integration histories of Afro-American males into Major League Baseball in the US and women of all ethnic backgrounds into Division I athletic programmes of the NCAA with the intent of developing propositions which could serve as a foundation for recommendations for the strategic management of the process of continuing integration of athletes with a disability into the United States Olympic Committee and its related national governing bodies. He identified 10 critical changes, three of which were essential components - law, war and economics - and a 10 point vertical integration action plan for the USOC and NGBs addressing the issues the study had highlighted, including active participation at all levels of athletes and experts from the field of sport for persons with a disability.

Ray Allard and Rebeccah Bornemann drew on their experience within Canadian based inclusion activities. The focus of this inclusion strategy was on Paralympic stream athletes into the mainstream sports systems, funded by the government. Their overview provided insight into areas where this has worked well and also where difficulties have been encountered. In the main, the response from main stream sports had been extremely encouraging, although some flexibility in approach and application had been called for to establish appropriate working relationships.

The presentations and discussion indicated that there had been positive, progressive steps taken within the area of inclusion at national elite level in the senior countries within the Paralympic Movement. The success rate of these activities has depended heavily on government cooperation and support through legislation and funding to provide professional programming resource at elite level. For these countries, the benefits that accrue from tapping into professional resource, financing of parallel or inclusive programmes and access to marketing, IT and technical expertise is already showing clear indications of higher achievement levels for athletes within such systems.

However, the need to address disparity in opportunity and professional resource support remains at grass roots development level both nationally and internationally. In addition, to complement and reinforce the achievements made, the IPC is called upon to ensure that policies, procedures and infrastructure exist to serve the more severely disabled and females equally well within the Paralympic Movement.

Integration / Development / Recruitments

Session B 4

Presenters: Anne Morash Johnson
                   Jack Benedick
                   Klaus Schüle et al. (Trevor Williams †)
                   Harald von Selzam

Moderator: Maura Strange

Anne Morash Johnson presented an overview of the opportunity levels provided within the programmes offered at the Casa Colina Centers for Rehabilitation, Pomona, California/USA. Casa Colina offers both competitive and recreational pursuit opportunities to persons with a disability. The Casa Colina Outdoor Adventure programme focuses on empowering persons with disabilities to experience both physical and emotional success. Activities are varied and include snow and water skiing, sailing, rock climbing, horse packing, dog sledding, scuba and white water rafting. Every effort is made to promote the value and benefit of high risk activities without endangering safety. Such opportunities are ensured for thousands of individuals through professional outfitters, rehabilitation personnel and trained volunteers.

Jack Benedick's presentation on integration of disabled athletes/sports focussed on the elite athletes in the sport of skiing at a national level in the US and internationally within the F.I.S. The introduction of a functional classification system for skiing facilitated inclusion strategies by allowing disabled skiing to be sport specific in its development and thus easily streamlined. On an international basis, many nations have now integrated, albeit at varying degrees and levels and many more are actively studying the feasibility of this incorporation. Within the US almost every ski area has some type of disabled skiing programme, ranging from rehabilitation and recreation to elite training centres, demonstrating the accommodation of opportunity at all levels as a prerequisite for sustained and healthy growth in participation levels. Additionally, active integration within competition programmes according to the "Golden Rule" supports credibility for disabled athletes' achievement. The recent introduction of a "Handicap Factor System" is levelling the playing field and creating a more competitive event where fewer medals are contended and thus going some way to dispel the "Special Olympics" image.

Klaus Schüle presented a study made in co-operation with Tarjja Kolkka, Walter Hubach and the late Trevor Williams, which demonstrated patterns of initial and continuing participation in wheelchair basketball in the United Kingdom and Germany. Comparison was made in the study of ways in which players from two of the world's leading wheelchair basketball nations first became involved in the sport and how this was pursued. Particular note was made in regard to the mediums used for introducing players to the sport and their social context. It was an important consideration of the study group to identify the influence of rehabilitation centres at the initial socialisation stage, i.e. what part was played by such institutions in the introduction of sport. In this respect it was shown that the German example centred more on rehabilitation as an introductory context, whereas in the UK the wheelchair basketball club situation was the dominant factor. Both Germany and the United Kingdom have moved to wheelchair basketball as a sport, rather than a rehabilitation activity. If rehabilitation centres are going to be more effective in this area, it was felt that sports knowledge and involvement of sports therapists from rehabilitation to sport can also be facilitated through contact persons such as current or ex-athletes.

Harald von Selzam through his experience in Paralympic Games organisation and bid situations asked the question "Separate or Together?" from an event management perspective. From data collected and consideration of both Olympic and Paralympic Games organisational and economic factors, the answer emerged that "together" provided the better option, i.e. as currently occurs with the

Paralympic Games closely following the Olympic Games, thus demonstrating a model of an overall Olympic celebration of sport.

Through close co-operation and integrated Organising Committees, many benefits and few disadvantages could be identified at sports political, operational, public relations, marketing and economic levels. In particular, the platform provided by the Olympic Games in promotional terms could not be ignored. Discussion therefore focussed on "fine tuning" the existing model to further enhance the Paralympic Games as part of the Olympic Festival. Visual impact strategies, both pre Games and during the event, were felt to be avenues that need further exploration and investment by the IPC. Informed media exercises incorporating high quality and dramatic images were considered to play an important role, particularly in promotional exercises in the pre-Games period.

It was stated that the Paralympic Movement must define the strategies to put us in a situation similar to the Olympic Games, where host broadcasting creates revenue rather than a cost factor for organisers to consider. So, the Paralympic Movement should be identifying why models work and making them work faster, more comprehensively and more consistently.

In comment, over the two sessions on Integration / Development / Recruitment, it would seem that the Paralympic Movement is focussing resource and attention to the elite end of our activity in an increasingly successful manner. However, perhaps the question should be asked whether strategies and mechanics to ensure sustained recruitment and sport and athletes development exist on as broad a base as is evidently necessary to support continued progress?

Integration / Development / Recruitment

Session B 7

Presenters: Karen DePauw
                   Claudine Sherrill
                   Heike Tiemann
                   Mary Hums / Anita Moorman

Moderator: Deena Scoretz

The participation of women in all aspects of disability sport is not equitable and needs to be improved. This statement, I'm sure, is not a surprise to anyone. The issue of women's participation was not only discussed in this session – it also came up in speeches during the opening ceremony and in presentations and questions throughout the conference. I understand that the organisers faced a dilemma when planning this programme: Is it effective to plan a specific session focusing on the participation of women? Or is it more effective to 'integrate' this topic area with other themes relating to development? I believe all those who participated in this session will agree that it **was** a good idea to focus time on this particular topic and that the discussions only managed to break the tip of a very large iceberg.

Before recapping the key findings and recommendations from this session, I would like to clarify the perspective that underlined the discussions: We do not have a problem with women in Paralympic sport. The key issue is dealing with the institution of sport or the sporting environment. It's important to re-frame our thinking, emphasising the responsibility of sport organisations to provide a sport environment were women have equitable opportunities.

The first speaker, Dr. Karen DePauw, provided a historical context for sport and marginality to discuss the connections between society and disability sport. Historical developments and factors were documented that have led to the under-representation of women, including:

- the predominately white, middle-class, physically disabled, male model of sport and therefore a lack of early sport experiences,
- the medical model of disability,
- a lack of female role models,
- lack of access to coaches and training programmes, and
- psychological and sociological factors.

Dr. DePauw identified three aspects relating to the link between disability sport and society: Sport is a reflection of society; sport is a reproduction of social values and, most importantly, it can be a site of resistance, where changes and transformations are possible. Transformations have no doubt already begun – there have been increases in the visibility and acceptance of all athletes with disabilities, but we have not yet reached a state where sport is the primary focus of an athlete's identity, instead of gender or disability.

What is necessary for further transformation to take place?

The first and fundamental ingredient is access. Are the doors open? The second speaker, Dr. Claudine Sherrill, reported evidence that many doors are **not** open to women with disabilities. Women's participation in the Paralympics decreased from 33% in Barcelona to 24% in Atlanta and nearly half of the participating countries did not have women represented in their teams. Those sports with the most women participating also had a greater number of women administrators and coaches. Some of the barriers arising out of Dr. Sherrill's qualitative research included a lack of knowledge about the possibilities, a lack of socialising agents, and a lack of finances. Resourceful solutions to these issues are certainly needed and it is important for men and women to work together to resolve gender inequities.

If the doors are open and programmes are accessible, are the people who are 'in' being accommodated? Are all individuals actively involved? Accommodation was presented as a second step toward social transformation and it was argued that it is generally the person with a disability who must adapt and accommodate. More accommodation is necessary on the part of the sport institution and sport context.

This type of adaptation can best be supported by knowledge surrounding the athlete and knowledge focusing on the context – the sport organisation. With respect to athletes, the research presented by Heike Tiemann identified issues and experiences particular to the female elite athlete with physical disabilities. Her research is of great relevance to service providers and all those working with female athletes with disabilities because it focused on the athlete's socialisation into disability sport and via disability sport. The socialisation agents and processes of women with congenital disabilities were significantly different from those with acquired disabilities. This emphasises the complexity and diverse nature of research in this area.

Turning our attention to the administrative side of sport, Dr. Mary Hums presented state-of-the art findings on the career paths of women working in the management of sport for people with disabilities. Data on the administrators – both men and women – working in disability sport is scarce and this study opened new areas of discussion and investigation. When compared with women working in an able-bodied professional sport organisation, these women were more 'cause-oriented' when discussing their career paths. Many were working in disability sport organisations to better their sport and thereby better the opportunities for the athletes. Other interview responses were more gender-neutral in comparison with administrators in traditional male-dominated sport. The importance of continuing research on this area – with new studies including male and female administrators with and without disabilities and international respondents, can significantly contribute to better recruitment of female sport administrators. This type of research can also lead to more effective sport organisations.

Concrete suggestions regarding women and disability sport:

- **work with female athletes with disabilities** – involve these athletes in planning and research and enhance opportunities for contact among athletes, between athletes and administrators, and between athletes and women with disabilities not yet involved in sport;

- **data collection and research** – accurate and complete information in all areas is needed; specific areas may include: participation statistics (in sport and administration), athletes' opportunities and services, different cultural contexts, socialisation factors, motivation factors, organisational structures, administrators in various types of positions from paid full-time to volunteer involvement, and links with other societal institutions and organisations;

- **be attentive to the unique needs of women** – for example, providing opportunities for child care during meetings and events in order to increase opportunities for women's involvement;

- **communication** – examples of good practice and success stories need to be communicated within the disability sport world and in society at large. During this congress session, a diverse and impressive range of successes were presented that could serve as models for further development;

- **networking** – forums for discussion at congresses and continued dialogue are essential.

The lively discussions generated in this session indicated that there is support and willingness to enhance women's participation in disability sport. Now it is time to take action.

Organization / Administration

Sessions B 3 and B 5

Presenters: Hans Lindström
Bob McCullough
Margret Kellner
Jennifer Banks
Walter Thompson
Fin Biering - Sørensen
David Grevemberg / Christian Lillieroos
Carol Mushett

Moderator: Patricia Longmuir

The sessions in the Organization and Administration section of the Conference generated a lot of discussion on a wide variety of ideas and opinions. The tremendous interest in these sessions suggests that the IPC should give strong consideration to enabling these topics to be discussed at future symposia, such as the Paralympic Congress in Sydney next year. Since the topics discussed in each session were significantly different, each session is summarized separately.

The first session examined the structure of, and relationships between organizations involved in disability sport. Internationally, the presentations discussed the IPC and the IOSDs, with specific presentations about ISMWSF and CP-ISRA. At the national level, discussions focused on an Australian model for athlete preparation prior to the Paralympics in Atlanta.

Hans Lindström highlighted the current roles of the IPC and the IOSDs and the potential for duplication and conflict as a result of the way in which these roles are currently defined. He called for another "Arnhem Conference" to get clear directions from the member nations as to the desired organizational structures and foci of control, particularly for the multi-disability sports.

Bob McCullough outlined the many factors which have created a need for change within the disability sport structure and how ISMWSF has responded in order to prepare for the new millenium. ISMWSF has agreed that the IPC will be responsible for all elite wheelchair sport, and believes that it should also do all multi-disability games in addition to the Paralympics. ISMWSF will do all developmental activities related to wheelchair sport, such as athlete recruitment, junior athlete programmes and coaching development.

Margret Kellner reviewed the development of CP-ISRA from the era of orientation through the era of development. She also outlined the CP-ISRA strategic plan for the future which focuses on working closely with other international federations to increase opportunities for individuals with cerebral palsy through advocacy, programme development, educational opportunities, and the development and refinement of the functional classification systems.

The paper by Jennifer Banks looked at a national level programme for athlete preparation and training. The Australian Paralympic Preparation Programme (PPP) had a tremendous impact on the success of the Australian team at the Paralympics in Atlanta. The PPP demonstrates how access to consistent support of the highest quality, and in all areas of training and preparation enables athletes to achieve their maximum potential.

It was clear from these presentations and the discussions which followed that there are important contributions made to disability sport by a variety of national and international organizations. All disability sport organizations have a similar focus. The top priority is providing the maximum benefit to the athletes. It is also clear that our collective experiences over the past decade have created a need to clarify goals, objectives, roles and responsibilities. Organizational changes to address these needs are planned or underway in all of the presenting organizations. From these presentations and discussions, two consistent themes emerged as recommended future directions:

1. The IPC and the IOSDs must continue to work closely in order to clarify and streamline their roles and structures, and

2. all organizations should consider the benefits of highly focused support, such as the PPP, for athletes in a variety of sports and all regions.

The second session examined a wide variety of support systems for disability sport. Two presentations looked at research, one at information technology, and one at the IPC Sport Technical Department itself.

Walter Thompson presented the need for a comprehensive research programme, coordinated through the IPC, for sport performance and management. He stated that it is critical that we bridge the gap between science and practice (athletes, coaches, etc.) so that scientists answer the questions that are of interest to athletes and coaches, and the athletes and coaches can use the research results to enhance performance. Important issues for the future which were identified in the presentation and discussion, included funding, creating a formal well-known research process, and getting people with disabilities meaningfully involved in all stages of research.

Fin Biering-Sørensen outlined the formal research process that has been implemented for the sport of swimming. A panel of scientists needs to review and approve all projects to ensure quality research. If such a review cannot be completed, the research should not be done since the quality of the work will be unknown. Swimming also has a process for non-scientists to bring research ideas to the review committee who will assist in getting the research done by qualified personnel. It was stressed that sport organizations should have responsibility for approving sport-specific research. The IPC should be responsible for approving sport-generic research. The importance of looking at the legal liability of review committee members if an approved project ultimately results in problems was raised during the discussion.

David Grevemberg and Christian Lillieroos spoke about the use of information technology to enhance teamwork and make organizations more effective in event management, data processing, information distribution, and general administration. The International Table Tennis Committee website was presented as a model of the successful use of information technology. Recommendations for the future included: having the IPC take the lead in being very proactive to ensure access to and training in information technology for all national Paralympic Committees in all regions, incorporating the use of information technology systems in all IPC functions, and developing disability sport specific information technology training. The discussion sounded a cautionary note that we cannot see information technology as the "ultimate answer" until it is universally accessible.

To conclude the session, Carol Mushett reviewed the IPC Sport Technical Department's goals for growth, quality, diversity, transparency, and accountability in Paralympic sport. She also discussed the Department's future initiatives to enhance sport administration and operations, diversify funding, enhance marketing, improve communication, coordinate the events calendar, and evaluate existing and new sport programmes.

In general, there appears to be the perception that past IPC structures are not optimal for the future support of disability sport. It is recommended that formal processes be created to ensure quality research, coordinated research activities, and sport-specific input into the relevance and appropriateness of sport-specific research. It is also recommended that the use of information technology be expanded for both sport management and administration. The IPC Sport Technical

Department has recognized the need for change and is developing strategies to enhance its effectiveness in these and other areas.

Organization / Administration

Session B 6

Presenters: Jonquil Solt
                    Robert Price
                    Abu Yilla

Moderator: Peter Downs

Jonquil Solt, Chairperson of the International Paralympic Equestrian Committee (IPEC), reported on the development and growth of Paralympic equestrian sport. The IPEC was set up in 1991, only two years after the formation of the International Paralympic Committee (IPC). After a slow start to its growth, by 1999 IPEC was in communication with over 40 nations. IPEC's rapid growth did not happen by accident. There were a number of key issues and events that contributed to the growth, including:

- equestrian sport has some unique attractions above other sports;

- people with a very diverse range of disabilities can take part, so opening up the market;

- men and women take part in equal terms;

- while dressage is the only Paralympic event, other events, such as vaulting, endurance riding and show jumping, attract significant numbers of competitors;

- the development of resource materials to complement a *Rule Book*, including a *Classification Manual* and a range of *Dressage Tests, brochures, videos, newsletters* and an *internet site;*

- making contact with key international bodies involved in

equestrianism and spreading 'word of mouth';

- conduct of education seminars and courses in 25 countries.

One of the key aspects of the success of IPEC is the openness of the sport to a wide variety of disability. Dressage tests are wide ranging, covering up to 26 prescribed movements. The four grades of impairment designed by IPEC allow people with different disabilities to compete on an equal basis. The riders with higher level of impairment compete in grades that have fewer prescribed movements. To ensure that riders comply with the grading system internationally IPEC have adopted the *Functional Profile System for Grading*. Judges of able-bodied events can attend conversion courses to accredit them to judge IPEC events. Since the formation of IPEC there have been several major achievements, including:

- an increase in the number of international competitions;

- an increase in the number of competing nations – 27 nations now 'widely practising the sport';

- maintenance of dressage as a Paralympic sport;

- the establishment of a network of classifiers, judges and technical delegates;

- an increase in the standard of competitors;

- an increase in the network of relevant organizations to support IPEC's growth.

IPEC has successfully developed the growth of a sport that is open to a wide range of people with a disability whilst still maintaining the basic purpose of the sport, to provide opportunities for people with a disability to reach their potential.

Bob Price presented a program of the Linkage Community Trust in Lincolnshire, UK, aimed at improving the health and fitness of students and residents with complex learning disabilities.

The Trust provides further education, residential care and employment opportunities for people with complex learning disabilities. The term 'complex learning disabilities' covers a wide range of disabilities, including moderate and severe intellectual disability, vision and hearing impairments, physical disability and emotional and behavioural disabilities. The common term in England for this range of disability is *learning disability*. The paper is divided into four parts.

1. Literature review

Literature supports the view that physical inactivity is associated with coronary artery disease. Causes of physical inactivity are more associated with motivational, emotional and temporal factors than access or facility related. There is a lack of research to investigate the long term benefits of physical activity for people with disabilities although it is reasonable to suspect that comparable health gains apply to people with disabilities. There is also a lack of research that examines the link between sedentary lifestyles and disability. Studies in USA and UK support the view that:

- people with learning disabilities have higher mortality rates, low levels of cardio-vascular fitness and higher levels of obesity;

- people with learning disabilities have lower levels of participation in physical activity to the general population.

In England there is evidence to suggest that people with learning disabilities in day and residential care settings do not have enough choices for moderate or vigorous physical activity to gain health benefits. There is some evidence that highlights the barriers that people with learning disabilities face when trying to access physical activity, including:

- primary barriers - unclear policy guidelines for day and residential care settings, including resourcing, transport, and staffing, participant income and expenditure;

- secondary barriers – how choice and rights are given, age appropriateness, segregated verses integrated physical activity.

From all this evidence Linkage is seeking to address the health and fitness needs of its students and residents by:

- raising their awareness and experience of health and fitness issues;

- enabling them to make more informed choices;

- providing a range of physical activity experiences;

- encouraging them to adopt more healthy lifestyles.

2. Linkage Community Trust

Linkage was established in 1976 to address the education and care needs of young people with complex learning difficulties. It has 200 students on a residential campus, 80 adults in long stay residential care facilities, 280 staff operating out of 30 properties. The College offers a broad curriculum that aims to create a stimulating and challenging educational environment. The residential care facilities aim to provide community-based care within a stimulating and challenging environment for a lifetime of a group of elderly and infirm residents. The care facilities also offers residential facilities for ex-college students who have no suitable home base. Individual programs are designed to equip people to live as independently in the community as possible.

3. Health and fitness

At present Linkage does not have a coordinated health and fitness curriculum. There are, however, a wide range of leisure activities offered to students and residents. Other incidental physical activity occurs but mostly on an ad hoc basis.

4. A new curriculum

In order to develop a health and fitness program 22 staff were invited to contribute to a curriculum. The curriculum addresses three key areas:

- healthy lifestyles – encouraging students and residents awareness of choices and the effect those choices have on healthy lifestyles; providing opportunities for students and residents to discuss issues of common interest;

- fitness – introducing a range of activities, including walking, swimming, cycling, keep-fit, tai chi and disco dancing; other lifestyle fitness opportunities will also be encouraged, including trying to develop an understanding as to why fitness is important;

- nutrition – utilizing a Health Education Authority model known as 'The Plate' to encourage people to adopt healthy eating habits.

5. Future possibilities

As the Health and Fitness curriculum takes shape, links will be established with local sports clubs and a 'buddy' type system encouraged to link people with an interest in sport and physical activity. An opportunity also exists for Linkage to seek recognition as Healthy Living Centre under the national Health Education Authority scheme.

Organization / Administration

Session B 8

Presenters: Majed Abdulfattah
                 José Luis Campo
                 Colin Higgs
                 Nina Kahrs, Nayinda Sentumbwe

Moderator: Peter Downs

Majed Abdul-Fattah of the Palestinian Sports Federation for the Disabled presented a community based rehabilitation program as a model for integrating sports activities. The needs of Palestinians with disabilities is largely overlooked in a country that has been ruled by the Israeli military for the past 32 years. The services sector generally is underdeveloped, particularly health and rehabilitation services effecting people with disabilities. A policy of segregation has prevailed over time that has influenced how the public view people with disabilities. During the 1980's a series of rehabilitation centers arose by necessity. Recognition as to the importance of mainstreaming began in the 1990's, particularly the establishment of a community based rehabilitation program (CBR). At this time sport for people with disabilities was introduced.

As generic sports clubs and organizations developed so too did sports organizations for people with disabilities. Structures for disability sport began to be developed. A lack of resources, policy direction and inaccessibility were barriers to development. Given these barriers at the local level a top-down approach was taken with the formation of the Palestinian Sports Federation of the Disabled (PSFD). In 1995 the CBR model was adopted by PSFD, particularly in recognition of the need to reach rural areas. Gradually, as the expertise gained through the CBR model developed, 12 disability sports organizations started up. Today, 2 of these organizations are integrated into mainstream clubs.

To assist in the mainstreaming of disability sport people with disabilities were targeted for positions on management committee's and were integrated into general assemblies. Specialist committee's were formed to deal with disability issues. Funding has been provided from local business. This is significant and encouraging for the future as other similar experiences in war-torn countries have resulted in mostly government backing. Mainstreaming has also occurred through the training of classifiers and judges at all levels.

There is a belief in Palestine that the current period of integration is highly significant for the broader society. PSFD are aware of their broader social responsibilities. Key to the broader philosophy is the empowerment of local providers and trainers. The strategy of inclusion is now taking over from integration. The movement toward inclusion continues despite a generally poor infrastructure, inadequate services and inaccessibility. PSFD continue to promote the rights of people with disabilities based on the social model of disability.

Nina Kahrs and Nayinda Sentumbwe reported on an initiative to develop sports activities for persons with visual impairments in Uganda. The Sporting with Visual Impairments project is an initiative of the Ugandan Mobility and Rehabilitation Program for Persons with Visual Impairments. Sport is one of the initiatives of the program. The Sporting and Visual Impairments project aims to make sport and adapted physical activity parts of all programs. The Mobility and Rehabilitation Program (MBR) was formed proceeding the 8th International Mobility Conference in Norway in 1996. The objectives and goals of MBR are:

- introduce, develop and promote sports and physical activities as a matter of choice for Ugandans with vision impairments;

- develop competence of service providers;

- use sport and physical activity to challenge stereotypes and negative attitudes toward people with vision impairments;

- provide a model for the development of disability sport and physical education.

A pilot project was developed as a first step toward achieving the above objectives. The project was conducted with the backdrop of little or no sporting opportunities for Ugandans with vision impairments. The pilot involved:

- information dissemination to people with vision impairments and able-bodied Ugandans about the sporting needs and athletic potential of people with vision impairment;

- imparting basic technical knowledge and skills to key personnel;

- introducing selected sports and activities;

- conduct of exhibitions and sport events, locally and nationally;

- establishing relevant organizations and networks to coordinate, promote and sustain activities.

The project started in 1997 through a sub-committee that identified specific target groups for involvement in particular activities. The primary target group was institutes of learning. There were several advantages to this approach, not least the ability to identify relevant personnel, the use of good facilities and desirable environments for people with vision impairments. The pilot activities were embraced with great enthusiasm by all concerned. A major activity was the conduct of a two day workshop to raise the awareness of disability sport held in April 1998. Subsequent two week courses have taken place in 1998 and 1999, attracting sixteen teachers.

By October 1998 the first Primary School Sports Championships for

Children with Visual Impairments was organized. As a result of this the Ministry of Education and the Uganda National Council of Sport are planning to organize a primary school sports competition for children with disabilities. These events are being established as regulars on the Ugandan sports calendar.

Several organizations have started to support people with vision impairments, notably the UNAB Kampala Sports club. Steps are now being taken to establish a Uganda Blind Sports Association. Support from IBSA has been critical to sustain the enthusiasm generated by these activities. Importantly, this initiative is generating interest from neighbouring African countries such as Zimbabwe, who are looking to adopt similar models.

Colin Higgs presented a Guyana Project for People with Disabilities, in which sport and recreation play a major role. Guyana has an ethnically diverse population of around one million. It has crippling economic problems and is the second poorest country in the western hemisphere. In terms of Official Development Assistance (ODA) the Canadian International Development Agency has similar goals to ODA, being:

- provision of basic human needs;

- advancement of women in development;

- infrastructure development;

- human rights, democracy and good governance;

- private sector development;

- the protection of the environment.

In general the needs of people with disabilities has a low priority.

People with disabilities are excluded from the very basic opportunities. The Guyana project has followed a model used by the Canadian Paraplegic Association in other countries where the CPA works with the NGO. Following a needs assessment a number of areas were identified that needed addressing:

- the establishment of a facility for the repair and maintenance and construction of wheelchairs;

- peer counseling;

- advocacy;

- employment readiness;

- barrier-free design;

- sport for persons with disabilities.

Workshop content was negotiated around these areas. The week long programs were organized and delivered by CPA and hosted by key local contacts. Evaluations regarded the workshops as successful, primarily as a result of responding to local needs. The involvement of people with disabilities as role models and leaders was also seen as a critical success factor, particularly given that successful people with disabilities are virtually unheard of in Guyana. Important lessons learnt during the project were:

- selecting the right leaders was critical to success;

- finding the appropriate venue;

- adapting materials for use in the workshops;

- identifying the reasons people went to the workshops and the role they fulfill afterwards.

It is critical that future international conferences consider developing countries more thoroughly. We need to consider technology and leading-edge practice and if they apply to the needs of athletes in developing countries. What may be an advance in one country may be a disadvantage in another. We also need to consider the cultural differences from one country to another, for example, in determining doping tests for women from developing countries. Good local coaches are needed and skilled classifiers. Appropriate facilities and mobility aids are required to assist participation. Finally, changes in societal attitudes are needed to encourage the participation of people with disabilities in sport.

Media / Marketing / Sponsoring

Session A 8

Presenters:	Gunther Belitz
	David Howe
	Robert Wanzel
	Reinhild Möller
	Jorge Vilela de Carvalho
Moderator:	Errol Marklein

The five presentations focussed on the following issues:

Gunther Belitz pointed out that the Paralympic Movement had come a long way from the times before Seoul '88 and had moved on quickly to the Games in Barcelona. Once Paralympic sport had stars and stories the media became generally interested. But there still is a need for more professionals to transport Paralympic sport to the media. To date the topic is still on the border line between the social and the sports page. It is our task to make the public aware of the difference between these two aspects. We need to make it easier for the public to understand disability sport and our motives.

David Howe stated that the media (journalists) were not yet deeply enough involved in Paralympic sport. He misses more research on how and in which way the media reported about sport for the disabled in the past and how the issue should be addressed in the future. He left the question open, whether the Paralympic Movement should or should not sell disability sport to the public.

Robert Wanzel called for more professional quality in all aspects of marketing sport for the disabled. He stressed the need to understand how to work with sponsors, i.e. the need to work together with them and to understand and please their needs. From this point of view,

Paralympic sport should sell its athletic philosophies and not try to get donations. The goal should be to promote the sport as sport. That needs professional thinking and a streamlining of the disability sport organisations.

Reinhild Möller saw the need to start at the grassroots. She felt that people with a disability helping able-bodied people could be a useful approach in this context. Once people had experienced that people with a disability can actually help or be role models for them, a different point of view would be created. The acceptance of people with a disability could be improved in the future, if this perspective were presented more offensively. The program "Disabled people help able-bodied people" could be considered the first step towards the "no prejudice" atmosphere required for marketing strategies.

Jorge Vilela de Carvalho presented a marketing campaign to promote the athletes who are going to Sidney and Athens. Athletes are presented as super athletes and this approach seems to attract the media greatly. The program is spread out over the next 6 years and is carrying the message to all communication agencies.

The presentations indicate that numerous activities are ongoing to promote disability sport and its philosophy, but those activities are very rarely combined in a program or strategy. It was general consent that advanced communication is needed in order to combine forces and to create a common image of disability sport. Once this has been accomplished, it will be easier to get sponsors, promoters and supporters for the Paralympic Movement and to reach the next level.

Conference Organization

Conference Committees

Conference President

Prof. Dr. Walter Tokarski

Scientific Committee

Prof. Dr. Gudrun Doll-Tepper (Chair)
Prof. Dr. Yagesh Bhambhani
Rebecca Bornemann
Prof. Dr. Jürgen Innenmoser
Prof. Dr. Joachim Mester
Dr. Christiane Peters
Dr. Karl Quade
Prof. Dr. Klaus Schüle
Dr. Horst Strohkendl
Prof. Dr. Yves Vanlandewijck
Dr. Markus Zimmer

Review Committee

Prof. Dr. Yagesh Bhambhani
Rebeccah Bornemann
Prof. Dr. Karen DePauw
Prof. Dr. Gudrun Doll-Tepper
Prof. Dr. Michael Ferrara
Deena Scoretz
Prof. Dr. Claudine Sherrill
Prof. Dr. Yves Vanlandewijck
Prof. Dr. Garry Wheeler

Organizing Committee

Werner Sonnenschein (overall coordination)
Michael Kröner (Secretary General)
Administrative and Volunteer Staff of the German Sport University

Conference Program – Schedule of Presentations

Date/ Time		Session A			Session B	
		Theme	Presenters		Theme	Presenters
Saturday 28 August						
19.00 - 22.00		Opening Ceremony followed by Buffet Dinner				
Sunday 29 August						
08.30 - 10.45	A1	Sport Performance – Exercise Physiology	Dr. Y. Bhambhani Dr. A. Schmid Dr. G. Frey Dr. M. Bernardi Mod.: Dr. D. Royer	B1	Classification I	Dr. H. Strohkendl Dr. Ch. Brunner Dr. J. Innenmoser Ms. N. Lorincz Mod.: Ms. R. Bornemann
		Coffee Break				
11.00 - 13.15	A2	Sport Performance – Advances in Training Techniques	Dr. K. Quade Mr. Ch. Nunn Dr. D. Daly Ms. S. Zimmermann Dr. T. Bradbury Mod.: Dr. Y. Vanlandewijck	B2	Integration/ Development/ Recruitment I	Mr. D. McCrae Dr. C. Rains Dr. T. Fay Mr. R. Allard Mod.: Ms. M. Strange
13.15 - 14.15		Lunch				
15.00 - 17.15	A3	Sport Performance – Technical Developments/ Equipment I	Dr. B. Burkett Dr. E. Forner Dr. Ch. Bohn Mr. R. Tinker Mod.: Dr. Y. Hutzler	B3	Organization/ Administration I	Mr. H. Lindström Mr. B. McCullough Ms. M. Kellner Ms. J. Banks Mod.: Ms. P. Longmuir
		Coffee Break				
17.30 - 19.00		Poster Presentations				
19.30		Dinner				
Monday 30 August						
08.30 - 10.45	A4	Sport Performance – Sports Medicine	Dr. M. Ferrara Dr. H. Stinus Dr. M. Riding Mod.: Dr. M. Zimmer	B4	Integration/ Development/ Recruitment II	Ms. A. Morash Johnson Mr. J. Benedick Dr. K. Schüle Mr. H. von Selzam Mod.: M. Strange
		Coffee Break				
11.00 - 13.15	A5	Ethics	Dr. Y. Chow Dr. G. Wheeler (1) Ms. J. Le Clair Dr. G. Wheeler (2) Mod.: Dr. G. Doll-Tepper	B5	Organization/ Administration II	Dr. W. Thompson Dr. F. Biering-Sørensen Mr. Ch. Lillieroos Ms. C. Mushett Mod.: Ms. P. Longmuir
13.15 - 14.15		Lunch				
15.00 - 16.30		Technical Demonstrations				
		Coffee Break				
17.00 - 19.00		Poster Presentations, Film Presentations				
19.30		Dinner				

Tuesday 31 August						
08.30 - 10.45	A6	Classification II	Dr. A. Kruimer Dr. R. Davis Mr. L. Worms Mod.: Ms. R. Bornemann	B6	Organization/ Administration III	Ms. J. Solt Dr. L. Olenik Dr. R. Price Dr. A. Yilla Mod.: Mr. P. Downs
Coffee Break						
11.00 - 13.15	A7	Sport Performance – Technical Developments/ Equipment II	Dr. L. van der Woude Dr. Y. Vanlandewijck Dr. R. Cooper Dr. K. van Breukelen Mod.: Dr. Y. Hutzler	B7	Integration/ Development/ Recruitment III	Dr. K. DePauw Dr. C. Sherrill Ms. H. Tiemann Dr. M. Hums Mod.: Ms. D. Scoretz
13.15 - 14.15	Lunch					
15.00 - 16.30	Round Table IOSD Presidents					
Coffee Break						
17.00 - 18.30	Sport Demonstration of Athletes with a Disability					
19.30	Dinner					
Wednesday 01 September						
08.30 - 10.45	A8	Media/ Marketing/ Sponsoring	Mr. G. Belitz Mr. D. Howe Dr. R. Wanzel Ms. R. Möller Mr. J. Vilela de Carvalho Mod.: Mr. E. Marklein	B8	Organisation/ Administration IV	Mr. M. Abdulfattah Mr. J.L. Campo Dr. C. Higgs Ms. N. Kahrs Mod.: Mr. P. Downs
Coffee Break						
11.00 - 11.45	Special Topics Session					
11.45 - 12.45	Lunch					
13.00 - 15.00	Synopses/ Conclusions					
15.00 - 15.30	Closing Ceremony					
15.45 - 19.00	Bus Transfer to the City Center- Sightseeing					
19.00	Dinner in a „Kölsch" Restaurant					

Acknowledgements

The German Sport University Cologne gratefully acknowledges the generous support and sponsorship which has made the VISTA '99 Conference possible:

Patronage

International Paralympic Committee (IPC)
International Council of Sport Science and Physical Education (ICSSPE)

Financial Support

Government of the Federal Republic of Germany
Government of the Federal State of North Rhine Westfalia
German Research Council (Deutsche Forschungsgemeinschaft)
International Paralympic Committee

Sponsorship

Toyota Deutschland GmbH

About the Editors

Dr. Gudrun Doll-Tepper is Professor of Sport Science at the Institute of Sport Science at the Free University of Berlin, Germany. She received her doctorate from the University of Berlin and her "habilitation" from the University of Frankfurt, Germany. She has authored and co-authored over 200 publications in sport science, sport pedagogy, and adapted physical activity and sport for persons with a disability. Dr. Doll-Tepper in President of the International Council of Sport Science and Physical Education, Chairperson of the International Paralympic Committee's Sport Science Committee, Invited Fellow of the European College of Sport Science, and a Member of the National Olympic Committee for Germany. In 1998 she received the William G. Anderson Commemorative Award for her contribution to the Paralympic Movement, the Alice-Profé-Award for her outstanding contribution to women in sport, and in 1999 the Distinguished Service Cross of the Federal Republic of Germany for her outstanding contribution to disability sport, physical education and sport science.

Michael Kröner is a senior student at the German Sport University where he specializes in rehabilitation/sport for persons with a disability. Paralyzed in 1992 after a car accident, he continued to practice competitive sport and took part in the 1998 Paralympic Winter Games in Nagano/Japan and in the 2000 Ski World Championships in Anzère-Crans Montana/Switzerland. Mr. Kröner served as Secretary General of the VISTA'99 Conference.

Werner Sonnenschein is head of the Office of International Affairs of the German Sport University. He has a broad international sport science administration background including an eight-year term of office as Secretary General of the International Council of Sport Science and Physical Education. He served as coordinator of the VISTA'99 Conference.